MICHAEL F. PALMER

PAUL TILLICH'S PHILOSOPHY OF ART

PAUL TILLICH'S PHILOSOPHY OF ART

BY

MICHAEL F. PALMER

WALTER DE GRUYTER · BERLIN · NEW YORK
1984

THEOLOGISCHE BIBLIOTHEK TÖPELMANN
HERAUSGEGEBEN VON
K. ALAND, C. H. RATSCHOW UND E. SCHLINK
41. BAND

Gedruckt mit Unterstützung der Alexander von Humboldt-Stiftung

Library of Congress Cataloging in Publication Data

Palmer, Michael F., 1945—
Paul Tillich's philosophy of art.

(Theologische Bibliothek Töpelmann ; 41. Bd.)
Bibliography: p. XI—XXI.
Includes indexes.
1. Tillich, Paul, 1886—1965.   2. Art—Philosophy—
History—20th century.   3. Christian art and symbolism—
History—20th century.   I. Title.   II. Series.
BX4827.T53P24 1983   261.5'7   83—15056
ISBN 3-11-009681-1

CIP-Kurztitelaufnahme der Deutschen Bibliothek

Palmer, Michael F.:
Paul Tillich's philosophy of art / by Michael F. Palmer. —
Berlin ; New York : de Gruyter, 1983.
(Theologische Bibliothek Töpelmann ; Bd. 41)
  ISBN 3-11-009681-1
NE: GT

Satz: Hagedorn, Berlin · Druck: Kupijai & Prochnow, Berlin · Einband: Fuhrmann, Berlin.

*To the memory
of my father*

PREFACE

In this book I have attempted to reconstruct Paul Tillich's Philosophy of Art, and inevitably the result is sometimes not so much what Tillich said as what I think he would have said. Thankfully, however, Tillich's work is not of the kind that makes such an undertaking altogether fanciful. It is true that he left us no major work on the subject; but what he did leave is a series of articles and lectures, spanning over forty years, which are remarkable in their consistency of argument and content. This, coupled with the 'systematic' and interlocking character of Tillich's thinking in general, makes it possible to fit the separate pieces of the jig-saw together.

One further point should be made. Tillich's central preocupation was with the relation between religion and culture, and thus with the construction of a theology which would overcome the 'destructive division' between the sacred and secular realms. The result is his famous 'theology of culture', which many commentators maintain is his greatest and most enduring intellectual achievement. And within this theology, art occupies a preeminent position. For, according to Tillich, it is in art that the convergence of these two realms may be observed. Thus he requires us to contemplate the work of painters, novelists and sculptors. We can learn, he says, more about culture and religion by studying the paintings of a Picasso or Munch than we can by reading the textbooks of theologians and sociologists. Art, therefore, does not stand on the fringes of Tillich's interest; rather, it is that activity which, more than any other, both explains and exemplifies the theology of culture itself.

My debts are many, but in particular I should like to express my thanks to Professor John Heywood Thomas of Nottingham University, who first introduced me to Tillich's work and supervised my early research, and to Professor Carl Heinz Ratschow of Marburg University, who was untiring in his advise and encouragement in the preparation of this book. I am also conscious of how much I owe to the Alexander von Humbold Foundation, under whose auspices this work was written.

Westerkirk 1983   Michael Palmer

CONTENTS

BIBLIOGRAPHY
I. BOOKS BY PAUL TILLICH

A History of Christian Thought (New York and Evanston: Harper & Row, 1968).

Biblical Religion and the Search for Ultimate Reality (Chicago: University of Chicago Press, 1955)

Das System der Wissenschaften nach Gegenständen und Methoden. Ein Entwurf (Göttingen: Vandenhoeck & Rupprecht, 1923). *GW,* I: 109–293.

Dynamics of Faith (New York: Harper & Row, 1958). Cited as *DF.*

Gesammelte Werke, ed. Renate Albrecht (Stuttgart: Evangelisches Verlagswerk). Cited as *GW.*

Love, Power, and Justice (New York: Oxford University Press, 1960).

Masse und Geist; Studien zur Philosophie der Masse (Berlin and Frankfurt: Verlag der Arbeitsgemeinschaft, 1922). *GW,* II: 35–90.

On the Boundary, with an Introduction by J. Heywood Thomas (London: Collins, 1967). This is a revision, newly translated, of Part I of *The Interpretation of History* (New York: Charles Scriber's Sons, 1936). Cited as *OB.*

Perspectives on Nineteenth and Twentieth Century Protestant Thought, ed. Carl E. Braaten (New York: Harper & Row, 1967).

Political Expectation, ed. J. Luther Adams (New York: Harper & Row, 1971).

Systematic Theology (London: James Nisbet. Vol. I, 1953; Vol. II, 1957; Vol. III, 1964). Cited as *ST.*

Systematische Theologie, Bd. I, trans. Renate Albrecht *et al.* (Stuttgart: Evangelisches Verlagswerk, 1956).

The Courage To Be (London: Collins, 1962). Cited as *CTB.*

The Interpretation of History, trans. N. Rasetzki and E. Talmey (New York: Charles Scribner's Sons, 1936). Cited as *IH.*

Theology of Culture (New York: Oxford University Press, 1964). Cited as *TC.*

The Protestant Era, trans. J. Luther Adams (Chicago: University of Chicago Press, 1957). Cited as *PE.*

The Religious Situation, trans. H. Richard Niebuhr (Cleveland and New York: Meridian Books, 1967). Cited as *RS.*

The Shaking of the Foundations (London: Penguin Books, 1966).

The World Situation (Philadelphia: Fortress Press, 1965).

Ultimate Concern: Dialogues with Students, ed. D. Mackenzie Brown (London:
S. C. M. Press, 1963).
What is Religion? trans. and ed. J. Luther Adams (New York, Evanston, and London: Harper & Row, 1969). Cited as *WR.*

II. ARTICLES BY PAUL TILLICH

'A Reinterpretation of the Doctrine of the Incarnation', *Church Quaterly Review,*
CXLVII, No. 294 (January–March 1949), pp. 133–148.
'Art and Ultimate Reality', *Cross Currents,* X, No. 1 (Winter 1960), pp. 1–13
'Authentic Religious Art', *Art Institute of Chicago* (Chicago, 1954), pp. 8–9. Written
jointly with Theodore M. Greene.
'Autobiographical Reflections', *The Theology of Paul Tillich,* ed. C. W. Kegley and
R. W. Bretall (New York: Macmillan, 1964), pp. 3–21.
'Between Utopianism and Escape from History', *Colgate Rochester Divinity School
Bulletin,* XXXI, No. 2 (May 1959), pp. 35–37.
'Christian Criteria for Our Culture', *Criterion* (Yale), I, No. 1, (October 1952),
pp. 1, 3–4.
Christianity and the Problem of Existence (Washington, D.C.: Henderson Services,
1951). Pp. 33 (mimeographed).
Das Dämonische (Tübingen: J. C. B. Mohr, 1926), p. 44. *GW,* VI: 42–71. E. T., *IH:*
77–122.
'Das religiöse Symbol', *Blätter für deutsche Philosophie* (Berlin), I, No. 4 (January
1928), pp. 277–299. *GW,* V: 196–212. Translated and revised in *Religious
Experience and Truth,* ed. S. Hook (New York: University Press, 1961), pp.
301–321.
'Der junge Hegel und das Schicksal Deutschlands', *Hegel und Goethe. Zwei Gedenk-
reden* (Tübingen: J. C. B. Mohr, 1932). *GW,* XII: 125–150.
'Der Mensch im Christentum und im Marxismus', *Schriftenreihe der Evangelischen
Arbeitsausschusses Düsseldorf,* H. 5 (Düsseldorf, 1953). *GW,* III: 194–209.
'Die christliche Gewissenheit und der historische Jesus'. Frament of an unpubli-
shed address (1911) in the Paul Tillich archive in Marburg University.
'Die Idee der Offenbarung', *Zeitschrift für Theologie und Kirche (Tübingen, 1927),*
VIII, No. 6, pp. 403–412.
'Die Kategorie des „Heiligen" bei Rudolf Otto', *Theologische Blätter* (Leipzig),
II, No. 1 (January 1923), pp. 11–12.
'Die Überwindung des Religionsbegriffs in der Religionsphilosophie', *Kant-Stu-
dien* (Berlin), XXVII, No. 3/4 (1922), pp. 446–469. E. T., The Conquest of the
Concept of Religion in the Philosophy of Religion'. *WR:* 122–154.

'Estrangement and Reconciliation in Modern Thought', *The Review of Religion*, IX, No. 1 (November 1944), pp. 5–19.

'Existential Analyses and Religious Symbols', *Contemporary Problems in Religion*, ed. H. A. Basilius (Detroit: Wayne University Press, 1956), pp. 35–55. Reprint in *Four Existentialist Theologians*, ed. Will Herberg (Garden City: Doubleday Anchor Boorks, No. 141, 1958), pp. 277–291.

'Existentialist Aspects of Modern Art', *Christianity and the Existentialists*, ed. Carl Michalson (New York: Scribner, 1956), pp. 128–147.

'Freedom in the Period of Transformation', *Freedom: Its Meaning*, ed Ruth N. Anshen (New York: Harcout, Brace, 1940), pp. 123–144.

'Gläubiger Realismus', *Theologenrundbrief für den Bund Deutscher Jugendvereine*, II (July–August 1927), pp. 3–13. *GW*, IV: 77-87.

'Honesty and Consecration', *Protestant Church Buildings and Equipment* (New York), XIII, No. 3 (September 1965), pp. 15–17.

'How much Truth is there in Karl Marx?' *The Christian Century*, LXV, No. 36 (September 1948), pp. 906–908.

'I'll always Remember. . . One Moment of Beauty', *Parade* (New York), 25.IX.1955, pp. 1–2.

'Kritisches und Positives Paradox. Eine Auseinandersetzung mit Karl Barth und Friedrich Gogarten', *Theologische Blätter* (Leipzig), II, No. 11 (November 1923), pp. 263–269. *GW*, VII: 216–225.

'Kult und Form', *Die Form* (Berlin), V, No. 23/24 (15 Dec., 1930), pp. 578–583.

'Marxism and Christian Socialism', *Christianity and Society* (New York), VII, No. 2 (1942), pp. 13–18.

'Marx and the Prophetic Tradition', *Radical Religion*, I, No. 4 (1935), pp. 21–29

'Marx's View of History', *Culture in History. Essays in Honor of Paul Radin*, ed. Stanley Daimond (New York: Columbia University Press, 1960), pp. 631–641.

'Natural and Revealed Religion', *Christendom*, I, No. 1 (Autumn 1935), pp. 159–170.

'Nietzsche and the Bourgeois Spirit', *Journal of the History of Ideas* (New York), VI, No. 3 (1945), pp. 307–309.

'Psychotherapy and a Christian Interpretation of Human Nature', *Review of Religion*, XIII, No. 3 (March 1949), pp. 264–268.

'Rechtfertigung und Zweifel', *Vorträge der theologischen Konferenz zu Gießen*, 39, (Gießen: Alfred Töpelmann, 1924), pp. 19–32.

'Rejoinder' to D. Moody Smith, *The Journal of Religion*, XLVI, No. 1, Part II (January 1966), pp. 191–194.

'Rejoinder' to R. P. Scharlemann, *The Journal of Religion*, XLVI, No. 1, Part II (January 1966), pp. 183–185.

'Relation of Metaphysics and Theology', *Review of Metaphysics*, X, No. 1 (September 1956), pp. 57–63.

'Religion and Culture', *Asian Cultural Studies* (International Christian University, Tokyo), No. 2 (1960), pp. 1–9.

'Religion and Secular Culture',*,The Journal of Religion*, XXVI, No. 2 (April 1946), pp. 78–86.

'Religion and the Visual Arts', Lecture given in Connecticut College (November 1955), pp. 2, 8–9 (mimeographed). Published as 'Existentialist Aspects of Modern Art', *Christianity and the Existentialists*, ed. Carl Michalson (New York: Scribner, 1956), pp. 128–147.

'Religionsphilosophie', *Lehrbuch der Philosophie*, ed. Max Dessoir, Bd. II: *Die Philosphie in Ihren Einzelgebieten* (Berlin: Ullstein, 1925), pp. 765–835. E. T., 'The Philosophy of Religion', *WR:27–121.*

'Religiöser Stil und religiöser Stoff in der bildenden Kunst', *Das neue Deutschland* (Gotha), IX, No. 9/12 (February–March, 1921), pp. 151–158.

'Religious Symbols and Our Knowledge of God', *Christian Scholar*, XXXVIII, No. 3 (September 1955), pp. 189–197. Reprinted as 'The Nature of Religious Language', *TC:* 53–67.

'Reply to Interpretation and Critism', *The Theology of Paul Tillich*, ed. C. W. Kegley and R. W. Bretall (New York: Macmillan, 1964), pp. 329–349.

'The Attack of Dialectical Materialism on Christianity', *The Student World* (Geneva) XXXI, No. 2 (1938), pp. 115–125.

'The Church and Communism', *Religion in Life*, VI, No. 3 (1937), pp. 347–357.

'The Meaning and Justification of Religious Symbols', *Religious Experience and Truth*, ed. S. Hook (New York: New York University Press, 1961), pp. 3–12.

'The Nature of Man', *Journal of Philosophy*, XLIII, No. 25 (December 1946), pp. 739–748.

'Theology and Architecture', *Architectural Forum*, CIII, No. 6 (December 1955), pp. 131–134. Reprinted as 'Theology, Architecture and Art', *Church Management*, XXXIII, No. 1 (October 1956), pp. 7, 55–56.

'The Problem of the Theological Method', *The Journal of Religion*, XXVII, No. 1 (January 1947), pp. 16–26.

'Theology and Symbolism', *Religious Symbolism*, ed. F. Ernest Johnson (New York: Harper, 1955), pp. 107–116.

'Theonomie', *Die Religion in Geschichte und Gegenwart*, ed. Hermann Gunkel *et al.*, (Tübingen: Mohr, 1931), pp. 1128–1129.

'The Present Theological Situation in the Light of the Continental European Development', *Theology Today*, VI, No. 3 (October 1949), pp. 299–310.

'The Relation of Religion and Health: Historical Consideration and Theoretical Questions', *Review of Religion*, X, No. 4 (May 1946), pp. 348–384.

'The Word of God', *Language: An Enquiry into its Meaning and Function*, ed. Ruth N. Anshen (New York: Harper, 1957), pp. 122–133.

'Über die Idee einer Theologie der Kultur', *Philosophische Vorträge der Kant-Gesellschaft*, No. 24 (Berlin: Reuther und Reichard, 1919), pp. 28–51. *GW,* IX: 13–31. E. T., 'On the Idea of a Theology of Culture', *WR:* 155–181.

'Über gläubigen Realismus', *Religiöse Verwirklichung* (Berlin: Furche, 1929), pp. 65–87. *GW,* IV: 88–106. Revised E. T., 'Realism and Faith', *PE: 66–82.*

What is wrong with "Dialectic" Theology?', *The Journal of Religion*, XV, No. 2 (April 1935), pp. 127–145.

'Zur Theologie der bildenden Kunst und der Architektur', *Kunst und Kirche*, Jg. 24 (1961), pp. 99–103.

III. SECONDARY BOOKS

Adams, J. L.: *Paul Tillich's Philosophy of Culture, Science, and Religion* (New York: Harper & Row, 1965).

Arnheim, R.: *Art and Visual Perception* (London: Faber & Faber, 1956).

Austin, J. L.: *How to do Things with Words* (Oxford: The Clarendon Press, 1962).

—: *Philosophical Papers* (Oxford: The Clarendon Press, 1961).

Barth, K.: *The Doctrine of the Word of God*, trans. G. T. Thomson (Edinburgh: T. & T. Clark, 1949).

Bell, C.: *Art* (London: Chatto and Windus, 1947).

Bonhoeffer, D.: *Act and Being*, trans. Bernard Noble (London: Collins, 1962).

Bosanquet, B.: *A History of Aesthetic* (London: George Allen and Unwin, 1922).

Brown, J.: *Subject and Object in Modern Theology* (London: S. C. M. Press, 1955).

Clayton, J. P.: *The Concept of Correlation: Paul Tillich and the Possibility of a Mediating Theology* (Berlin: de Gruyter, 1979).

Delekat, F.: *Immanuel Kant* (Heidelberg: Quelle & Meyer, 1966)

Dube, W.-D.: *The Expressionists* (London: Thames & Hudson, 1972).

Ebeling, G.: *Theology and Proclamation: A Discussion with Rudolf Bultmann*, trans. John Riches (London: Collins, 1966).

Edschmid, K.: *Frühe Manifeste; Epochen des Expressionismus* (Hamburg: C. Wegner, 1957).

Eliot, T. S.: *Selected Essays* (New York: Harcourt, Brace, 1950).

Fechter, P.: *Expressionismus* (München: R. Piper, 1914).

Fleming, W.: *Art and Ideas* (New York: Holt, Rinehart & Winston, 1970).

Gilot, F. (with Carlton Lake): *Life with Picasso* (London: Penguin Books, 1965).

Gombrich, E. H.: *Art and Illusion* (London: Phaidon Press, 1960).

—: *Meditations of a Hobby Horse* (London: Phaidon Press, 1963).

Greene, T. M.: *The Arts and the Art of Criticism* (Princeton: Princeton University Press, 1947).

Hamilton, K.: *The System and the Gospel* (London: S. C. M. Press, 1963).

Hartlaub, G. F.: *Kunst und Religion. Ein Versuch über die Möglichkeit neuer religiöser Kunst* (Leipzig, Wolff, 1919).

Hegel, G. W. F.: *Hegels theologische Jugendschriften*, ed. Herman Nohl (Tübingen: J. C. B. Mohr, 1907). E. T., *On Christianity: Early Theological Writings*, trans. T. M. Knox, with an introduction, and fragments translated by Richard Kroner (Gloucester, Mass.: Peter Smith, 1970).

—: 'Vorlesungen über die Ästhetik', *Werke* (Berlin: Duncker & Humblot, 1843), X.

Hick, J.: *Philosophy of Religion* (Englewood Cliffs, N. J.: Prentice-Hall, 1963).

Hospers, J.: *Meaning and Truth in Arts* (Chapel Hill, University of North Carolina Press, 1970).

Johnson, R. C.: *Authority in Protestant Theology* (Philadelphia: The Westminster Press, 1959).

Kähler, M.: *Der sogenannte historische Jesus und der geschichtliche biblische Christus* (Leipzig: A. Deichert, 1892). E. T., *The So-called Historical Jesus and the Historic, Biblical Christ*, trans. and ed. C. E. Braaten, with an Introduction by Paul Tillich (Philadelphia: The Fortress Press, 1964).

Kandinsky, W.: *Über das Geistige in der Kunst* (München: R. Piper, 1912).

Kant, I.: *Gesammelte Schriften*, Bd. IV (Berlin: Georg Reimer, 1903). E. T., T. K. Abbott, *Kant's Critique of Practical Reason and Other Works on the Theory of Ethics* (London: 1909).

Keefe, D. J.: *Thomism and the Ontological Theology of Paul Tillich* (Leiden: E. J. Brill, 1971).

Kelsey, D.: *The Fabric of Paul Tillich's Theology* (New Haven and London: Yale University Press, 1967).

Kierkegaard, S.: *Concluding Unscientific Postscript*, trans. D. Swenson (Princeton: Princeton University Press, 1944).

Killen, R. A.: *The Ontological Theology of Paul Tillich* (Kampen, Netherlands: J. H. Kok, 1956).

Kraemer, H.: *Religion and the Christian Faith* (London: Lutterworth Press, 1956).

Langer, S.: *Feeling and Form* (London: Routledge & Kegan Paul, 1953).

Lankheit, K. (ed.): *Der Blaue Reiter* (München: R. Piper, 1912; Dokumentarische Neuausgabe von K. Lankheit, 1965).

—: *Der Turm der blauen Pferde* (Stuttgart: Philipp Reclam jun., 1961).

Lewis, B. I.: *George Grosz: Art and Politics in the Weimar Republic* (Madison: The University of Wisconsin Press, 1971).

Lukács, G.: *The Young Hegel* (London: Merlin Press, 1975).

Lynton, N.: *Concepts of Modern Art* (London: Penguin Books, 1974).

Marc, F.: *Briefe aus dem Feld* (Berlin: Helmut Rauschenbusch Verlag, 1948).

Marcel, G.: *The Philosophy of Existence* (Chicago: Henry Regnery, 1952).

Marx, K.: *Der Historische Materialismus*, ed. Alfred Kroner (Leipzig, 1932)

McKelway, A. J.: *The Systematic Theology of Paul Tillich* (London: Lutterworth Press, 1964).

Myers, B. S.: *Expressionism: A Generation in Revolt* (London: Thames & Hudson, 1963).

O'Malley, J. B.: *The Fellowship of Being* (The Hague: Martinus Nijhoff, 1966).
Pauck, W. and M.: *Paul Tillich: His Life and Thought* (London: Collins, 1977).
Ramsey, I. T.: *Models and Mystery* (London: Oxford University Press, 1964).
Richards, I. A.: *Principles of Literary Criticism* (New York: Harcourt, Brace, 1950).
— (with C. K. Ogden): *The Meaning of Meaning* (London: Kegan Paul, 1936).
Rowe, W. L.: *Religious Symbols and God* (Chicago and London: The University of Chicago Press, 1968).
Schardt, A. J.: *Franc Marc* (Berlin: Rembrandt Verlag, 1936).
Schiller, F. von: *Sämtliche Werke*, XII (Säkular Edition, Stuttgart and Berlin: Cotta, 1905).
Schmitz, J.: *Die apologetische Theologie Paul Tillichs* (Mainz: Matthias-Grünewald-Verlag, 1966).
Selz, P.: *German Expressionist Painting* (Berkeley and Los Angeles: University of California Press, 1957).
Smart, A.: *The Assisi Problem and the Art of Giotto* (Oxford: Clarendon Press, 1971).
Stevenson, C. L.: *Ethics and Language* (Yale: Yale University Press, 1943).
Sydow, M. von: *Die deutsche expressionistische Kultur und Malerei* (Berlin: Furche-Verlag, 1920).
Tate, A.: *Reason in Madness* (New York: Putnams, 1941).
Tavard, G. H.: *Paul Tillich and the Christian Message* (New York: Scharles Scribner's Sons, 1962).
Thomas, J. H.: *Paul Tillich: An Appraisal* (London: S. C. M. Press, 1963).
Tillich, H.: *From Time to Time* (New York: Stein & Day, 1973).
Troeltsch, E.: *Der Historismus und seine Überwindung* (Berlin: Rolf Heise, 1924).
E. T., *Christian Thought: Its History and Application* (London: University of London Press, 1923).
Walden, H.: *Einblick in Kunst – Expressionismus, Futurismus, Kubismus* (Berlin: Verlag Der Sturm, 1924).
—: *Expressionismus: Die Kunstwende* (Berlin: Verlag Der Sturm, 1918).
Worringer, W.: *Abstraktion und Einfühlung. Ein Beitrag zur Stilpsychologie* (München: R. Piper, 1907).
Zuurdeeg, W. F.: *An Analytical Philosophy of Religion* (London: George Allen & Unwin, 1959).

IV. SECONDARY ARTICLES

Adams, J. L.: 'What Kind of Religion has a Place in Higher Education?', *Journal of Bible and Religion*, XII (1945), pp. 185–192.
Aldwinckle, R. F.: 'Tillich's Theory of Religious Symbolism', *Canadian Journal of Theology*, X, No. 2 (April 1964), pp. 110–117.

Alston, W. P.: 'Tillich's Conception of a Relegious Symbol', *Religious Experience and Truth*, ed. S. Hook (New York: New York University Press, 1961), pp. 12–26.

Arnheim, R.: 'Experimentell-psychologische Untersuchungen zum Ausdrucks-problem', *Psychol. Forsch.*, (1928), II, pp. 2–132.

—: 'The Gestalt Theory of Expression', *Psychological Review*, LVI, No. 3 (May 1949), pp. 156–171.

Ayers, R. H.: '"Myth" in Theological Discourse: A Profusion of Confusion', *Anglican Theological Review*, XLVIII, No. 2 (April 1966), pp. 200–211.

Barth, K.: 'Ein Briefwechsel mit Adolf von Harnack', *Theologische Fragen und Antworten* (Zollikon/Zürich: Evangelischer Verlag, 1957), pp. 7–31.

—: 'Mozart', *Religion and Culture: Essays in Honour of Paul Tillich*, ed. Walter Leibrecht (New York: Harper, 1959), pp. 61–78.

Bohning, E.: 'Goethe's and Schiller's Interpretation of Beauty', *The German Quaterly*, XXII, No. 4 (November 1949), pp. 185–194.

Clarke, B. L.: 'God and the Symbolic in Tillich', *Anglican Theological Review*, XLVIII, No. 3 (July 1961), pp. 302–311.

Clayton, J. P.: 'Is Jesus Necessary for Christology? An Antimony in Tillich's Theological Method', *Christ, Faith and History*, ed. S. W. Sykes and J. P. Clayton (Cambridge: Cambridge University Press), pp. 147–163.

Cross, W. O.: 'Some Notes on the Ontology of Paul Tillich', *Anglican Theological Review*, XIV, No. 4 (October 1957), pp. 297–310.

Donnell, C. A.: 'The Problem of Representation and Expressionism in Post-Impresionist Art', *British Journal of Aesthetics*, XV, No. 3 (Summer 1975), pp. 226–238.

Dowey, E. A.: 'Tillich, Barth, and the Criteria of Theology', *Theology Today*, XV, No. 1 (April 1958), pp. 48–58.

Dulles, A. R.: 'Paul Tillich and the Bible', *Paul Tillich in Catholic Thought*, ed. T. A. O'Meara and C. D. Weisser (London: Darton, Longman and Todd, 1965), pp. 109–132.

Fenton, J. Y.: 'Being-itself and Religious Symbolism', *The Journal of Religion*, XLV, No. 2 (April 1965), pp. 75–86.

Ferré, N. F. S.: 'The Fabric of Paul Tillich's Theology', *Scottish Jorunal of Theology*, XXI, No. 2 (June 1968), pp. 157–169.

Ford, L. S.: 'The Three Strands of Tillich's Theory of Religious Symbols', *The Journal of Religion*, XLVI, No. 1 (January 1966), pp. 104–130.

—: 'Tillich's Implicit Natural Theology', *Scottish Journal of Theology*, XXIV, No. 3 (August 1971), pp. 257–270.

—: 'Tillich's One Nonsymbolic Statement: *A Propos* of a Recent Study by Rowe', *Journal of the American Academy of Religion*, XXXVIII, No. 2 (June 1970), pp. 176–182.

Forster, K.: 'Paul Tillich and St. Thomas', *Paul Tillich in Catholic Thought*, ed. T. A. O'Meara and C. D. Weisser (London: Darton, Longman and Todd, 1965), pp. 97–105.

Hammond, G. B.: 'An Examination of Tillich's Method of Correlation', *Journal of Bible and Religion*, XXXII, No. 3 (July 1964), pp. 248–251.

Hartshorne, C.: 'Tillich's Doctrine of God', *The Theology of Paul Tillich*, ed. C. W. Kegley and R. W. Bretall (New York: Macmillan, 1964), pp. 164–195.

Hick, J. H.: 'Article Review' of Tillich's *Systematic Theology*, Vols. I and II, *Scottish Journal of Theology*, XII, No. 3 (September 1959), pp. 286–297.

—: 'The Idea of Necessary Being', *The Princeton Seminary Bulletin*, LIV, No. 2 (November 1960), pp. 11–21.

Holmer, P. L.: 'Paul Tillich and the Language about God', *Journal of Religious Thought*, XXII, No. 1 (January 1965–1966), pp. 35–50.

—: 'Paul Tillich: Language and Meaning', *Journal of Religious Thought*, XXII, No. 2 (April 1965–1966), pp. 85–106.

Hook, S.: 'The Atheism of Paul Tillich', *Religious Experience and Truth*, ed. S. Hook (New York: New York University Press, 1961), pp. 59–64.

Johnson, R. C.: 'A Theologian of Synthesis', *Theology Today*, XV (April 1958), pp. 36–42.

Loomer, B. M.: 'Tillich's Theology of Correlation', *The Jorunal of Religion*, XXXVI, No. 3 (July 1956), pp. 150–156.

McCollough, T. E.: 'The Ontology of Tillich and Biblical Personalism', *Scottish Journal of Theology*, XV, No. 3 (September 1962), pp. 266–281.

McDonald, H. D.: 'The Symbolic Theology of Paul Tillich', *Scottish Journal of Theology*, XVII, No. 4 (December 1964), pp. 414–430.

Mollegen, A. T.: 'Christology and Biblical Critism in Tillich', *The Theology of Paul Tillich*, ed. C. W. Kegley and R. W. Bretall (New York: Macmillan, 1964) pp. 230–245.

Niebuhr, R.: 'Biblical Thought and Ontological Speculation in Tillich's Theology', *The Theology of Paul Tillich*, ed. C. W. Kegley and R. W. Bretall (New York: Macmillan, 1964), pp. 216–227.

O'Connor, E.: 'Paul Tillich: An Impression', *Paul Tillich in Catholic Thought*, ed. T. A. O'Meara and C. D. Weisser (London: Darton, Longman and Todd, 1965), pp. 25–41.

Palmer, M. F.: 'A Reply to Some Interpretations of Tillich's Christology', *The Heythrop Journal*, XVII, No. 2 (April 1976), pp. 169–177.

—: 'Can the Historian Invalidate Gospel Statements? Some Notes on Dialectical Theology', *The Downside Review*, XVII, No. 2 (January 1977), pp. 11–18.

—: 'Hartshorne's Critique of Tillich's Theory of Religious Symbolism', *The Heythrop Journal*, XVII, No. 4 (October 1976), pp. 379–394.

—: 'Paul Tillich's Critique of Bultmann's Christology', *The Heythrop Journal*, XX, No. 3 (July 1979), pp. 279–289.

—: 'The Certainty of Faith and Tillich's Concept of the *Analogia Imaginis*',
Scottish Journal of Theology, XXV, No. 3 (August 1972), pp. 279–295.

Peters, E. H.: 'Tillich's Doctrine of Essence, Existence, and the Christ', *The Journal
of Religion*, XLIII, No. 4 (October 1963), pp. 298–299.

Putnam, L. J.: 'Tillich, Revelation, and Miracle', *Theology and Life*, IX, Winter
1966), pp. 363–368.

Richards, I. A.: 'Science and Poetry', *A Modern Book of Esthetics*, ed. Rader (London:
Kegan Paul, 1926), pp. 270–285.

Rome, S. and B.: 'Interrogation of Paul Tillich', *Philosophical Interrogations*, (New
York: Holt, Rinehart and Winston, 1964), pp. 357–409.

Rosenthal, K.: 'Myth and Symbol' *Scotish Journal of Theology* XVIII, No. 4
(December 1965) pp. 411–434.

Scharlemann, R. P.: 'Tillich's Method of Correlation: Two Proposed Revisions',
The Journal of Religion, XLVI, No. 1, Part II (January 1966), pp. 92–103.

Schmalenbach, F.: 'The Term *Neue Sachlichkeit*', *Art Bulletin*, XXII, No 3, pp.
161–165.

Sclafani, R. J.: '"Art", Wittgenstein, and Open-Textured Concepts', *Journal of
Aesthetics and Criticism*, XXIX, No. 3 (Spring 1971), pp. 333–341.

Siegwalt, G.: 'La théologie systématique de P. Tillich', *Revue d'Histoire et de Philosophie Religieuse*, XLI (1961), pp. 173–192.

Simpson: M.: 'Paul Tillich: Symbolism and Objectivity', *The Heythrop Journal*,
VIII, No. 3 (July 1967), pp. 293–309.

Taubes, J.: 'On the Nature of the Theological Method: Some Reflections on the
Methodological Principles of Tillich's Theology', *The Journal of Religion*,
XXXIV, No. 1 (January 1954), pp. 12–25.

Thomas, J. H.: 'Some Comments on Tillich's Doctrine of Creation', *Scottish Journal
of Theology*, XIV, No. 2 (June 1961), pp. 113–118,

—: 'The Correlation of Philosophy and Theology in Tillich's System', *London
Quaterly and Holborn Review*, Sixth Series, XXVIII, No. 1 (January 1959), pp.
47–54.

—: 'The Problem of defining a Theology of Culture, with reference to the Theology of Paul Tillich', *Creation, Christ & Culture*, ed. R. W. McKinney (Edinburgh: T. & T. Clark, 1976), pp. 272–287.

—: 'Tillich on Philosophy and Theology', *Union Seminary Quaterly Review*, VIII,
No. 3 (March 1953), pp. 10–16.

Ulrich, J.: 'Goethes Einfluß auf die Entwicklung des Schillerschen Schönheitsbegriffes', *Jahrbuch der Goethe-Gesellschaft* (Weimar: Verlag der Goethe-Gesellschaft, 1934), pp. 165–212.

Urban, W. M.: 'Tillich's Theory of the Religious Symbol', *Journal of Liberal
Religion*, II, No. 2 (Summer 1940), pp. 34–36.

Veatch, H.: 'Tillich's Distinction between Metaphysics and Theology', *Review of
Metaphysics*, X, No 3 (March 1957), pp. 529–533.

Waismann, F.: 'The Resources of Language', *The Importance of Language*, ed. M. Black (Englewood Cliffs, N. J.: Prentice Hall, 1962), pp. 107–120.

—: Verifiability', *The Theory of Meaning*, ed. G. H. R. Parkinson: (Oxford: Oxford University Press, 1968), pp. 35–60.

Weigel, G.: 'Contemporaneous Protestantism and Paul Tillich', *Theological Studies*, XI, No. 2 (June 1950), pp. 177–202.

—: 'Recent Protestant Theology', *Theological Studies* (1953), pp. 573–585.

ABBREVIATIONS FOR THE WORKS
OF PAUL TILLICH

CTB   *The Courage To Be* (London: Collins, 1962)

DF   *Dynamics of Faith* (New York: Harper & Row, 1958)

GW   *Gesammelte Werke,* ed. Renate Albrecht (Stuttgart: Evangelisches Verlagswerk)

IH   *The Interpretation of History,* trans. N. Rasetzki and E. Talmey (New York: Charles Scribner's Sons, 1936)

OB   *On the Boundary,* with an Introduction by J. Heywood Thomas (London: Collins, 1967). This is a revision, newly translated of Part I of *IH*

PE   *The Protestant Era,* trans. J. Luther Adams (abridged ed.; Chicago: University of Chicago Press, 1957)

RS   *The Religious Situation,* trans. H. Richard Niebuhr (Cleveland and New York: Meridian Books, 1967)

ST   *Systematic Theology* (London: James Nisbet. Vol. I, 1953; Vol. II, 1957; Vol. III, 1964)

WR   *What is Religion?* trans. and ed. J. Luther Adams (New York, Evanson, and London: Harper & Row, 1969)

CHAPTER ONE
EXPRESSIONISM AND THE
CATEGORY OF EXPRESSIVENESS
I. RELIGIOUS ART AND EXPRESSIONISM

In his short autobiographical sketch *On the Boundary* Paul Tillich
writes:

> Art is the highest form of play and the genuinely creative realm of
> the imagination. Though I have not produced anything in the field of
> the creative arts, my love for the arts has been of great importance to my
> theological and philosophical work.[1]

In tracing the development of this love, Tillich tells us that his father,
a superintendent of the Prussian Territorial Church, although caring
little for architecture and the visual arts, was a keen musician and even
composed a little, thereby maintaining 'the musical traditions associated
with the evangelical ministry'.[2] Tillich's interests were to be otherwise.

---

[1] *OB:* 26. The notion of art as play, with which Tillich begins, is a recurrent
theme in German aesthetics and probably stems from Schiller's use of the
term 'play-drive' *(Spieltrieb)* to characterize the artist's voluntary acceptance of rules. A man is 'nur da ganz Mensch, wo er spielt'. *Sämtliche Werke*
(Säkular Edition, Stuttgart & Berlin: Cotta, 1905) XII, p. 59. Bernard
Bosanquet, in his *A History of Aesthetic* (London: George Allen & Unwin,
1922), suggests that Schiller was here dependent on Kant *(Ibid.,* pp. 294—
295), although another possible influence is Goethe. Cf. J. Ulrich, 'Goethes
Einfluß auf die Entwicklung des Schillerschen Schönheitsbegriffes', *Jahrbuch
der Goethe-Gesellschaft* (Weimar: Verlag der Goethe-Gesellschaft, 1934) XX,
pp. 165—212; and Elizabeth Bohning, 'Goethe's and Schiller's Interpretation
of Beauty', *The German Quarterly*, XXII, No. 4 (November 1949)
pp. 185—194. Interestingly, the idea of art as play is central also to Karl
Barth's famous essay on 'Mozart' in *Religion and Culture: Essays in
Honour of Paul Tillich* (New York: Harper, 1959).

[2] *OB:* 26.

For not only was he unmusical—and appears to have remained so until late in life—but at an early age developed a 'passion' for architecture, one which expressed itself later in 'the admiration of and pilgrimage to great architecture, and in the feeling of inner fulfilment in places where good architecture surrounded me'.[3] There are, he suggests, environmental reasons for this. Until his fourteenth year, Tillich lived in the parish house of Schönfliess, a small town in eastern Brandenburg, medieval in character and built around an old Gothic church. The close proximity of the house to the church not only had, it appears, an influence on Tillich's decision to become a theologian but also accounts for his even earlier ambition to become an architect.

> In my early life I wished to become an architect and only in my late
> teens the other desire, to become a philosophical theologian, was vic-
> torious. I decided to build in concepts and propositions instead of stone,
> iron and glass. But building remains my passion, in clay and in thought
> and as the relation of the medieval cathedrals to the scholastic systems
> shows, the two ways of building are not so far from each other. Both
> express an attitude to the meaning of life as a whole.[4]

During this same period, Tillich's 'longing for art' turned also to literature, in particular to the classic Schlegel translations of Shake-speare. Here begins his life-long infatuation with *Hamlet*, a play which he later called 'this most precious work of secular literature viewed existentially'[5], and which explains in part his 'instinctive sympathy today for what is called existentialism'.[6] Neither Goethe nor Dostoevsky had a similar impact, the former expressing 'too little of the boundary situation ... it did not then seem to be existential enough'.[7] Later Tillich was to revise this opinion of Goethe, and included him among those other poets—George, Hofmannsthal, Rilke and Werfel—who had moved him deeply and contributed to his own theological development. This interest in poetry, he admits, was largely due to the influence of

---

[3] 'Honesty and Consecration', *Protestant Church Buildings and Equipment* (New York) XIII, No. 3 (September 1965) p. 15.

[4] *Ibid.*

[5] Quoted by James Luther Adams, *Paul Tillich's Philosophy of Culture, Science and Religion* (New York: Harper & Row, 1965) p. 66.

[6] *OB*: 27. Other references to Hamlet are in *CTB*: 46, 66, and *ST*, 3; 345.

[7] *Ibid.*

his wife, Hannah, who herself wrote verses.[8] Tillich concludes, however, that literature 'contains too much philosophy to be able to satisfy fully the desire for pure artistic contemplation'.[9]

And yet, despite Tillich's evident love of architecture and literature, it is clear from his autobiographical account that it is to *painting* that we must turn for the decisive influence on his aesthetics. Again, he provides us with an explanation of why this should be so, suggesting that the reason lies in the circumstances surrounding his discovery of the pictorial arts. For Tillich's appreciation of painting began in the trenches during the First World War and thus belongs to the most shattering and formative period of his life. During his four years of military service as an army chaplain, Tillich survived the offensives at Verdun, Amiens and Aisne-Marne, received the Iron Cross, sustained two nervous breakdowns, and emerged with a consciousness of suffering and death from which, so his biographers record, he never fully recovered.[10] Throughout this time painting provided him with his principal means of relaxation and escape, an inevitable reaction, he tells us, 'to the horror, ugliness and destructiveness of war. My delight even in the poor reproductions obtainable at the military bookstores developed into a systematic study of the history of art. And out of this study came the experience of art...'[11] Then, during his last furlough of the war, Tillich visited the Kaiser Friedrich Museum in Berlin. There he saw Botticelli's 'Madonna with Singing Angels', the picture hanging alone on a wall opposite the entrance. The setting itself was dramatic and the painting's impact on him enormous: ever afterwards Tillich was to speak of it as a moment of 'revelation', as an experience in which he had been grasped not only by the beauty and power of visual art but by the reality of the absolute. Over forty years later he referred to this event as follows:—

> Ich stand vor einem der runden Madonnenbilder von Botticelli. Und in einem Moment, für den ich keinen anderen Namen als den der Inspiration weiß, eröffnete sich mir der Sinn dessen, was ein Gemälde offenbaren kann. Es kann eine neue Dimension des Seins erschließen, aber nur dann,

---

[8] *Ibid.*, p. 30. Many of her poems are included in her biography of her husband, *From Time to Time* (New York: Stein and Day, 1973).

[9] *Ibid.*, p. 27.

[10] Wilhelm and Marion Pauck, *Paul Tillich: His Life and Thought* (London: Collins, 1977) p. 51.

[11] *OB: 27—28.*

wenn es gleichzeitig der Kraft hat, die korrespondierende Schicht der Seele zu öffnen. Es war naturgemäß für einen Theologen, die Frage zu stellen: Wie verhält sich diese Inspiration zu dem, was in der theologischen Sprache Inspiration genannt wird? Wie verhält sich die ästhetische zu der religiösen Funktion des menschlichen Geistes? Wie verhalten sich die künstlerischen Symbole — und alle künstlerischen Schöpfungen sind Symbole (so naturalistisch ihr Stil auch sein mag) — zu den Symbolen, in denen Religion sich ausdrückt?[12]

This account introduces us, without further ado, to some of the central questions with which Tillich's aesthetic is concerned. How is religious art to be distinguished from other styles? What, for example, is the relation between artistic inspiration and religious inspiration, or between the symbolic language of art and the symbolic language of theology? Now what is surprising here is not that Tillich asks these questions—as he says, they are the proper questions for a theologian to ask—but that it should have been a Botticelli that provoked this response, given that Botticelli belongs to that style of Renaissance art usually abhorred by Tillich. Here, admittedly, we have a picture that one would normally call religious because of the scene it depicts: a doleful Madonna holds the Christ-child, she is surrounded by eight handsome angels carrying flowers, a divine crown hovers above her. And yet it is precisely this type of painting, despite its evident beauty and theme, that is repeatedly condemned as a 'non-religious style dealing with religious contents', as the kind of thing suitable only for church magazines and the offices of ministers, and which is, moreover, 'dangerously irreligious... something against which everybody who understands the situation of our time has to fight'.[13]

---

[12] 'Zur Theologie der bildenden Kunst und der Architektur', *Kunst und Kirche*, Jg. 24 (1961) pp. 99—103. *GW*, IX: 345. Also published in *Auf der Grenze* (Stuttgart: EVW, 1962). The Botticelli is more generally known as the *Raczinski tondo*. It was painted circa 1477, is of tempera on a poplar panel, measures 135 cm. in diameter, and is presently No. 102 A in the Staatliche Museum Gemäldegalerie in Berlin. Tillich refers to it again in 'I'll always Remember... One Moment of Beauty', *Parade* (New York), 25. ix. 1955, p. 2, and in *OB*: 28.

[13] 'Religion and the Visual Arts.' Lecture given in Connecticut College, November 1955, pp. 2, 8—9 (mimeographed). Published as 'Existentialist Aspects of Modern Art' in *Christianity and the Existentialists*, ed. Carl Michalson (New York: Scribner, 1956) pp. 128—147.

The point of Tillich's attack lies in the last of these quotations, with the phrase 'the situation of our time'. The types of religious art we normally associate with special religious symbols—like portraits of the Christ or of the Holy Virgin and Child, and which we find in the canvases of a Raphael or Rubens—are not religious because their contents are recognizably religious. For religion, as we shall see, deals primarily with a specific dimension of *reality*, with an area of life of actual validity, whereas these pictures present us with *idealizations* of human and natural forms, with a degree of balance, harmonization and proportion that is entirely at odds both with modern man's understanding of himself, and, more importantly, with any understanding of the world as it really is. Hence Tillich's general condemnation of the so-called religious art of the Renaissance:—

> In der Renaissance, die christlicher Humanismus ist, ist die Form idealer Vollkommenheit zugleich Antizipation jenseitiger Erfüllung. Die Schönheit der Renaissance-Bilder nimmt — oft auch thematisch angedeutet — das wiedergewonnene Paradies vorweg. Idealismus ist antizipierte Eschatologie. Er ist Vorwegnehmen dessen, was nur als Gegenstand der Erwartung möglich ist.
>
> Auf dieser Basis sind zahllose religiöse Bilder entstanden. Aber sind die Madonnen und Kreuzigungen und Auferstehungen und biblischen Geschichten der Renaissance-Maler wirkliche Schöpfungen religiöser Kunst? Sie sind es nicht! Sie sind Visionen menschlicher Vollendung...'[14]

This goes some way towards explaining what Tillich means by a religious picture. Clearly, on the evidence of the preceding quotation, a painting is not religious because its subject is; because, let us say, it depicts the temptations of a saint, the crucifixion of Christ, or the Madonna with the infant Jesus. To put the matter another way, we may have a picture that is religious even though it deals with no overtly religious theme. What does, however, appear to be a minimal requirement is that religious art must in some sense be 'realistic', that is, attuned to the 'situation of our time'. What, then, we may ask, is the character of this situation to which a picture must correspond if it is to be deemed religious?

Tillich gives a partial answer to this question in one of his surveys of art. The article opens with the almost obligatory condemnation of high Renaissance portraiture, part of which I have already quoted.[15]

---

[14] 'Zur Theologie der bildenden Kunst und der Architektur', *GW*, IX: 349.
[15] 'Religion and the Visual Arts', p. 2.

Then follows a fairly succinct interpretation of various styles, including accounts of artists like Jan Steen, Cézanne, Van Gogh, Munch, Picasso, Braque, Chagall, Chirico and Sutherland, Nolde and Rouault. This survey suggests that a picture is called religious when it attempts, however partially, to understand the nature of the human predicament, or rather when it seeks, however tentatively, to reveal the basic structures of reality without recourse to any beautifying process. And the picture that emerges is a dismal one. A 'Still Life' by Cézanne indicates the disappearance of idealism and the consciousness of the 'disrupted forms of our existence'; Van Gogh's 'Night Cafe' portrays 'in beautiful colours ... the horror of emptiness'; Munch paints pictures of 'horror, a shock of that which is uncanny'; and Picasso's 'Guernica' is an 'immediate horror', while Braque's 'Table' reveals the 'dissolution of the organic realities...'.[16]

After such remarks one it tempted to conclude that a picture is religious the more unpleasant it gets; and that, irrespective of its theme or lack of one, it will be considered religious if, like the Picasso, it acknowledges 'the human situation in its depth of estrangement and despair'.[17] Here, indeed, we have a quite specific definition of the 'situation of our time', one which, by its very choice of words, reveals an indebtedness to the familiar categories of modern existentialism. And it is these categories which, at this initial stage at least, provide Tillich with the means of judging whether a certain style is religious. For to say that a picture incorporates elements like despair or estrangement, doubt or meaninglessness, is to say also that this picture achieves a definite and recognizable contemporaneity with our situation: not because it reflects a fashionable development in modern philosophy, but because, like this philosophy, it speaks to us about conditions and feelings which we ourselves recognize as accurate descriptions of our own experience. It is in this sense that the realism and the religious character of a work of art are linked. Inasmuch as the artist has had the power and insight to portray the nature of the human predicament, he has fulfilled the first and minimal requirement for a religious picture.

We have in former centuries painters who did very similar things. We have it in the mannerist period, after Michelangelo. We have it in some of the Baroque pictures. We have it in people like Goya. We have

16 *Ibid.*, pp. 4—6.
17 *Ibid.*, p. 5.

it in those great demonic pictures by Breughel and Bosch where elements of the psychological as well as the natural reality are brought into the picture without a naturalistic connection with each other, without a system of categories into which they are put. This is the decisive element in all existentialism. The essential categories of time, space, causality, substance, have lost their ultimate power. They give no meaning to our world ... Mankind does not feel at home in this world anymore. The categories have lost their embracing and overwhelming and asserting power. There is no safety in the world ... Things are displaced. Displaced persons are a symbol of our time, and displaced souls are the reality in all countries. This large scale displacement of our existence is expressed in these pictures.[18]

The extent to which Tillich's aesthetics requires and incorporates an existentialist doctrine of man will be analysed in the next chapter. For the moment, however, three features of his discussion so far are of more immediate interest. The first can be dealt with briefly and refers again to the Botticelli. It can be assumed, hopefully without too much psychological juggling, that Tillich's reaction to the portrait of the Madonna and Child was occasioned largely by the *contrast* it presented to Tillich's own recent war experiences; that, in other words, the shock produced by this picture was caused more by its *denial* of the less harmonious, less integrated, more disruptive and dislocated aspects of reality, than by its recognition of them. And yet, for all that, the Botticelli is still called a 'revelation'. Now if this is not to be taken as a straightforward contradiction of the former demand for realism in religious art, then it remains for Tillich to show how such an equation can be made, given this previous requirement. To the list of questions asked by Tillich in relation to the Botticelli, we may therefore add the following: How can such a portrait be considered a medium of revelation, if it has a distinctly religious theme but belongs to a style of art generally condemned as irreligious? Or conversely: Is there any class of picture (or school of painting) that can never in any sense be considered religious? These questions represent major problems in Tillich's philosophy of art, to which we shall return.

The second feature of Tillich's argument that I wish to mention has to do with his selection of those painters generally considered more religious than other. If my understanding of Tillich's reaction to the

---

[18] *Ibid.*, pp. 7—8.

Botticelli is correct—if, that is, we should view it in terms of the conflict between a reality experienced and a reality idealized—then it becomes much less difficult to see why he should have turned to artists like Munch and Van Gogh as truly religious painters, and why he should have deprecated the sentimentalism of a Guido Reni or Hoffmann. For art is religious not because it reflects a particular disposition on the part of the artist, nor because it provides us with the nearest approximation to a 'photographic' account of external or objective phenomena, but because it presents an image of reality which probes *beneath* the surface reality, because it reveals to us the structure of the disrupted society and speaks to us, albeit pictorially, of notions like guilt and loneliness, ugliness and death, as well as of beauty and courage. It is on this basis that Tillich claims that it is 'not an exaggeration to ascribe more of the quality of sacredness to a still-life by Cézanne or a tree by Van Gogh than to a picture of Jesus by Uhde'[19]—the point of this remark being that here, with these painters, we find a more profound account of nature and the human predicament. The general effect of such painting may certainly be dismal; but, remembering that Tillich's study of art began in the trenches, it is perhaps understandable that he should have accepted this image rather than any other. As indeed one might expect, Tillich's choice of painter and theme to describe the 'situation of our time' has a good deal to do with his own biography.

It is, however, the third and final feature of Tillich's discussion that is unquestionably the most important of the three. If his selection of the so-called religious artists depends on the kind of thematic similarities already mentioned, then it comes as no surprise to learn that many of these painters should have been associated, either directly or indirectly, with a particular artistic movement—in this case, with the movement commonly known as 'Expressionism'; and that Tillich's first acquaintance with expressionist art should come immediately after the war, the introduction being made by his childhood friend, the art historian Eckart von Sydow.[20] Thus Van Gogh and Cézanne, together with Gauguin, are invariably cited as the three great precursors of Expressionism, largely through their controlled deformation of natural forms and intense colouring to produce a powerfully communicative art; Braque and Picasso, although normally referred to as Cubists, were called

[19] *RS:* 89.

Expressionists in an exhibition held in Berlin in April 1911; Munch's hallucinatory imagery and his use of woodcuts prefigured a good deal of later German expressionistic work, while the scandal following the rejection of his pictures in the *Verein Bildender Künstler* ('Society of Fine Artists') in 1889 was a significant factor in the later formation of the Berlin Secession of Expressionists under the leadership of Max Liebermann; Emil Nolde, himself deeply influenced by Munch, is generally regarded as the most powerful representative of the Dresden group of Expressionists, known otherwise as *Die Brücke* (among them Ernst Ludwig Kirchner, Erich Heckel, Karl Schmidt-Rottluff and Fritz Bleyl), while Chagall, Rouault and Sutherland have also, though less obviously, been included in the membership. Even the other artists named by Tillich—Dürer, Bosch, Goya, Michelangelo—have been described as forerunners of Expressionism, marked as they are by 'expressionistic qualities and particularly by an apocalyptic anxiety that appeals strongly to our century'.[21]

In fact there is no doubt that, of all the various art forms open to Tillich throughout his life, it was Expressionism (especially in its German phase) that had the most profound and lasting impact on him, one which was never exceeded in intensity or duration by any other style of painting. Tillich himself is quite emphatic on this point[22], and the extent of his preference can be seen throughout his writings. All Tillich's surveys of art contain a favourable, almost laudatory account of Expressionism, the description itself often tailored to incorporate Tillich's own conclusions, so leaving us with the impression not only that we are here dealing with a gradation of types or heirarchy of artistic styles in which Expressionism is pre-eminent, but that the conclusion could not have been reached without a prior knowledge of expressionistic techniques. A good example of this can be seen if we turn to the book *Masse und Geist* (1922), which contains perhaps the most

---

[20] See Pauck, *op. cit.*, p. 75. Sydow's *Die deutsche expressionistische Kultur und Malerei* (Berlin: Furche-Verlag, 1920) is reviewed by Tillich in his important article 'Religiöser Stil und religiöser Stoff in der bildenden Kunst', *Das neue Deutschland*, Jg. 9 (1921) pp. 151—158. GW, IX: 312—323.

[21] Norbert Lynton, 'Expressionism', *Concepts of Modern Art* (London: Penguin Books, 1974) p. 34.

[22] *OB*: 28.

remarkable survey of all. In the section entitled 'Masse und Persönlichkeit' (written in 1920) Tillich analyses different types of mass movement
in modern society, the distinctive feature of this study being that it
makes almost no reference to political, economic or ideological factors,
but proceeds on the basis of the treatment of masses in the paintings of
various historical periods.[23]

The first period examined is the early Gothic painting of masses,
in which the crowd is completely dominated by the idea it represents,
whether it be the idea of a crowd of followers (as in a 'Carrying of the
Cross') or of a group of worshippers (as in a 'Birth of Christ'). Everything individual is suppressed: '*ein* Gesichtsausdruck, *eine* Kopfhaltung,
eine Körper- und Gewandlinie, *eine* Lichtstärke macht sie einander
gleich. Und keiner tritt ganz hervor'.[24] Three-dimensional space, which
accentuates the individuality of persons, is not used. Even the leader,
be it Christ or Pilate, the Madonna or a King, is given little individual
characterization, but is seen simply as the centre of gravity, the mediator
of the revelation or representative of the supernatural idea that pervades
the whole canvas. Here, in short, we may speak of the 'mystical
conception of the masses' *(der mystische Begriff der Masse).*[25]

All this changes in late Gothic or early Renaissance art. Pictures
like a 'Mocking', an 'Arrest' or a 'Peasants' Feast', plus the use of
three-dimensional space, signify the discovery of the individual and
the loss of the earlier 'communal feeling'. Even the Christ has become
one among many, often surrounded or even obscured by other figures.
The previous unity of the supernatural idea is lost in the nominalism of
the period, the particular is ascending the throne, and the old medieval
society is decomposing. This is the age of social revolution and the
Peasants' Revolt, in which the 'realistic mass' has replaced the mystical
mass *(Es ist die realistische Masse, die die mystische ablöst).*[26]

---

[23] *Masse und Geist; Studien zur Philosophie der Masse* (Berlin & Frankfurt:
Verlag der Arbeitsgemeinschaft, 1922). *GW*, II: 35—90. 'Masse und Persönlichkeit' appeared in *Die Verhandlungen des 27. und 28. Evangelisch-So-
zialen Kongresses.* Hrsg. W. Schneemelcher (Göttingen: Vandenhoeck und
Ruprecht, 1920) pp. 76—96.

[24] *GW*, II: 36.

[25] *Ibid.*, p. 37.

[26] *Ibid.*, p. 38.

Passing over Tillich's discussion of Baroque art—which is seen, as in the case of Rubens, to reflect the shift towards the inner personal convictions of faith and an urban, aristocratic society—we come finally to his analysis of modern art, here treated under the headings of Impressionism and Expressionism. Impressionism is 'die Stilform des individualistischen Bürgertums der zweiten Hälfte des 19. Jahrhunderts'. A 'Boulevard' by Monet, a 'Coffee House' by Degas, reveal the individual's subordination to the primacy of nature—but not of nature in its metaphysical meaning but rather in its surface appearance. Everything is a study in light, colour and movement; every object is but a vision of the moment: interesting, piquant, but still only a piece of the landscape. Form is all and has become the technique and rationale of the age. This determines the treatment of masses. They, like nature itself, are objects not subjects, and have become the focus of formal technology, of education and agitation. This, then, is the period of social reform and Marxism, or, as revealed in Impressionist painting, the epoch of the 'technological mass' *(die Masse als Objekt der Impression und der Technik).*[27]

And what of Expressionism? Before the end of the 19th century, Tillich continues, but primarily in the first decade of the 20th, a new spirit of revolt has begun to emerge, a reaction in the name of a deeper, less superficial meaning in life. It is, moreover, a movement not only initiated by the painter, but one which finds its supreme exposition in painting. The artist thus achieves a doubly prophetic status: he both announces and reveals the new depths of meaning in the world. This is Expressionism. It is true that, stylistically speaking, things appear in their outward shape to be even more disintegrated than they were with the Impressionists; but this is not decay, so much as a new perception into the depth or 'essentiality' of visible forms. Expressionism, therefore, is a 'new mysticism' *(eine neue Mystik)*, creating simultaneously a new inner experience of things and a new style. This can be seen in expressionist pictures of the masses. People appear alike, a 'dull something' *(ein dumpfes Etwas)* presses down upon them, while a new two-dimensional space deprives them of all individuality. At one moment, indeed, the masses seem reduced to animality, to a level of existence without hope of redemption; but then, at the next, they are raised above

---

[27] *Ibid.,* pp. 38—39.

humanity to new ecstatic and visionary heights. Now the masses have become the subject again; they have no leader, yet their suffering is the prelude to a new birth and a new leader. This is the period of the First World War, of the Russian 'soul-chaos' and the communist martyrs. Thus, with the advent of Expressionism, with its exhibition of a new power in the structure of things, the end of the survey is united with its beginning. For here a new 'mystical mass' has come into being: the mystic element being neither supernatural nor directed from above, but rather breaking out of the depths of the soul and remaining in the reality of the world. This, then, as revealed by the creativity of the Expressionists, is a unique age and a new movement: the 'masses of the immanent mysticism' *(die Masse der immanenten Mystik).*[28]

Tillich's account of Expressionism is, to be frank, considerably less intelligible than the earlier sections of his survey. No paintings are named to support the argument, and although Expressionism is said to depict the oscillation of the mass between a state of abject misery and ecstatic heights, we are given no clue as to the cause or nature of this transition. Similarly, at one moment we are told that the mass is once again the subject, but at the next that their plight prefigures the appearance of a new leader, which would presumably entail some abdication of authority on their part. And what, we may ask, is this 'dull something' that presses down on the people? It would be convenient to conclude that this is an indication of Tillich's early existentialism: the absence of any description of the oppressive force reminding us of Kafka's *The Trial,* in which the hero, Joseph K, knows neither the reason for his arrest, the name of his accusers, nor the verdict of the court. The difficulty with this interpretation is that Tillich's introduction to existentialism is generally placed around 1925—when he was a fellow professor with Martin Heidegger at the University of Marburg—while the section 'Masse und Persönlichkeit' pre-dates this by some five years.

Yet, despite these obvious obscurities, Tillich's survey leaves us in no doubt as to the position occupied by Expressionism. For unlike the Gothic, Renaissance, Baroque and Impressionist styles, Expressionism is not merely the reflection of an historical period, the 'mute revealer' of an epoch, but is arrayed in the robes of a prophet. The spirit of revolt of which Tillich speaks may well be visible in Nietzsche's philosophy

---

[28] *Ibid.,* p. 40.

or the social theory of Marx, but it is the expressionist painter, above all else, who announces the new age with prophetic force. This immediately raises Expressionism to a level generally unattainable by previous styles, and then only in the isolated cases of genius.

And much the same is claimed for Expressionism in relation to the 'new insight' it communicates. For unlike Impressionism, for example, which finds its meaning in surfaces and never raises itself above the middle-class morality to which it belongs, Expressionism rejects the art of the capitalist society and functions at a level *below* that of external appearances. Not only, in other words, has Expressionism had the demand for truth placed upon it, but it has responded to this demand with a revolutionary fervour unsurpassed by other artistic movements, stripping nature of its objective form and destroying the outer actuality of things and processes in its attempt to reveal the dimension of depth, the 'immanent mysticism' of reality itself.

In 1921 Tillich, by then *Privatdozent* at the University of Berlin, developed these ideas in his classroom lectures, often comparing the pictures of the modern artist with ancient Greek philosophy, particularly Parmenides and Heraclitus.[29] The painting that absorbed him most was Franz Marc's 'Turm der blauen Pferde' ('Tower of the Blue Horses'). Marc, an Expressionist associated with the group known as *Der Blaue Reiter* (which included Kandinsky, Macke, Jawlensky, Klee, Gabriele Münter and Marianne von Werefkin), was six years older than Tillich and had been killed in March 1916 at Verdun. Significantly enough, he had wished originally to be a theologian, the religious element continuing to dominate his work. There is, he wrote, 'one great truth ... that there is no great, pure art without religion, that the more religious art

---

[29] 'Zur Theologie der bildenden Kunst und der Architektur', *GW*, IX: 345—346. Tillich's interest in Marc was not purely artistic but had more definite political associations. The Berlin university buildings stood opposite the art gallery, then housed in the old imperial palace. One day, during the course of his lectures, Tillich witnessed streetfighting between the intelligentsia and the 'lower petty bourgeoisie', the latter protesting against an exhibition of modern art which included Marc's work. From then on Tillich linked Marc with the anti-bourgeois struggle, admitting that, largely for that reason, Marc's pictures continued to have a symbolic significance for him quite apart from their artistic merit. 'Art and Ultimate Reality', *Cross Currents*, X, No. 1 (Winter 1960) p. 10.

has been, the more artistic it has been'.[30] Following this programme, Marc made an intensive study of animal anatomy, believing the human form too ugly to depict and that only the 'animalization of art' could contain the symbolism, pathos and mystery of nature. This was the spirit in which he produced the famous animal pictures of 1911, of which 'Turm der blauen Pferde' is one. Marc's style became increasingly bold and abstract, his pictures of a deer, a horse or a tiger reducing natural shapes to geometrical structures, the animals themselves achieving a oneness with nature from which man was excluded. 'We no longer cling to reproduction of nature', he proclaimed in 1912, 'but destroy it, so as to reveal the right laws which hold sway behind the beautiful exterior'.[31] It was this latter point that Tillich emphasized in his Berlin lectures: that, for example, Marc's 'Yellow Horses', by its destruction of natural forms and colours and by its stylistic simplicity, had gained an insight into the inner truth of things; that what was presented here was more than the picturing of particular horses, so much as the whole reality or 'essence' of horses as such, the singular representatives of the entire species. For Tillich as for Marc, these paintings provided a 'breakthrough of content in form and colour' *(Durchbruch des Gehalts in Form und Farbe).*[32]

We find, therefore, in Marc's consciously religious art, the general character of Expressionism exemplified, the term 'breakthrough' conveniently covering the two aspects of the movement so far mentioned: first, its radical break with bourgeois artistic attitudes; and second, the form-breaking quality of its style. If we now link these two characteristics to what Tillich has said already about the need for realism in religious art—this demand itself, we remember, being expressed in terms of the rejection of superficiality and the need for a more profound perception into the nature of the human predicament—we thus arrive at Tillich's final and most important classification of Expressionism,

---

[30] Quoted by Wolf-Dieter Dube, *The Expressionists* (London: Thames & Hudson, 1972) p. 125. The standard work on Marc is Alois J. Schardt's *Franc Marc* (Berlin: Rembrandt Verlag, 1936). For an analysis of 'Der Turm der blauen Pferde', see Klaus Lankheit's monograph of the same name (Stuttgart: Philipp Reclam Jun., 1961).

[31] Wolf-Dieter Dube, *op. cit.,* p. 132.

[32] Franz Marc, *Briefe aus dem Feld* (Berlin: Helmut Rauschenbusch Verlag, 1948) p. 75. Quoted in Pauck, *op. cit.,* p. 77.

namely, that in Expressionism this demand for realism is met; that in Expressionism, both in the nature of its insights and the character of its techniques, we have the prototype of a genuine religious art; that, in a word, 'Religious art is Expressionistic'.[33] This, then, is the culmination of Tillich's analysis of Expressionism, the association between this movement and religious art being recognized within the identity of a definition. And the consequences are significant. For if religious art is expressionistic art, then this entails that the 'immanent mysticism' revealed by the Expressionists is a religious perception into the nature of the world, and that the form-destructive method of their style is necessary for its disclosure; it also means that if Tillich's philosophy is to show the true nature of religious art, then it must incorporate these two insights since both are implied in the definition he himself has set up. And such, indeed, is the case, the concept of 'new mysticism' figuring prominently in his doctrine of God, the concept of 'form-breaking style' determining his own notion of the 'breakthrough', which dominates his theory of revelation.[34]

The extent of this identification between religious art and Expressionism can best be seen by turning to one final survey, included in Die Religiöse Lage der Gegenwart, first published in 1926 and later translated as The Religious Situation in 1932.[35] This book, Tillich's first major success in Germany and America, is, as he admits, dedicated to an artist friend because its central concept, 'belief-ful realism', is dependent on his study of art, particularly of the movement that succeeded Expressionism and known as 'New Realism'.[36]

The Religious Situation is an attempt to understand the nature of present society on the basis of the faith expressed in the various interpretations of life which this society offers. Tillich begins by saying that what we are witnessing is not so much the decline of the West but the

---

[33] 'Theology, Architecture and Art', Church Management (October 1956) p. 55. Reprinted from 'Theology and Architecture', Architectural Forum (New York) CIII, No. 6 (1955) pp. 131—134.

[34] OB: 28.

[35] Die religiöse Lage der Gegenwart (Berlin: Ullstein, 1926). E.T., The Religious Situation, translated and introduced by H. Richard Niebuhr (New York: Henry Holt, 1932; edition used: New York: Meridian Books, 1956).

[36] OB: 28.

revolt against the 'spirit of capitalist society': this phrase designating a fundamental attitude towards the world, not a particular class or party of men.[37] The capitalist faith is described as a belief in the self-sufficiency of the human and finite world, closed against 'invasions of the eternal' and possessed of a ruthless, impersonal activity which seeks to subordinate the world of nature and mind to human control and bourgeois custom. Mathematical natural science, technique and capitalist economy are the three great representative products of this period, undergirding capitalist ambitions and producing an attitude of human domination with little or no respect for personal individuality.[38] All this is expressed in education, politics, religion and the arts, notably in the novels of Zola and Flaubert. By the end of the 19th century, so Tillich concludes, and as the tragic lives of Nietzsche, Strindberg and Van Gogh bear witness, all opposition to the prevailing capitalist mood was quite impossible.

But that situation has now been destroyed, partly by war and revolution but principally by a reawakened 'recognition of the sacredness of personality ... of faith in human rights and human worth'.[39] What is now revealed in the present situation is an attitude of faith which believes that a 'living structure cannot be composed out of its parts but can only grow forth out of an original, creative source', and which rejects, therefore, the capitalist view of the intrinsic, intra-worldly value of the life-process.[40] In science Einstein, Planck and Bohr, in psychology Freud, in philosophy Bergson, Simmel and Husserl, in the study of history Troeltsch and Spengler, in ethics the educational reformers and the youth movement, in literature George, Dehmel, Werfel and the rediscovery of Dostoevsky—all are representative of the belief that the bourgeois picture of a self-sufficient world is meaningless. What has emerged instead is a fundamentally different apprehension of reality, one which, although conceding individuality and uniqueness to observable phenomena, is not interested in the conditioned forms of existence for their own sake but for their power in expressing the profounder levels of being, the universal and unconditioned significance

---

[37] *RS: 27.*
[38] *Ibid.,* p. 42.
[39] *Ibid.,* p. 49.
[40] *Ibid.,* p. 59.

of things. *This is the attitude of 'belief-ful realism' (Gläubiger Realismus).*

As we might expect, it is at this point that Tillich introduces his survey of modern art. Art, he says, provides the best indication of the character of a *spiritual* situation because, unlike science and philosophy, its 'immediate task is not that of apprehending essence but that of expressing meaning'.[41] The stylistic classifications that follow are predictable—Impressionism being assigned to the bourgeoisie, Expressionism to the revolutionaries—but the terminology used has altered to conform to the analysis of 'belief-ful realism'. Thus Impressionism is described as a 'metaphysics of a finitude which postulates its own absoluteness', preoccupied with the brilliant but scientific representation of the momentary impressions of external nature, and so excluding any 'breakthrough' to the eternal.[42] Expressionism, on the other hand, offers us an 'objective metaphysic', evoking the abyss of Being and the 'inner expressive force of reality'. Here, too, the selfcontained finitude of capitalist civilization is 'broken through', Cézanne restoring to things 'their real metaphysical meaning', Van Gogh revealing the 'creative dynamic in light and colour', Munch showing the 'cosmic dread present in nature and mankind'.[43] The later styles of futurism, cubism and constructivism have developed these expressionist insights, refusing to conform to the bourgeois ethic and using planes, lines and cubes with 'an almost mystical transparency'.

> In this case as in expressionism in general the self-sufficient form of existence was broken through. Not a transcendent world is depicted as in the art of the ancients but the transcendental reference in all things to that which lies beyond them is expressed.[44]

Although this would appear to be a clear example of the attitude of 'belief-ful realism', Tillich adds, somewhat surprisingly, that the most precise formulation of its principles is not found in Expressionism itself but in the artistic style that succeeded it. This is the movement known as 'New Realism' or 'New Objectivity' *(die neue Sachlichkeit),* the term being coined by Gustav Friedrich Hartlaub, the distinguished director of the Kunsthalle in Mannheim, to cover the work of George

---

[41] *Ibid.,* p. 85.
[42] *Ibid.,* pp. 86—87.
[43] *Ibid.,* p. 87.
[44] *Ibid.,* p. 88.

Grosz, Otto Dix and Max Beckmann in the 1920s.[45] Here we find not only the same stress on the spiritual significance of natural forms, but, as the name suggests, a more direct and less sophisticated representation of objects than that found in the more romantic imagery of Expressionism. At first it seemed that the New Realism was the antithesis of the expressionist movement, restoring confidence in capitalist traditions; but in fact it was an even mightier opponent, 'carrying the battle into the camp of the enemy and employing his own best weapons against him'.[46] In this new style the metaphysical reference of things is reaffirmed, together with a new and positive evaluation of the objects depicted.

Tillich makes much of this distinction between the two styles, upsetting, it would seem, the previous pre-eminence of expressionistic art. His argument, however, is extremely unsatisfactory, both on internal and historical grounds[47]; and it is significant that the only writings which maintain it are those of the 1920s, when presumably Tillich was most susceptible to the new movement; thereafter he reverts to his classification of religious art as expressionistic, never mentions New Realism in his later surveys, and frequently describes Expressionism in precisely the same terms as those formerly used for New Realism.[48] Even the essays of the 1920s are inconsistent in their account of this distinction. We are told, for example, that the realism of the New Objectivity is entirely different from the realism of the Expressionists; but Tillich provides no supportive evidence and then proceeds to describe New Realism as a radicalization of the attack on bourgeois superficiality inaugurated by Expressionism.[49] Elsewhere he claims that it is only with the 'sudden and immediately evident' appearance of New Realism that we can speak of the beginning of a 'belief-ful realism'; but then, in the

---

[45] *Ibid.*, p. 90. Hartlaub's first use of the term appears in a circular letter dated May 18, 1923, quoted by Fritz Schmalenbach, 'The Term *Neue Sachlichkeit*', *Art Bulletin*, XXII, No. 3 (September 1940) p. 161. It is interesting that Hartlaub's own attempt to define the nature of religious art, in his *Kunst und Religion. Ein Versuch über die Möglichkeit neuer religiöser Kunst* (Leipzig: Wolff, 1919), is reviewed by Tillich in 'Religiöser Stil und religiöser Stoff in der bildenden Kunst'.

[46] *Ibid.*, p. 91.

[47] For the historical reasons, see below pp. 25—30.

[48] Compare, for example, 'Protestantism and Artistic Style', *TC:* 74—75, with the articles listed below in n. 50.

[49] *RS:* 90.

same paragraph, he remarks that the success of the *new* movement
depended on its *assimilation* of the two strongest motifs of Expressionism:

> Der empirische Realität der Dinge wurde wieder aufgesucht, aber
> nicht um ihrer selbst willen, sondern als Ausdruck des objektiven Ge-
> haltes, der inneren Mächtigkeit der Dinge.[50]

This suggests that Tillich's association in the 1920s with the style
known as New Realism should not be seen as a denial of expressionist
aims, so much as an allegiance to the one contemporary movement
in which he saw the basic presuppositions of Expressionism being maintained and extended. For both styles can be called 'realistic' because
they seek to reveal the spiritual meaning of reality by using its given
forms, asserting that it is possible to seek for the ultimate power of
reality *within the concreteness of its structures;* and both can be called
'belief-ful' because they claim that the ultimate meaning and power
thus sought cannot be derived from the whole of reality and cannot
be apprehended by the scientific or conceptual processes *belonging to
the whole of reality.* In each case the capitalist myth of progress is
destroyed in the perception that meaning is not innate; that there is no
such thing as the self-sufficiency of the temporal order; and that all
time and every civilization receive their true meaning from the relation
to eternity, to the unconditioned source of all meaning. 'The closed
circle of finite existence which is represented by faith in progress has
been broken; the presence of the eternal in time and history has been
recognized'.[51]

Let us now try summarize the argument so far. Tillich's three
surveys have reviewed a number of different movements in the visual
arts—Gothic, Renaissance, Baroque, Impressionism, Expressionism,
Cubism, New Realism etc.—and the problem we have been dealing with
can best be set under the general heading of the 'problem of style': of
saying what style is, of distinguishing one artistic style from another,

---

[50] 'Über gläubigen Realismus', *Religiöse Verwirklichung* (Berlin: Furche, 1929)
pp. 66. *GW*, IV: 88—106. Revised E.T., 'Realism and Faith', *PE:* 66—82.
Cf. 'Gläubiger Realismus', reprint from *Theologenrundbrief für den Bund
Deutscher Jugendvereine, II* (July—August 1927) pp. 3—13 (*GW*, IV:
77—87). In the E.T., Tillich replaces the term 'belief-ful realism' with
'self-transcending realism'.
[51] *RS:* 82.

of seeking a definition of religious style. Style, it would appear, incorporates various elements, the first and most obvious being that it is the product of the artist's creative imagination. Tillich's surveys make clear, however, that this does not mean that style is simply the reflection of the artist's subjectivity—carrying, as it were, the distinctive imprint of a phase or evolution in his perceptions of reality; style is also the simultaneous exemplification of other, more generic styles—the style of the artist's school, tradition and, above all, cultural and historical situation—and it is primarily the deciphering of these contextual styles that enables us to establish the particular tradition to which a painter belongs. Every style, therefore, is a commentary both on its own histori-cal period and its own contemporary interpretation of man and his world, even though the artist himself is usually unaware of this inter-pretation. 'Thus, a contemporary Picasso will be in the individual style, and more specifically in the current style, of Picasso himself; it will also be in the expressionistic Western European tradition; and it will be, in its own way, expressive of the mid-twentieth century'.[52]

All these elements are contained in religious art. Like every other style, the religious style is a perspective or standpoint, which, although expressed by the individual artist, is not the product of individual arbitrariness. Religious art, that is to say, is a genuinely creative act issuing from within the circle in which the artist moves: the representa-tive, as it were, of the spiritual insights or needs to be found within the history and cultural groups upon which this circle depends. This, we remember, determined Tillich's survey in *Masse und Geist:* the transitions in art reflect the transitions in historical periods, and from an analysis of the religious character of the one we can evaluate the religious character of the other. But how is religious style to be distinguished? This question is complicated by certain peculiarities basic to religious art. It is, for instance, disinterested in the exact representation of external phenomena; unlike the naturalistic styles it contains no figurative or narrative form which could be assessed in terms of its accuracy in depicting certain objects or events. Similarly, religious style is not primarily concerned with the subjective disposition of the artist nor with the development of his skills; unlike Impressionism, therefore,

[52] 'Authentic Religious Art', *Art Institute of Chicago* (Chicago: 1954), written jointly with Theodore M. Greene, pp. 8—9.

it rejects the subordination of nature to individual self-assertiveness or technical expertise, regarding both as products of the capitalist society it repudiates. However, the most remarkable feature of religious style is this: that its nature cannot be attributed to any explicit use of the familiar symbols of religion; and that the use of such material does not guarantee either artistic integrity or significant religious expressiveness. In *The Religious Situation* the reason given for this is largely historical: the religious art of the bourgeois society has so reduced the traditional symbols of religion to the level of middle-class morality that any attempt to derive inspiration from them is now impossible. Even the Expressionists failed conspicuously in this regard. The modern religious consciousness, so Tillich remarks, must therefore find new ways of expressing itself, without recourse to traditional religious symbolism.[53]

This conclusion sets new boundaries to Tillich's argument, since now it appears that there is no special religious sphere of culture—such, for example, as the church and its practices—the mere portrayal of which would constitute religious art. But how, therefore, is the 'religious' aspect in religious art to be defined? And how, once this definition has been reached, will it determine the choice of subject to be portrayed and the artistic method to be employed?

As we have seen, art is religious when it seeks to reveal, through the ordinarily encountered forms of reality, the transcendental reference of these forms to the eternal, to that which lies beyond the particularity of concrete things. All Tillich's surveys converge at this point, whether it be in the analysis of the 'situation of our time', 'immanent mysticism' or 'belief-ful realism'. Put differently, we can say that what distinguishes religious style from any other—what constitutes its expressiveness— is its perception of the 'dimension of depth', of the hidden ground and meaning of every situation and every object. It is this insight which determines both the subjects and method of religious art. For if we are concerned here with the expression of that which is the ultimate power and meaning of *all* encountered reality, then it follows that *any* reality, so encountered, can function as the means of religious expression. Accordingly the artistic choice of subject is limitless: a portrait, a landscape, a still-life, a nude, an historical event—all could form the basis of the religious perception as all are pictures of actual or potential

---

[53] *RS:* 89.

elements within our experience. In Tillich's argument, therefore, the objectivity *(Sachlichkeit)* of existent things is raised to a new dignity as a *requirement* of revelation.[54]

The artistic method of religious art is determined in a similar fashion. If the *unconditioned* meaning of existence is manifested in and through the *conditioned* forms of existence, then we must say that religious style is expressive of that which transcends those situations and objects from which the subject-matter of all artistic styles is derived. Hence no natural thing or event can become the vehicle of revelation through what it is in itself, but only through its manifestation of that which is both implicit within and distinct from it as the ground of its being and meaning. The spiritual interpretation of reality requires, therefore, the destruction of the natural forms of reality under the power of that which they express; or, more exactly, it rejects any artistic method which, like the use of three-dimensional space or perspective, ascribes independent status or significance to objective phenomena.[55] For the meaning of things is not innate to the things themselves, nor is it bound to the technical or subjective forms of their representation; rather, meaning has a transcendental reference, one which determines the basic methodological principle of religious art: *that in religious style there can be no equation between that which is expressed and the means of expression.*

II. RELIGIOUS ART AND THE CATEGORY OF EXPRESSIVENESS

Many of the points summarized here will be dealt with more extensively in subsequent chapters. For the moment, however, I want to turn to one final aspect of Tillich's discussion so far. As we have seen, Tillich's various replies to the questions concerning the nature, scope and method of religious art are set within his analysis of Expressionism. Each of the three surveys concludes with an account of Expressionism; each of these accounts is paralleled by a discussion of a particular

---

[54] So, in his article 'Kult und Form', Tillich sets up three prerequisites for religious art: that it must be determined by the daily life, by *our* particular situation, and by reality. *Die Form*, V, No. 23—24 (December 1930) pp. 578—583. *GW*, IX: 324—327.

[55] *RS*: 89.

concept; and each of these concepts provides the basis for an analysis of religious style. By this means we arrived at the definition of religious art as 'expressionistic'. But in one sense, of course, this definition is misleading since other artists of other periods (Dürer, Bosch, Goya, Michelangelo) are called religious painters. What justifies the definition, therefore, is not that religious style is restricted to a particular development in 20th century art, but that in this movement we find the nature and method of religious art exemplified. The religious style, in other words, has no prescribed historical boundaries, since what we are dealing with is a perception into the nature of reality, which, in principle at least, is accessible to all.

Precisely the same point is made in Tillich's use of the phrase 'the situation of our time'. This phrase, we remember, was used to distinguish between two types of picture. The first type possesses religious content but lacks religious style (i.e., it uses the familiar symbols of the religious tradition — a 'Cross', a 'Madonna and Child' — but presents a beautification or idealization of human and natural forms); and the second type lacks religious content but possesses religious style (i.e., it uses the material of ordinarily encountered reality — a 'Café', a 'Table' — in order to reveal the dimension of depth in reality). Religious art, so defined, is realistic to the extent that it expresses the artist's search for ultimate meaning and significance in terms of his everyday experience. But here too the phrase 'the situation of our time' is misleading, since it is clearly not designed to limit religious art to the art contemporaneous with our own historical period. So, in the same survey, we read that the greatest of all German religious pictures is the famous Isenheim altarpiece by Grünewald (painted *circa* 1515), and that this shows 'that expressionism is by no means a modern invention'.[56]

The conclusion to be drawn from this is extremely significant. Although religious art is defined in terms of its *power to express*, we must now say that *that which it expresses* cannot itself be defined in terms of the cultural or historical changes which determine artistic style. Put otherwise, the expressionist-religious style contains a unique and invariable perception into the ultimate referent of reality, one which

---

[56] 'Religion and the Visual Arts', p. 9. This was in fact a common view held by the Expressionists themselves. See Peter Selz, *German Expressionist Painting* (Berkeley & Los Angeles: University of California Press, 1957) pp. 16—17.

is locatable within but not associable with the various cultural or historical changes to which every artist and every style is subject. This, indeed, indicates the essentially *non-progressive* character of religious art: it is not dependent on the artist's acquisition of new experiences or new facts, but is rather the presentation of such facts and experiences within the singular perspective of ultimate meaning. Thus, for example, we can call both Goya and Picasso 'expressionists', but cannot thereby speak of a cultural identity between early 19th and 20th century Spain. Here too the variable is the means of expression, not that which is expressed. To be sure, religious art must speak in terms accessible to us; but the intelligibility of the language—or rather our recognition of the images depicted—is not the defining quality of religious style. For when we speak of 'the situation of *our* time', we are referring to that spiritual interpretation of reality, which, through *characteristic* of our modern situation, is not *peculiar* to it.[57] We are, more precisely, denoting the artistic presentation of the facts and circumstances of our age in the light of that which, as the *eternal* referent of all things, cannot be restricted to the changing imagery of our own historical or cultural epoch.

In other words, then, it is the *category of expressiveness* which provides the criterion of judgment between religious and non-religious art, not the relation of a special style to a special movement. The expressive element is the irreducible and determining factor in religious art; and only those styles which offer the spiritual understanding of reality denoted by the term 'expressive' can be called religious, irrespective of their period or tradition. Once again, therefore, the definition of religious art *as* expressionistic art is confirmed, but this time with an important shift of emphasis: the specific principle of interpretation, which Expressionism exemplifies, is itself dissociable from that movement. And this conclusion points us in another direction. For the question now is whether this definition can be established without any reference to Expressionism at all.

At first sight, of course, this question appears manifestly absurd; but it appears less so if we are speaking here not of Tillich's use of the term

---

[57] This, of course, appears to be an unduly optimistic interpretation of our present situation. Tillich later accepted this criticism, particularly after the Second World War, but insisted that religious art requires this interpretation.

'expressionism' but of the particular interpretation and method to which that term refers. Then we may legitimately ask: from whence is the category of expressiveness derived? Is it, for example, a *retrospective* judgment of other styles made, as the term suggests, on the basis of Tillich's study of Expressionism? Or is it a category initially determined by his *theological* delineation of the nature of religious insight and later *confirmed* in Expressionism? Are we dealing here with a certain style that *reveals* a particular interpretation of reality, or with a particular interpretation of reality *corroborated* in a certain style?

The most direct way of tackling this question is to ask whether Expressionism ever incorporated, consciously or otherwise, the kind of religious art prescribed by Tillich. The answer, however, is complicated by one fact: that Expressionism never was the kind of cohesive movement that Tillich's surveys suggest. The name itself is of doubtful origin, some ascribing it to the title Julien-Auguste Hervé gave to his nature studies shown in Paris in 1901, others to Paul Cassirer's alleged remark about a painting by Pechstein during a meeting of the hanging committee of the Berlin Secession. All we can say for certain is that in the Berlin exhibition of 1911 the term covered Matisse, the Fauve, Picasso and Braque, and that it was thereafter appropriated by the critic Hermath Walden in his periodical *Der Sturm*, even though Schmidt-Rottluff and Marc were unhappy with the description. Kirchner rejected it altogether, Kandinsky mentions it only once in a footnote in his *Über das Geistige in der Kunst*, and Walden's own *Expressionismus* (subtitled 'the turning-point in art') took it as a convenient synonym for the European avant-garde in general.[58]

But much more significant is that such vagueness about the meaning and use of the term 'expressionism' reflects a fundamental uncertainty about the programmatic character of the movement as a whole. In part the reason for this lay in the extreme fragmentation of the artistic scene created by the German federalist system. In the widely separated parts of Germany, groups of artists and independent museum directors, unhampered by any single authority such as existed in Paris or London, could foster individualistic ideas and methods. By 1900 Berlin was the

---

[58] See Kandinsky, *Über das Geistige in der Kunst* (München: R. Piper, 1912) p. 96; and Hermath Walden, *Expressionismus: Die Kunstwende* (Verlag Der Sturm: Berlin, 1918). Kandinsky's footnote is quoted below in n. 70.

main cultural centre; but other cities—Munich, Cologne, Dresden, Hannover—had international reputations, had their own academies, their own avant-gardists and reactionaries. The conservative camps, led by the Kaiser's representative, Anton von Werner, were quick to denounce any departure from 'official art' as subversive and degenerate, and the press made considerable capital out of the heated exchanges that ensued. This forced artists into affiliations that did not necessarily spring from any specific ideology, and gave to Expressionism the character of a political protest, even though few of its painters were activists and few of their paintings concerned with political issues or social strategy. Expressionism, in other words, although certainly an anti-establishment reaction at the turn of the century, *never was a movement coordinated on the basis of defined principles.* This explains why the various 'Secessions' that rose during the 1890s attempted to include *any* style that had a revolutionary impulse, and why *Die Brücke,* as its name suggests, sought to attract every iconoclastic and fermenting tendency to itself. The primary objective was to get through to a public unable to respond to the nymphs, heroes and allegories sanctioned by Kaiser Wilhelm; and this *Die Brücke* did, with bright colours and assertively primitive forms, but without at first any direct social comment or any presentation of their own needs or anxieties. Indeed, in terms of Tillich's classification of Expressionism as an anti-bourgeois movement, it is worth remembering that no group was so anxious to make itself known to a wider market, and that the woodcut was not merely an artistic device but a means of rapid and inexpensive self-advertisement.[59]

The extreme heterogeneous character of Expressionism also defies any easy classification of its method. Tillich's own account closely follows the first monograph written on the subject, Paul Fechter's *Der Expressionismus* (1914).[60] Fechter took the movement to apply to the whole gamut of international tendencies considered post-Impressionism and anti-Impressionism, thus including Cubism in France and Futurism

---

[59] For the historical background to Expressionism, see Bernard S. Myers, *Expressionism: A Generation in Revolt* (London: Thames & Hudson, 1963) pp. 15—19.

[60] Paul Fechter, *Expressionismus* (München: R. Piper, 1914). Cubism and Futurism are discussed on pp. 30—41 and 42—46 respectively.

in Italy. His conclusion, which Tillich supports, was that the true discovery of the movement lay in its realization that the rules of art need
not depend on the formal representation of objects, on the need to
obtain an impression of their external appearance; that abstract composi-
tions could be as effectively expressive as subject pictures, and that
indeed the subject could be abandoned altogether. This conclusion
justified the description of Braque and Picasso as expressionists since
both had explored the expressive power of colour and shape, space and
texture, and both had used 'low content' subject material—landscapes,
still-lifes—for that purpose.

And yet, even within these limits set by Fechter, it is difficult to
maintain hard and fast distinctions. Indeed, Tillich's own muddle
between Expressionism and New Realism is a good example of what
happens when one makes the attempt. The art of George Grosz and
Otto Dix could not have existed without the precedent of *Die Brücke* and
Der Blaue Reiter graphics[61], and if their pictures are said to represent
a return to a naturalism opposed to the obscure abstracts of, say, Klee
and Kandinsky, then this can hardly be justified in relation to the
majority of expressionist painters, whose work by the 1920s was, if
anything, too conventionally accepted as part of the modern scene.[62]
Neither Kirchner's 'hieroglyphs' nor Mueller's nudes can be considered
anti-naturalistic, since in each case the use of two-dimensional form was
designed to present natural objects with the greatest possible economy
and simplicity; Schmidt-Rottluff, although experimenting with Cubist
techniques in 1912, was never willing to forego the power of explicit
statement or to represent an idea without an object; and Pechstein, by
remaining so loyal to naturalistic representation, became successful to
the point that, by 1915, he was second only to Picasso in public esteem.

---

[61] For the expressionist influences on Grosz, see Beth Irwin Lewis, *George
Grosz: Art and Politics in the Weimar Republic* (Madison: The University
of Wisconsin Press, 1971) pp. 15—19.

[62] In 'Art and Ultimate Reality' Tillich is even more confusing. He tells us
that in Berlin in the 1920s he saw a Kandinsky similar to his 'Improvisation',
and that this picture 'at that time was very near to my own religious
thinking' (*Ibid.*, pp. 6—7). Although it is impossible to trace the particular
picture concerned, it probably belongs to the 1911—1913 group—see
Kandinsky's 'Improvisation No. 19' and 'Dreamy Improvisation'—which
where then considered the highpoint of expressionist abstraction!

Indeed, the Cubists themselves provide an interesting comment on the distinctions Tillich is seeking to introduce. The classical phase of Cubism sought a very careful balance between representation and abstraction, and this we can see in Picasso's great masterpiece, the *Demoiselles d'Avignon* of 1907; but when Braque and Picasso attempted later to heighten the realistic element by the techniques of *papier collé* and *collage*, this was done not to reduce the obscurity of their art but to increase it![63]

The basic question remains, however, whether the expressionist style, even in Fechter's open-ended description of it, can be called a religious style. Can it be said, to follow Tillich, that the Expressionists, by their destruction of natural form and colour, sought to discover the universal significance of the realities they thus negated? Now it is certainly true that many Expressionists were preoccupied with religious themes. In the case of Schmidt-Rottluff and Jawlensky, for example, their experiences during the First World War and the psychological shock it produced made the question of the transcendental reference of reality of paramount importance; Nolde, doubtless inspired by his intensely pietist background, produced between 1911 and 1913 a series of religious paintings, one of which, *Pentecost,* made such an impression on Tillich that he later admitted having derived some of his ideas from it (although no details are given)[64]; and Marc, whom we have already discussed, was to give the most precise definition of the religious aims of art: 'durch ihre Arbeit ihrer Zeit Symbole zu schaffen, die auf die Altäre der kommenden geistigen Religion gehören und hinter denen der Erzeuger ver-

---

[63] In conversation with Françoise Gilot, Picasso explained that 'the purpose of the *papier collé* was to give the idea that different textures can enter into a composition to become the reality in the painting that competes with the reality in nature. We tried to get rid of 'trompe l'oeil' to find a 'trompe l'esprit' ... If a piece of newspaper can become a bottle, that gives us something to think about in connection with both newspapers and bottles, too. This displaced object has entered a universe for which it was not made and where it retains, in a measure, its strangeness. And this strangeness was what we wanted to make people think about because we were quite aware that our world was becoming very strange and not exactly reassuring'. Francoise Gilot and Carlton Lake, *Life with Picasso* (London: Penguin Books, 1965) p. 70.

[64] 'Art and Ultimate Reality', p. 10.

schwindet'.[65] Any of these artists could, and in Marc's case evidently did, form models for Tillich's analysis of religious art; but to say that these artists indicate a *general tendency* within Expressionism is to give that movement a degree of cohesiveness that its variform character cannot support. Thus Schmidt-Rottluff was to proclaim that the movement had no 'new programme' and was vigorously to resist any attempt at stylistic or thematic classification; Nolde admitted that his pictures proceeded from no clearly conceived idea, while his *Pentecost* was so detested by the Berlin Secession that it led to the formation of a splinter group, the *Neue Sezession;* and even Marc, for all his personal religious fervour, was later to write to Kandinsky that a fine summary of expressionist aims was to be found in Wilhelm Worringer's *Abstraktion und Einfühlung:* a book which has little to do with religious matters, but which stresses that all art is basically *subjective* and that the most important element in artistic creation is *intuition.*[66]

If Tillich was right, therefore, to describe Expressionism as an association of revolutionaries, this association itself tends to resist the kind of overall interpretation offered by the terms 'immanent mysticism' and 'belief-ful realism'. For the preoccupation with protest and drama, with the drive towards self-expression unimpeded by conventions, not only frustrated the Expressionists' own attempts at stylistic classification —which largely accounts for the comparatively short lifespan of the Secessions and the wholesale defections to other groups—but also, and much more significantly, fostered the cult of the strong artistic personality, of the artist concerned primarily with the transmission of his *own* personal experiences and according to his *own* individual dictates. And this in turn provides us with an alternative interpretation of the expressionist method: namely, that the relegation of the subject-matter by compositional or figurative distortion was required, not because this style is thereby expressive of that which transcends the subject-matter as its ultimate reference, but because in this way *no meaning other than that intended by the artist and perceived by the spectator could be*

---

[65] *Der Blaue Reiter* (München: R. Piper, 1912; Dokumentarische Neuausgabe von Klaus Lankheit, 1965) p. 31. Many of the movement's early proclamations are included in Kasimir Edschmid's *Frühe Manifeste; Epochen des Expressionismus* (Hamburg: C. Wegner, 1957).

[66] Wilhelm Worringer, *Abstraktion und Einfühlung. Ein Beitrag zur Stilpsychologie* (München: R. Piper, 1907) pp. 1—33.

attributed to the canvas. Put differently, the hallmark of expressionistic art is its *anti-naturalistic subjectivism:* the attempt by the painter to express the world of his inner experience and the freshness of his sensations in their simplest form. And, as Schmidt-Rottluff remarked, there is nothing essentially new in this. For the campaign of introspection, which delineates Expressionism above all else, and the emotional power and vitality which accompany it, have their antecedents in the art of Goya, Blake, Delacroix and Friedrich; that is, in the romantic and paradoxical supposition that the discovery of the individual as an unrestrained and creative personality could produce universal truths.[67]

It is, therefore, only with extreme caution that we can speak of Expressionism as an influence on Tillich's 'category of expressiveness'. This category certainly contains a method found in expressionistic art; and on that basis alone who is to say that Tillich did or did not derive a certain methodology from his study of Expressionism? His own suggestion, we should remember, is that he did; but if this be so, then we can at least reply that this method is the expressionist technique in its most basic form, adopted, it would seem, with little appreciation of the heterogeneous character of the movement that subscribed to it.[68] But, for our present purposes, still more significant is the use to which this method is put. Tillich's view, to repeat, is that this method both reveals and is illustrative of a quite specific spiritual interpretation of reality, one which justifies the definition of religious art as expressionistic. Yet this argument is difficult to maintain for two reasons: first, and more generally, because the variegated character of the movement resists such classifications—to the point, indeed, where some scholars argue that there never was a movement called 'Expressionism'[69]; and second, and more exactly, because the method itself, so far as we can define it, points more to an assumption of the artist's own self-assertive individuality than to any preoccupation on his part with eternal values. Indeed we may go further and say that, if anything, study of the expressionist method leads us in an altogether different direction to that

---

[67] Cf. Norbert Lynton, *op. cit.,* p. 35; Bernard S. Myers, *op. cit.,* pp. 14—17; and Peter Selz, *op. cit.,* pp. 19—21.

[68] *OB:* 28. In Ch. IV I shall try to show that even this dependence on the expressionist method is questionable since it could equally arise from Tillich's analysis of revelation and religious symbols.

[69] Cf. Norbert Lynton, *op. cit.,* p. 38.

intended by Tillich. Tillich claims that the prophetic character of expressionist art lies in its perception that the meaning of natural objects is not innate to the objects themselves but grounded in an ultimate source of meaning; but a more accurate assessment would be that, for the Expressionist, the meaning of such objects is sustained by the value he himself attributes to them and wishes to communicate to the onlooker, and that accordingly the presupposition of an ultimate meaning is legitimate only in so far as it reflects the painter's own subjective disposition. This alternative reading not only accounts for the absence among Expressionists of any commonly accepted principle by which reality can be interpreted, but also explains the logic behind the method they commonly adopt. For in the deliberate distortion of external nature by their economy of line and heightening of colour, these artists seek to express *the experience that nature itself has aroused in them.* Thus when Kandinsky and Walden speak of the 'spiritual' in art, they are not, as Tillich's argument would suggest, preoccupied with an interpretation of reality *sub specie aeternitatis* but with the demand to connect the visual material in art to the inner life of the artist; or rather with the attempt to extend the limits and expressive power of their medium through a presentation of nature controlled by and infused with the painter's own emotional demands, *whether they be religious or not.*[70]

The fact, indeed, that Tillich's surveys take no account of this last possibility—that the 'category of expressiveness' is determined by a definition of the expressionist method which *implies* the interpretation of reality peculiar to religious art—indicates perhaps more clearly than anything else that Tillich has here superimposed on Expressionism a *theological judgment of their style;* that he has, on the basis of his definition, deduced from the presence of the method that it must operate

---

[70] In his footnote, Kandinsky writes of 'der Neigung, die Natur nicht als äußerliche Erscheinung darzustellen, sondern überwiegend das Element der *inneren Impression,* die kürzlich *Expression* genannt wurde, kundzugeben' (*op. cit.,* p. 96). Walden is even more explicit in his *Einblick in Kunst — Expressionismus, Futurismus, Kubismus* (Berlin: Verlag Der Sturm, 1924): 'Kunst ist die Gestaltung des geistigen Erlebnisses ... Der Künstler malt, was er schaut mit seinen innersten Sinnen, den Ausdruck, die Expression seines Wesens ... Der Eindruck von außen wird ihm der Ausdruck von innen. Er ist Träger und Getragener seiner Visionen, seiner inneren Geschichte' (*ibid.,* p. 68).

within a *theological perspective*. But this definition, as I have tried to show, cannot be maintained as it applies to Expressionism. For although there may well have been members of the movement who would have subscribed to the spiritual interpretation of reality offered by Tillich, it is highly doubtful whether even they would have accepted this interpretation as the single reason why the movement adopted the method it did, as that which defines the movement as such. Similarly, it may well be that this interpretation does indeed require the expressionist method—a point to which we shall return; but the study of Expressionism has demonstrated that this argument is not necessarily reversible, that that method must require that interpretation. A much more likely account of its style is that it allowed the artist to dissociate himself from the formal representation of objects and so to give free rein to the expression of his own individual response to nature, *not* that he perceived therein a means of expressing the transcendent referent of everything that is. Tillich, of course, is well within his rights to see more in the expressionist method than many, if not all, of its exponents realized, and so to view it from the theological perspective of 'immanent mysticism' or 'belief-ful realism'; but in seeking to impose this perspective as the defining characteristic of the movement—as that which not only distinguishes it from its predecessors but constitutes, as it were, its collective greatness—he is introducing an art-historical judgment which an analysis of Expressionism does not support.

With this conclusion in mind, it only remains for us to determine more exactly why Tillich should have placed Expressionism within this perspective. This we can do by turning to his article 'Über die Idee einer Theologie der Kultur'.[71] This essay, the first to establish Tillich's theological reputation in Germany, was written in 1919 for the *Kant-Gesellschaft* of Berlin, and so presumably completed within months of his introduction to Expressionism by Eckart von Sydow. Indeed, for that very reason, it is perhaps not entirely fortuitous that the analysis of Expressionism, brief in itself, should be introduced only at the conclu-

---

[71] 'Über die Idee einer Theologie der Kultur', *Philosophische Vorträge der Kant-Gesellschaft*, No. 24 (Berlin: Reuther & Reichard, 1919) pp. 28—52. *GW*, IX: 13—31. E.T., 'On the Idea of a Theology of Culture', *What is Religion?* translated and introduced by James Luther Adams (New York & London: Harper and Row, 1969) pp. 155—181.

sion of the main argument, as in fact a 'particularly impressive example' of certain principles already defined.[72]

Tillich has provided his own account of the historical background to this article. He tells us that, on his return from the First World War, he found 'a deep gap between the cultural revolution and the religious tradition in central and eastern Europe'.[73] The Lutheran, Roman and Greek Catholic churches rejected the cultural and political revolutions, the revolutionary movements repudiated the churches' right to pronounce on any secular matters, such as science, politics and the arts. It was, Tillich continues, 'very obvious for those of us who had spiritual ties with both sides that this situation was intolerable and, in the long run, disastrous for religion as well as for culture'.[74] The attempt was made, therefore, to close the gap between the sacred and secular realms, partly by founding political movements with strong religious affiliations[75], and partly by redefining the relation and character of these two realms in such a way that the *mutual immanence of religion and culture within each other could be established*. Tillich's essay remains the classic formulation of this latter attempt, written, he remarks, 'with the enthusiasm of those years in which we believed that a new beginning, a period of radical transformation ... had come upon us, in spite of breakdown and misery'.[76]

Tillich begins by drawing a fundamental distinction between the empirical sciences and, what he calls, the 'systematic cultural sciences' (to which both theology and art belong). In the former the progress of scientific enquiry can establish whether certain judgments about reality are correct, and to these judgments one's own individual attitude is subordinate; but in the latter the alternative 'right or wrong' does not apply because here 'the standpoint of the systematic thinker belongs to the heart of the matter itself'.[77] Thus in theology and the arts there is literally no limit to the attitudes which can be adopted—we can have, for example, a Catholic or modern Protestant view in dogmatics,

---

[72] *Ibid.*, p. 169.
[73] 'Religion and Secular Culture', *The Journal of Religion*, XXVI, No. 2 (April 1946) p. 79.
[74] *Ibid.*
[75] *Ibid.*
[76] *Ibid.*, p. 80.
[77] 'On the Idea of a Theology of Culture', *WR:* 155.

or a Gothic or Baroque style in aesthetics—since in each case the nature
of the discipline is determined not by abstract reasoning but by the
standpoints expressed by individuals, and expressed, moreover, in a
creative relation to the cultural groups and history to which those
individuals belong. This conclusion is decisive for Tillich's characterization of theology. Theology is not the science of one particular object,
which we call God, nor is it the scientific presentation of a special
complex of revelation; it is rather the *concretely normative* science of
religion, concerned with the particular forms in which the religious
attitude manifests itself.[78]

This immediately raises the question of the relation of religion
to culture. Religion has 'the peculiarity of not being attributable to
any particular psychic function', and none of those theories which
assigned religion either to the theoretical sphere (Hegel), to the practical
sphere (Kant) or to the realm of feeling (Schleiermacher) has survived.
Religion, on the contrary, is an *attitude of the spirit* which combines all
three elements in a complex whole.[79] Culture, however, can be divided
into two distinct spheres: the theoretical, which includes the aesthetic
and intellectual functions, and the practical, which includes the individual and socioethical functions. If we now conjoin these two analyses
of religion and culture, we arrive at the following conclusion: that
religion, although culturally operative only in relation to a theoretical
or practical attitude, cannot itself be equated with those theoretical or
practical acts in which it appears; that, indeed, the attitude of the
spirit is actualizable in *all* spiritual and cultural areas, and that 'in
every sphere of cultural life there is now a special circle, a special
sphere of influence of "the religious"'.[80] And it is precisely this contention, Tillich admits, that has provoked the great conflicts between church
and state, between art and the cultic, between science and dogma; that
has widened the 'deep gap' between the sacred and secular realms, and
created thereby a double truth, a double morality and a double justice.
This 'double existence', he proclaims, 'must be abolished at all costs; it
is intolerable as soon as it enters consciousness, for it destroys consciousness'.[81]

---

[78] *Ibid.*, p. 157.
[79] *Ibid.*, p. 160. *GW*, IX: 17.
[80] *Ibid.*, p. 161.
[81] *Ibid.*, p. 162.

Tillich's solution lies in his redefinition of the concept of religion. This is the turning-point of his article, and I quote the passage in full:—

Religion is directedness toward the Unconditional. Through existing realities, through values, through personal life, the meaning of unconditional reality becomes evident; before which every particular thing and the totality of all particulars—before which every value and the system of values—before which personality and community are shattered in their own self-sufficient being and value. This is not a new reality, alongside or above other things: that would only be a thing of a higher order which would again fall under the No. On the contrary, it is precisely through things that that reality is thrust upon us which it at one and the same time the No and the Yes to every thing. It is not a being, nor is it the substance or totality of beings; it is—to use a mystical formula—that which is above all beings which at the same time is the absolute Nothing and the absolute Something. But even the predicate "is" already disguises the facts of the case, since we are here dealing not with a reality of existence, but with a reality of meaning, and that indeed is the ultimate and deepest meaning—reality which shakes the foundation of all things and builds them up anew.[82]

The reason why, therefore, one cannot speak of special religious spheres of culture is that, following this redefinition of the concept of religion, *all such spheres have in principle ceased to exist.* If it is in the nature of the religious attitude that it is orientated towards that which, as the unconditioned reality, negates the entire cognitive sphere as it affirms it, then clearly this attitude cannot assign to itself a special cognition, object or epistemology whereby the unconditional is expressed; and equally, if it is the task of culture to realize the individual forms of meaning, to arrange them within a theoretical or practical system, then that which is revealed in religion as the ultimate ground of meaning is the hidden presupposition of every cultural endeavour. In a word, *every religious act is culturally formed and every form of culture is implicitly religious.* The mutual immanence of religion and culture is thus affirmed in a cultural synthesis of the two, that is, in a *theology of culture* which overcomes the culture-destroying antagonism between science and dogma by 'a science religious in itself', and which replaces the distinction between art and the cultus by an *art religious in itself.*[83]

---

[82] *Ibid.*, pp. 162—163.
[83] *Ibid.*, p. 168.

Significantly enough, it is at this point that Tillich introduces Expressionism as a 'particularly impressive example' of the argument so far advanced, taking precedence over other examples drawn from philosophy, ethics and politics; and once again it is the method adopted by Expressionism that leads to this conclusion: the form-breaking character of its style is clearly most appropriate for the revelation of that which, following the redefinition of religion, *shatters* the attitude of self-sufficiency and *shakes* the foundation of all things.[84] But still more important is that the progression of Tillich's argument leaves us in no doubt as to why he should have superimposed on Expressionism a theological judgment of its art. For him, Expressionism is the classic representative of the theology of culture. Expressionism, we might even say, is the *theology of culture at work.*

Nor should we be surprised by this. As we have seen throughout this chapter, Expressionism, on Tillich's view at least, denies that religious art is constituted by its picturing of a special sphere of the 'religious' in culture, and maintains instead that what is religious is the presupposition of culture itself, thereby justifying the revelation of ultimate meaning through any cultural form and in the absence of any overtly religious theme. *Religious art is religious by virtue of what it expresses not by virtue of what it depicts.* Similarly we can say of the 'category of expressiveness'—of the principle which incorporates both the method and interpretation of reality by which religious art is determined—that it is that category of the cultural synthesis proposed by Tillich which is devoted to the manifestation of the divine in the artistic act and its creations; that it is the criterion of aesthetics within the theology of culture. Accordingly it is to the theology of culture that we must turn for the further development of Tillich's philosophy of art.

---

[84] *Ibid.*, p. 169.

CHAPTER TWO
TOWARDS A THEOLOGY
OF CULTURE
I. SYNTHESIS AND THE THEORY OF MEANING

The aim of Tillich's aesthetics is to delineate the function and meaning of art within a philosophy of religion which proposes a synthesis between religion and culture, this synthesis being more generally known as the theology of culture. According to Tillich, Expressionism, by the spiritual interpretation of reality it offers, provides us with the classic formulation of the theology of culture within the visual arts, and, for that reason, gives its name to the definition of religious style. Thus we may say that the formula 'religious art is expressionistic' is a paraphrase of the central proposition of the theology of culture: that within the synthesis outlined by this theology the mutual immanence of religion and culture is in principle established.

This brief summary of the argument presented in the preceding chapter indicates the place from which Tillich's aesthetic theory now develops, that is, from the *demand for synthesis*. Indeed, it is perhaps no exaggeration to say that the primary intention of Tillich's entire philosophy of religion is to find that point at which religion and culture conjoin, and from there to effect a 'synthetic solution' within the so-called theology of culture. As he writes, 'the way of synthesis is alone genuine and legitimate'[1],—a remark which, by expressing the basic need to overcome the dangerous dualism between religion and culture, points to the necessity of an interpretation of reality that will

---

[1] 'Religionsphilosophie', *Lehrbuch der Philosophie*, ed. Max Dessoir, Bd. II: *Die Philosophie in ihren Einzelgebieten* (Berlin: Ullstein, 1925) pp. 765—835. *GW*, I: 297—364. E.T., 'The Philosophy of Religion', *WR:* 30. That Tillich is a theologian of synthesis has been noted by many commentators. See particularly, R. C. Johnson, 'A Theologian of Synthesis', *Theology Today*, XV (April 1958) pp. 36—42; Kenelm Forster, 'Paul Tillich and

reveal the underlying unity of all aspects of the spiritual and cultural life. The same demand for synthesis can be seen if we turn away from the contrast 'religion and culture' to the still more familiar contrast of 'holy and profane', the distinction that Tillich calls the 'foundation of every philosophy of religion and culture'.[2] On the basis of this polarity we can define the church and society as those two distinct sociological realities in which, respectively, the holy is allegedly presented and the profane appears. The way of synthesis, however, rejects this opposition: it recognizes the 'logical consistency' of the contrast but 'denies its factual truth' by establishing that point at which the holy may be considered the universal presupposition of human existence in all its functions.[3] The theology of culture, in other words, effects the synthesis by disclosing the extent to which religion, far from being a *special* function of man's spiritual life, is a dimension implicit within all areas of human activity, including those cultural activities from which it is normally dissociated. Just as every religious act, whether in organized religion or private worship, is culturally formed, so there is no cultural creation without the dimension of the holy expressed in it. This, then, is an interpretation of the holy in which its position *beside* the profane is abolished.

> The "alongsidedness" must not be permitted to stand; that is, religion and theology must not remain alongside the other functions and sciences. The synthesis . . . can be attained only if the normative science of religion is in some sense a normative cultural science in general, and only if religion is presented not as one function alongside others but as *an attitude in all the other functions.*[4]

Before coming to an account of the synthesis, one final point should be made, namely, that the theology of culture is Tillich's rebuttal of the charge that, in defining religious art as expressionistic, he has superimposed on Expressionism a theological and, for the most part, unwar-

---

St. Thomas', *Paul Tillich in Catholic Thought*, ed. T. A. O'Meara and C. D. Weisser (London: Darton, Longman and Todd, 1965) p. 97; Gustave Weigel, 'Contemporaneous Protestantism and Paul Tillich', *Theological Studies*, XI, No. 2 (June 1950) pp. 177—202; and Gerard Siegwalt, 'La théologie systématique des P. Tillich', *Revue d'Histoire et de Philosophie Religieuses*, XLI (1961) pp. 191—192.

2 'Church and Culture', *IH:* 220.

3 *Ibid.*, p. 221.

4 'The Philosophy of Religion', *WR:* 34 (my emphasis).

ranted evaluation of its art. For if, according to the synthesis, the religious attitude is inherent in all cultural functions—thus including art itself—Tillich could reply that the theological terms he has employed refer solely to that aspect of every art that is religious *a priori*, and that therefore the various styles and intentions of the artists concerned make no difference whatever to the appropriateness of this terminology. In this case, the phrase 'theology of art' would not denote the theological perspective through which works of art *could* be viewed—and which we may or may not consider legitimate—but rather that area of artistic creativity which is *necessarily religious and without which the artistic process itself would be unintelligible.* If, therefore, the concepts 'immanent mysticism' and 'belief-ful realism' are indeed justifiable descriptions of the religious attitude, then these concepts can, with equal justification, be applied to those artistic images *which express the same attitude*. In neither case would we be dealing with two separate histories —with the history of theology and the history of art—but with the various conceptual and artistic forms in which this singular attitude has been expressed.

With these remarks in mind, we turn now to the synthesis itself. The theology of culture can be approached from two angles, each of which reflects an interesting change of emphasis in Tillich's thinking. The first has to do with a *theory of meaning*, which is presented substantially in his earlier works, the second with a *theory of being*, which we find primarily in his *Systematic Theology*, notably in the discussion of the doctrine of God and revelation. This change can be seen, to give a brief example, in Tillich's classifications of the nature of philosophy. In his *Das System der Wissenschaften* (1923), philosophy is described as the 'theory of the principles of meaning'[5], whereas in the first volume of the *Systematic Theology* (1951), philosophy is said to deal 'with the structure of being in itself'.[6] Without developing this point, it is nevertheless important to note that at no stage in his theology does Tillich depart from the view that the problems of meaning and being are interrelated problems. Thus we shall see that the climax of the theology of culture is reached when the ontological ground of being is identified

---

[5] *Das System der Wissenschaften nach Gegenständen und Methoden. Ein Entwurf* (Göttingen: Vandenhoeck & Ruprecht, 1923). *GW*, I: 109—293. 'Philosophie ist Lehre von den Sinnprinzipien' (*Ibid.*, p. 232).

[6] *ST*, 1: 25.

as the unconditioned *presupposition* of every act of meaning.[7] By beginning, therefore, with the theory of meaning we are introducing a formal and not material distinction between the two theories, one which enables us to analyse the synthesis precisely at the point where Tillich's discussion of religious art left off. For we remember that in all his surveys the element which distinguishes religious style from every other —what constitutes its expressiveness—was primarily its perception of the unconditioned *meaning* manifested in and through the conditioned forms of existence. The following account, then, is no more than an extension of the argument that meaning has a transcendental reference.

For Tillich 'the field in which culture and religion meet is the common directedness toward the unity of meaning'.[8] In the essay 'On the Idea of a Theology of Culture' we have seen already how Tillich locates his definition of religion within the theory of meaning. Religion, to repeat, is an attitude of the spirit directed towards the ultimate *reality of meaning*.[9] In the same article, culture was described as having two aspects, the theoretical and the practical. Tillich's intention is now to show how every cultural activity contains a reference to meaning, and how the meaning implied in culture presupposes the ultimate referent of meaning to which religion refers.

In his *Das System der Wissenschaften* Tillich develops his argument at some length. There are, he says, three main types of science: the science of thinking (logic and mathematics, *die Denkwissenschaften*), the science of existence (the empirical sciences, *die Seinswissenschaften*), and the sciences of 'spirit' *(die Geisteswissenschaften)*.[10] The last named refer to the cultural or normative sciences, which have as their object activities like epistemology, aesthetics and metaphysics in the theoretical sphere, and jurisprudence, political science and ethics in the practical sphere. What distinguishes the cultural normative sciences from the other two is that, whereas in the sciences of thinking thought is directed towards the concept of *validity* and thus possesses an axiomatic certainty lacking in other kinds of knowledge, and whereas in the empirical sciences thought is directed towards existence with a view to *describing* it correctly, in the cultural sciences the object of knowledge is neither

---

[7] See Ch. IV, pp. 126—127.
[8] 'The Philosophy of Religion', *WR:* 60.
[9] 'On the Idea of a Theology of Culture', *WR:* 62—63. See above, p. 35.
[10] *Das System der Wissenschaften, GW,* I: 120—121.

a priori nor pre-given but *created,* born in the creative process of spirit *(Geist).*[11]

The cultural sciences, therefore, involve the creative-spiritual activities. In this definition it is the notion of 'spirit' which establishes the connection between culture and the theory of meaning. *Geist* depends on two other concepts, thought *(Denken)* and being *(Sein),* which constitute the essential components of the act of knowledge, namely, the act as such and that towards which it is directed, the thinking and that which is intended or thought.[12] The peculiarity of *Geist,* however, is that it is not reducible to either of these two elements but involves both. For *Geist* is the self-determination of thinking in being *(die Selbstbestimmung des Denkens im Sein),* the form of 'thought-in-being' *(die Form des seienden Denkens),* the *synthetic* act of knowledge in the existential dimension.[13]

Quite what Tillich means by this can be explained if we refer back to the sciences of thinking and existence. In the former, knowledge is directed towards those universal concepts or laws to which every object must accomodate itself, if only because these concepts or laws are the forms of thought itself: the rules of logic and mathematics are thus framed apart from the specifics of existence and neglect the particularities of being; in the latter, however, the self-sufficiency of thought is replaced by a form of knowledge subject to these particularities, the empirical sciences being determined by the causal context in which objects are observed and by the permanent process of verification in relation to them. In the 'sciences of spirit', on the other hand, thought is able to free itself both from the attitude of the empiricist, which is subservient to reality, and from the attitude of the logician, which is divorced from reality. *Geist,* that is to say, can project itself into the existential order, having the power to become a part of existence by creating something in existence, something which, once created, it can observe and evaluate.

> Dadurch macht es sich selbst zu einem Objekt neben anderen Objekten. Das Denken stellt sich unter all die Bedingungen und Bestimmungen, die dem Sein zukommen, in die das Denken das Sein aufgelöst hat. Das Denken wird ein Stück Existenz. Wenn wir fragen, wo sich dieses

---

[11] *Ibid.,* pp. 213—214.
[12] *Ibid.,* p. 210.
[13] *Ibid.*

existierende Denken befindet, so können wir nur antworten: Im "Inneren" der bewußten Wesen, für uns vor allem im Geistesleben *der Menschheit.*[14]

Geist, therefore, is the dynamic power of *creativity* in the human personality, and man is *das geistig-Individuelle* in and through whom the theoretical and practical acts of the cultural sciences originate and develop. Culture itself, to put the matter another way, is the creation of the generative activity of man as the individual 'spirit-bearing' form *(die individuelle geisttragende Gestalt);* it is the result of the 'productive' character of the conscious being, in which no single psychic function but rather the whole personality, with its capacities for thinking, feeling and willing, acts in the creation of something new.[15] In this activity of of the spirit, thought frees itself from its dependence on the forms of pure thought and pure being and constructs something which cannot be deduced either from the structural laws of mind or from the observable objects of sense. Thus 'freedom' is a presupposition of the creativity of *Geist.*[16] If we now ask what it is that constitutes the free human act of creation in the realm of spirit, the answer is provided in the *theory of meaning:* 'Das Erkenntnisziel der Geisteswissenschaften ist *der Sinnbegriff . . . Die Akte der geisttragenden Gestalt sind sinngebende Akte'.*[17]

With this conclusion Tillich's argument arrives at its destination, albeit by a somewhat circuitous route. Every spiritual act is an act of meaning *(Sinn). Geist* is creative in the realm of meaning, and presupposes a link between meaning and being which logic disregards by divorcing the notion of validity from reality and which empiricism overlooks in its rejection of the freedom of spirit from reality. More generally we can say that the principles of the theory of meaning are not derived from the sciences of thought and being but from the *function of the consciousness in the spiritual act.* This, we should add, explains Tillich's earlier remark that the difference between the empirical sciences and the systematic cultural sciences is that in the latter 'the standpoint of the systematic thinker belongs to the heart of the matter itself'.[18] For, following the concept of *Geist* and regardless of the various

---

[14] *Ibid.,* p. 120 (my emphasis).
[15] *Ibid.,* pp. 212, 210 & 121.
[16] *Ibid.,* p. 210.
[17] *Ibid.,* p. 222 (my emphasis).
[18] 'On the Idea of a Theology of Culture', *WR:* 155. See above, p. 33.

theories of knowledge we may adopt, of how we may construe the relation between subject and object, spirit is by definition the actualization of meaning (Sinnvollzug) brought to expression in the individual personality.[19] In other terms, the attribution of meaning by man to some aspect of the existential order is precisely that creative-spiritual activity by which the cultural sciences are established. Thus the reality in which the 'spirit-bearing form' lives and creates is meaningful reality, the culture itself; and every cultural science, in both its theoretical and practical subdivisions, represents the creative synthesis of thought and being in the human consciousness. This points to the two-fold character of the Geisteswissenschaft: that it is both productive of and created by the act of meaning in the spiritual act; that it is both the prius and posterius of the spiritual creation. 'Sie lebt von den Schöpfungen, die sie mitschafft ... sie ist die systematische Form des sich selbst bestimmenden Denkens'.[20]

Having determined in this way that the theory of meaning stands at the centre of any proper understanding of the origin and function of the cultural sciences, Tillich now applies the theory extensively in his analysis of their form. For our purposes, it is sufficient to notice that Tillich offers a tripartite classification of the 'elements' of the Geisteswissenschaften: first, the theory of the principles of meaning (die Sinnprinzipienlehre, which is philosophy); second, the theory of the material of meaning (die Sinnmateriallehre, which is the history of thought from the viewpoint of the historical actualization of the principles); and third, the normative system of meanings (die Sinnormenlehre, which is systematics).[21] In the study of religion, this three-fold scheme appears

---

[19] 'The Philosophy of Religion', WR: 56.
[20] Das System der Wissenschaften, GW: I: 220.
[21] Ibid., pp. 230—245. This same classification is proposed by Ernst Troeltsch, to whom Das System der Wissenschaften is dedicated. Cf. Troeltsch, Der Historismus und seine Überwindung (Berlin: Rolf Heise, 1924) p. 28. E.T., Christian Thought: Its History and Application (London: University of London Press, 1923) p. 81. What Tillich has to say about Troeltsch's 'religious a priori', the category designating the special function of religion, is relevant to the argument at hand.
Was gemeint ist, ist deutlich. Es soll ein Gültiges gegenüber dem bloß Tatsächlichen, und es soll ein Eigentümlich-Religiöses gegenüber dem bloß Kulturellen festgehalten werden. Das Suchen nach der religiösen Wesenheit im platonisch-kantischen Sinne leitet Troeltschs Arbeit. Es ist nur merk-

as the *philosophy of religion*, which is the theory of the religious function and its categories; as the *cultural history of religion*, which attends to the individual realizations of the concept of religion in history; and as *theology*, which has been defined already as the normative and systematic presentation of the concrete realization of the concept of religion.[22] As is the case with every cultural science, these three elements belong inseparably together and are in continual interaction. What distinguishes religion, however, is that, although susceptible to the normal divisions of the *Geisteswissenschaften*, it cannot be treated as one science among others since it alone possesses a relevance for all spheres and disciplines of the cultural sciences. This, then, is the turning-point in Tillich's theory of meaning and recalls once more the main problem of the synthesis: of how and in what way the normative science of religion can be considered the normative cultural science in general. In what respects do the principles of meaning in the spiritual acts of the *Geisteswissenschaften* presuppose the ultimate principle of meaning in the spiritual act of religion?

As we have seen, the attribution of meaning by the human consciousness in the spiritual act constitutes the common characteristic in the theoretical and practical spheres of culture. All the cultural sciences, in all the diversity of their interests, are brought to a focus in the dialectic of thought and being, which operates as the inner tension or 'dynamic' of the spiritual act, and in the creative activity of man as the 'spirit-bearing form' in existence. This conclusion, however, could be •interpreted as saying no more than that *Geist* is a subjective concept,

---

würdig und doch nicht zufällig, daß Troeltsch über die methodische Forderung nicht hinausgekommen ist, daß wir eine deutliche, inhaltliche Charakterisierung der religiösen *a priori* vergeblich suchen. Wird die Religion zu einer Funktion neben anderen gemacht, so ist der ihr innewohnende Anspruch auf Unbedingtheit unerfüllt geblieben, und es läßt sich keine zugängliche inhaltliche Bestimmung für sie finden. Und wird die Religion primär als Geistesfunktion gewertet, so kann zwar ein formales Geltungsbewußtsein gesichert werden, aber der Anspruch auf Transzendenz im überformalen Sinne bleibt unerfüllt. Das bedeutet aber in beiden Beziehungen: Das Unbedingte ist dem Bedingten geopfert' (*Kant-Studien*, Jg. 29, 1924), pp. 351—358. *GW*, XII: 167—168. Cf., *Perspectives on Nineteenth & Twentieth Century Protestant Thought*, ed. C. E. Braaten [New York: Harper & Row, 1967] pp. 230—234.

[22] 'The Philosophy of Religion', *WR:* 32—33.

that the ascription of meaning implies the dominance of the individual attitude. This is for example the way in which the concept is treated by nominalism and pragmatism. Nominalism, says Tillich, regards all concepts as subjective constructions, as words or fictions, which have meaning for life in general but no objective truth; and pragmatism, orientated as it is towards the technological attitude, considers concepts to be no more than acts of object-manipulation, significant primarily in the dynamics of power relations.[23] Tillich, we recall, has already provided a partial answer to these positions in his earlier attack on the 'spirit of capitalist society'; but the argument developed now is no duplication of that presented in *The Religious Situation*. For whereas the concept of 'belief-ful realism' was introduced as an *alternative* to the bourgeois attitude—the perception that meaning has a transcendental reference being *contrary* to the ethic of self-sufficiency—Tillich now insists that the awareness of meaning itself implies this perception, that in every spiritual act the orientation is necessarily towards the unconditioned meaning. The previous alternative, in other words, has here given way to a requirement.[24]

Tillich begins by saying that in every act of meaning lies an awareness 'of the interconnection of meaning in which every separate meaning stands and without which it would be meaningless'.[25] This interconnection of meaning contains 'the silent presupposition of the meaningfulness of the whole, the unity of all possible meanings, i.e., faith in the meaning of life itself'.[26] Meaning, therefore, is always a 'system of meanings', and the 'system of all possible systems of meaning we call objectively *world*, subjectively *culture*'.[27] From this we can say that the concept of meaning requires a concept of system, and that accordingly cultural science is concerned with the formation of a system, with the attempt to prevent the degeneration of the single meaning into a meaningless aphorism by securing its position in relation to other meanings, by placing it within a unique and creative perception of reality. If, however, we now go one stage further and ask whether

---

[23] *Ibid.*, pp. 47—48.
[24] See above, Ch. I, pp. 15—17.
[25] 'The Philosophy of Religion', *WR:* 57.
[26] *IH:* 221.
[27] *Ibid.*, p. 222. See also *Das System der Wissenschaften*, GW, I: 223.

reality is meaningful because we perceive it as such, Tillich replies
that every act of meaning, whether ascribing meaning to an element
within the world or to the world itself, depends on the presupposition of
an *unconditioned meaningfulness within that act itself*. The unconditioned meaning 'bears the meaning of each single meaning as well as the
meaning of the whole. That is, it is the basis of meaning'.[28]

> Die Akte der geisttragenden Gestalt sind sinngebende Akte. Das ist
> nicht so zu verstehen, als ob eine an sich sinnlose Wirklichkeit durch die
> Akte der geisttragenden Gestalten sinnvoll würde. Solche pragmatische
> Auffassung ist dem Wesen des Geistes fern. Vielmehr sind die sinngeben-
> den Akte sinnerfüllende Akte. Der dem Seienden in all seinen Formen
> innewohnende Sinn kommt in den geistigen Akten zu sich selbst, der
> Sinn der Wirklichkeit verwirklicht sich im Geistigen. Alles Sein steht
> unter dem Gesetz der unbedingten Form, aber allein im Geist wird das
> Unbedingte als Unbedingtes, als Geltung erfaßt. Im Geist erfüllt sich der
> Sinn des Seins.[29]

When fully understood, therefore, the *Geisteswissenschaften*, although
meaning-activities of the spirit, are not subjective creations but point
beyond thought and existence and beyond themselves to the unconditioned meaning, to that which is at the same time the meaning inherent
in all forms of thinking and being. This unconditional basis of each
meaning is transcendent in regard to every meaning, and cannot accordingly be grasped as such in any single act of meaning by the individual;
it cannot be determined by any specific form of thought or by the
totality of all thought-forms; it cannot be identified with any form
of existence or by all the forms of existence together. In this way the
concept of meaning—and by extension the structure and function of the
cultural sciences—presupposes an unequivocally valid ground of meaning,
which is itself independent of any subjective psychological construction.
In traditional language, this ground of meaning which surpasses all that
is conceivable is called *God*, and the direction of the spirit which turns
towards him is called *religion*.[30]

Thus culture, as the creative activity of the spirit orientated towards
the unconditional meaning, is *implicitly religious*. Every cultural act
contains a religious attitude in so far as it is directed towards the

---

[28] *Ibid.*
[29] *Das System der Wissenschaften, GW*, I: 222.
[30] *IH*: 222.

Unconditional in the theoretical and practical spheres of the functions of the spirit. Conversely, religion is neither a supplement to or synthesis of the functions of culture: it is not a new value inserted into a system of values but rather that attitude of the spirit pointing to the *presupposition of every value and every cultural form*.[31] By this means an essential unity is established between religion and culture. In every act of meaning faith in the absolute meaning is disclosed; every cultural science is thus a revelation of its own presupposition. In Tillich's words: 'culture is a form of expression of religion, and religion is the substance of culture' *(die Kultur ist Ausdrucksform der Religion, und die Religion ist Inhalt der Kultur)*.[32] With this remark, which Tillich tells us is the central proposition of his theology of culture, the synthesis is attained within the sphere of meaning. For with it both religion and culture are driven to the point where each must apprehend itself as an expression of the same attitude, as either the explicit or implicit reference to the Unconditional as the transcendent ground of meaning.[33]

Enough has now been said about Tillich's theory of meaning for us to return to his philosophy of art. On the basis of the argument so far, the following definition of art may be proposed: *Art is a medium of the unconditional meaning in the life of the spirit*. This definition depends on three subsidiary propositions: first, that aesthetics belongs to the theoretical division of the cultural sciences; second, that art, as a cultural activity, contains a reference to meaning; and third, that in every reference to meaning the unconditionality of meaning is presupposed. Hence the aesthetic act entails the revelation of ultimate meaning. In terms of the synthesis, this same conclusion can be better expressed by reference to the concept of spirit or *Geist*. The cultural sciences have to do with spiritual acts; in every spiritual act the

---

[31] 'Religion ... is not one meaning-function alongside others. This follows immediately from its character as directedness toward the Unconditional. That which is the basis of all functions of meaning cannot itself be one of these functions. Rather, the relation is such that the meaning-functions come to fulfilment in meaning only in relatedness to the unconditional meaning, and that therefore the religious intention is the presupposition for successful meaning-fulfilment in all functions.' 'The Philosophy of Religion', *WR:* 73.

[32] *Ibid. GW*, I: 329.

[33] *PE:* xiii.

orientation is towards the unconditioned meaning; since both religion and art are spiritual activities, in each the focus of concern is *identical*. Strictly speaking, therefore, the judgment that art is religious in itself cannot be a theological judgment superimposed on art since the dimension to which theology refers is the one dimension implied in all areas of artistic creativity. That art, in other terms, is the actualization of the religious attitude in the theoretical sphere of cultural life follows from the fact that the religious attitude alone is the all-embracing attitude incorporated within every form of cultural expression. Thus we may conclude that, at the point where the synthesis between religion and art is achieved—that is, in their common directedness towards the ultimate meaning—art is religious in the same way that religion is religious, and that any legitimate designation of the religious perspective—for example, 'belief-ful realism' or 'immanent mysticism'— is simultaneously a legitimate description of the artistic perspective.

What, then, is the difference between religion and art, or, more generally, between the holy and profane? From the viewpoint of the synthesis just proposed, there can, of course, be no distinction since all theoretical and practical acts of meaning are directed to the absolute alone. Tillich accepts, however, that the intelligibility of terms like 'holy' and 'profane' requires the possibility of making some distinction, and that by this means we may establish an initial difference between them of *intention*.

> There is the possibility of so directing one's mind to single meanings, that the act of faith, although implicitly concurring, is excluded from one's consciousness. That is the profane, unbelieving, worldly attitude; just so is it possible, while excluding the single forms of meaning and their relationships, to direct oneself to the absolute meaning. That is the holy, believing, religious attitude. The first is directed toward the single meaning and its fulfilment in the system of meanings of world. In the second, the single meaning is only a medium, a symbol, a vessel of the absolute meaning.[34]

This distinction between the holy and profane is directly reflected in the distinction between religion and culture, since here too the division between them is recognized primarily in their differing intentions. 'Religion is directedness toward the Unconditional, and culture is

---

[34] *IH:* 224—225.

directedness toward the conditioned forms and their unity'.[35] Religion, that is, relates acts of meaning to their unconditioned presupposition, and culture relates them to the meaningful world it knows. Thus, despite the truth of religion that every cultural act contains the unconditioned meaning, what distinguishes culture is that it is unaware of this fact, that none of its acts of meaning are achieved with a consciously religious attitude. 'Culture as culture is therefore substantially, but not intentionally, religious'.[36]

This conclusion tells us more about the relation between religious and secular art. In religious art the artist's intention is to reveal the unconditioned meaning through the medium of encountered reality. This is a *conscious act*, in which, to use the language of 'belief-ful realism', the artist presents a 'spiritual interpretation of reality' whereby the transcendent meaning of all meanings is expressed. In secular art, however, the artist focuses on the particularity of concrete things and seeks to establish their individual meaning in the system of finite meanings. But notwithstanding this difference, no art can be essentially profane but only consciously profane. For no matter what the intentions of the poet, painter or novelist may be—no matter how forthright he may be in his denial of the religious perspective—the dimension of the holy is implied within his work. Secular art, that is to say, is the exclusion from the consciousness of that ultimate level of meaning entailed in every aesthetic act. In this sense, then, *all* art is religious irrespective of the personality or allegiances of the artist. Even in secular art the denial of religion is never absolute.

This same line of reasoning helps us to classify the subject-matter of religious art. The subjects of artistic expression—the themes, situations or objects pictured by the artist—fall into two groups: there are those by which the artist seeks to reveal nothing other than the unconditioned ground of meaning, and there are those which are portrayed by him without any explicit sense of their ultimate reference. The first are the media of religious expression, the second of cultural expression. This does not mean that the subjects of religious art are not part of the culture but rather that they are religious by intention; the subjects of all other aesthetic acts are not so by intention, although they are in

---

[35] 'The Philosophy of Religion', *WR:* 59.
[36] *Ibid.*

actuality. Because every attributive act of meaning therefore presupposes the unconditional basis of meaning, every artistic expression of a particular subject, no matter what that subject may be or include, is either an explicit or tacit expression of meaning in its ultimate dimension. In a word, the apprehension of meaning in itself, and irrespective of the artist's choice of subject-matter, entails the religious attitude.

This recalls the definition proposed at the end of the last chapter, namely, that religious art is religious by virtue of what it expresses not by virtue of what it depicts.[37] Religion is not a special function of man's spiritual life, the mere portrayal of which would constitute religious art, but is the experience of a quality in all areas of human activity, including the aesthetic functions. The consequence of this is extremely significant. An art that is open to the ultimate meaning is not necessarily one in which the majority of artists are actively religious, nor does it belong necessarily to an age of prescribed religious objects. Indeed, on Tillich's theory of meaning, it is quite possible that the number of true religious artists can be greater in a so-called 'irreligious' period than in a 'religious' one. The requirement of religious art is rather that the artist should be turned towards and receptive to the ultimate meaning, that the demand for unconditional meaning should permeate and guide his own creative work. For such an artist, the holy is not a problem but a presupposition; and for him there is no profane subject, no profane history and no profane world.

In many ways this account of Tillich's aesthetics in relation to his theory of meaning raises more problems than it solves. Religion, we have seen, is the substance of culture, and, by implication, of art as well. This has already told us something about the structure of art, notably that art as an act of meaning is directly or indirectly a medium of unconditional meaning. But to what extent, we may ask, would an analysis of the formal properties of art, of those elements that go to make up the artistic act as such, reinforce this interpretation? What is called for, in other words, is not so much an argument depending on the definition of art as a cultural science or spiritual act, but one which proceeds on the basis of an exact account of the nature of art itself. Thereafter the question would be whether the nature of faith corresponds to the nature of art, and whether Tillich's 'theology of art' does or does

---

[37] See above, p. 36.

not provide us with an appropriate vocabularly of aesthetics. In a similar fashion, the proposition that culture (and so art) is a form of expression of religion has told us something about the intentions of the artist and his subject-matter. But this being so, in what respects may we speak of art in terms of the concept of revelation? For if, to give one example, religious art does not depend on the picturing of religious objects, how are we to explain those canvases which duplicate pictorially the Christian affirmation that Jesus was the Christ, and which maintain accordingly that the gospels are the reliable sources of this event? This problem becomes more acute when we remember that Tillich's aesthetics covers not only the visual arts but also literature. In the biblical narratives are we dealing with a portrait informed and created by the historical figure it depicts, or with one in which the significance attributed by the evangelists outweighs any question of the importance that figure had in real life? If the latter is the case, then has not the artistic imagination here produced a religion?

Tillich's replies to these questions introduce us to some of the major sections of his philosophy of art, each of which will be discussed in later chapters. So, in Chapter Three, we shall look at Tillich's analysis of the structure of the art object, and, in Chapter Four, at his account of art in terms of the concept of revelation and at the Christology required by this account. For the rest of this chapter, however, I want to return to a problem left unresolved in Chapter One.

The problem has to do with Tillich's demand for realism in religious art. This demand, we remember, was summarized by the phrase 'the situation of our time', according to which a fundamental prerequisite of religious style was established. To quote an earlier remark, a picture is called religious when 'it speaks to us about conditions and feelings which we ourselves recognize as accurate descriptions of our own experience'.[38] These descriptions incorporated categories familiar in the existentialist doctrine of man—*viz.*, despair and estrangement, doubt and meaninglessness—and the extent to which an artist employed them decided the degree to which his work was religious. Using these criteria, therefore, Tillich was able to distinguish between the more and the less religious painters (between Van Gogh and Uhde), this distinction further reminding us that a picture is not religious because its subject is.

---

[38] See above, p. 6.

Matters were complicated, however, by Botticelli's 'Madonna with Singing Angels'. For whereas the idealistic style of this picture would normally consign it to the second group of paintings, Tillich's own preference for it appeared to contradict that classification. In what sense, then, could the Botticelli be called a non-realistic but nevertheless religious picture? And this question prompted another: Is there any artistic style than can never be called religious?[39]

It is not hard to see how Tillich's theory of meaning multiplies our difficulties at this point. For if, to follow the theory, every art-form is implicitly religious, the second of these questions has been answered in such a way that the religious character of a style cannot be determined by its realistic or non-realistic elements. For example, although we may deplore Hoffmann's sentimental portraits of Jesus, we cannot say that these pictures are not religious because all aesthetic acts are acts of meaning and every act of meaning presupposes ultimate meaning. We may object to the meaning attributed to Jesus in a Hoffmann canvas, but we cannot deny the fact of its attribution, which is sufficient for the argument at hand. Indeed, by arguing in this way, it would seem that we may dispense altogether with the criterion of realism in the classification of religious art and use it merely to determine the subject-matter of a particular style: that some styles are concerned with descriptions of the human predicament and some are not. But in either case it no longer matters what is depicted—be it a sunflower or a crucifixion—since whatever is the object of the artistic imagination is, by virtue of that fact alone, located within the sphere of religion.

How, then, are we to co-ordinate these two aspects of Tillich's philosophy of art, the category of realism with the theory of meaning? One way is to look more closely at the description of 'the situation of our time' which Tillich, in his first survey, deemed necessary for religious style, and more particularly at the primary concept by which the realism of that description is determined. This is the concept of estrangement, a concept central to Tillich's *theory of being*. Expressed otherwise, therefore, estrangement is that category of Tillich's theory of being which ensures that the language of religious art incorporates the language of the world as it is; and to that extent, as we shall see, it determines a whole range of further stylistic classifications.

---

[39] See above, p. 7.

II. THE THEORY OF BEING: ESTRANGEMENT AND THE CATEGORY OF REALISM IN RELIGIOUS ART

So central is the *ontological* concept of estrangement to Tillich's thinking that no part of his philosophy, and certainly not his philosophy of art, can be adequately undertood without it. One of the most important examples of this fact is to be found in the *Systematic Theology*, where the use of the concept is necessary to the method employed by Tillich. This is the so-called 'method of correlation', and it too plays a significant part in Tillich's aesthetics.[40]

Briefly put, Tillich's correlative method is an exercise in apologetics: it aims to relate and adapt the Christian message to the modern situation in such a way that the unique character of that message is retained. Apologetic theology, he says, is 'answering theology': 'it answers the questions implied in the "situation" in the power of the eternal message and with the means provided by the situation whose questions it answers'.[41] Accordingly, correlation seeks to explain 'the contents of the Christian faith through existential questions and theological answers in mutual interdependence'[42]; it recognizes both that man 'cannot receive an answer to a question he has not asked', and that he has asked 'in his very existence ... questions which Christianity answers'.[43] Thus the first

---

[40] For more details on the method of correlation, see Tillich, 'The Problem of Theological Method', *The Journal of Religion*, XXVII, No. 1 (January 1947) pp. 16—26; Bernard M. Loomer, 'Tillich's Theology of Correlation', *The Journal of Religion*, XXXVI, No. 3 (July 1956) pp. 150—156; Guyton B. Hammond, 'An Examination of Tillich's Method of Correlation', *Journal of Bible and Religion*, XXXII, No. 3 (July 1964) pp. 248—251; and Jacob Taubes, 'On the Nature of the Theological Method: Some Reflections on the Methodological Principles of Tillich's Theology', *The Journal of Religion*, XXXIV, No. 1 (January 1954) pp. 12—25. The most substantial critique of the method is by J. P. Clayton: *The Concept of Correlation: Paul Tillich and the Possibility of a Mediating Theology* (Berlin: De Gruyter, 1979).

[41] *ST*, 1: 6. This distinguishes apologetic from 'kerygmatic' theology. If the 'unchangeable truth of the message (kerygma) over against the changing demands of the situation' is emphasized, then that theology is kerygmatic. *ST*, 1: 4.

[42] *ST*, 1: 68.

[43] *ST*, 2: 15 & *ST*, 1: 73.

duty of the theologian is to analyse the existential situation from which the questions arise; he must seek a common ground between the one who asks and the one who answers by listening to the questions asked *before* answering them in terms of the message.

Correlation, however, imposes a second duty upon the theologian, namely that he should work not only as a philosopher but more exactly as an ontologist. Analysing the existential situation is, Tillich continues, the principal role of philosophy, philosophy here being described as 'that cognitive approach to reality in which reality as such is the object'.[44] But this analysis also reveals that the questions asked here are fundamentally ontological questions: questions, that is, about being and non-being, ontological anxiety and the ambiguities of life. Philosophy, therefore, must 'answer in ontological terms'.[45] So the theologian, in first seeking the questions put by the situation, must work as a philosopher, and must, moreover, phrase the answers given in Christian revelation in ontological terms if they are to be relevant to that situation.[46] In this sense, correlation, as Scharlemann has described it, speaks a 'theontological language': the questions implied in human existence, and elaborated in ontological terms, determine the meaning and the theological interpretation of the answers as they appear in the classical religious

---

[44] *ST*, 1: 22.

[45] *Ibid.*, p. 24.

[46] Theology therefore is fundamentally an ontological enquiry. 'This makes the division between philosophy and theology impossible, for, whatever the relation of God, world, and man may be, it lies in the frame of being; and any interpretation of the meaning and structure of being as being, unavoidably has consequences for the interpretation of God, man, and the world in their interrelations.' 'Philosophy and Theology', *PE:* 86. Cf. 'Relation of Metaphysics and Theology', *Review of Metaphysics,* X, No. 1 (September 1956) pp. 57—63. J. Heywood Thomas, in a series of articles, contends that this relation between philosophy and theology is nothing more than a tautology in the sense that 'if anything is theology then what makes it theology also makes it philosophy'. 'The Correlation of Philosophy and Theology in Tillich's System', *London Quarterly and Holborn Review,* Sixth Series, XXVIII (January 1959) p. 52. See also 'Tillich on Philosophy and Theology', *Union Seminary Quarterly Review,* VIII, No. 3 (March 1953) pp. 10—16; and *Paul Tillich: An Appraisal* (London: S.C.M. Press, 1963) pp. 42—43. Cf. H. Veatch, 'Tillich's Distinction between Metaphysics and Theology', *Review of Metaphysics,* X, No. 3 (March 1957) pp. 529—533.

concepts.[47] As our author remarks: 'In respect to content the Christian answers are dependent on the revelatory events in which they appear; in respect to form they are dependent on the structure of the questions which they answer'.[48]

This conclusion immediately establishes the necessity of the concept of estrangement to Tillich's method. For if, as Tillich contends, estrangement is the basic characteristic of the universal human condition, every question asked by man and every answer provided by Christianity will be determined by this fact. The answers implied in the Christian faith are meaningful only in so far as they are in correlation with questions concerning the whole of our existence, with the existential questions implied in the situation of estrangement. Accordingly, each of the five parts of Tillich's *Systematic Theology* follows this dialectic pattern: each makes an analysis of the state of estrangement from which the existential questions arise, and each seeks to demonstrate that the symbols used in the Christian message are the answers to these questions. One side deals with what man is in his estranged existence (with what he should not be), while the other deals with man as he essentially is (with

---

[47] R. P. Scharlemann, 'Tillich's Method of Correlation: Two Proposed Revisions', *The Journal of Religion*, XLVI, No. 1, Part II (January 1966) pp. 93 & 102. Tillich, in his 'Rejoinder', accepts this formulation (*Ibid.*, p. 184).

[48] *ST*, 1: 72. It is at this point that the difference between Tillich and Barth is most instructive. Barth declares that revelation is in no way dependent on man and so emphasizes the 'Word of God' which stands over against the human situation and is thrown at it 'like a stone'. Tillich, while agreeing that the content of revelation is given to man as an objective reality and not produced by philosophical or theological reflection, maintains that revelation is dependent on the cultural situation of the day, to which it must relate. No doctrine of revelation which is divorced from man's reception of it is therefore possible. This basic difference is presented in detail in Tillich's 'Die Überwindung des Religionsbegriffs in der Religionsphilosophie', *Kant-Studien*, XXVII, No. 3/4 (1922) pp. 446—469. E.T., 'The Conquest of the Concept of Religion in the Philosophy of Religion', *WR:* 122—154. Accordingly Tillich characterizes Barth's position as 'undialectical'. See 'Kritisches und Positives Paradox — Eine Auseinandersetzung mit Karl Barth und Friedrich Gogarten', *Theologische Blätter*, II, No. 11 (November 1923) pp. 263—269; and 'What is Wrong with "Dialectic" Theology?' *The Journal of Religion*, XV, No. 2 (April 1935) pp. 127—145. Cf. E. A. Dowey, 'Tillich, Barth, and the Criteria of Theology', *Theology Today*, XV, No. 1 (April 1958) pp. 43—58.

what he ought to be). This, says Tillich, corresponds to the Christian distinction between the realm of creation and the realm of salvation.[49]

Even on the basis of this brief outline, we can see already how Tillich's correlative use of estrangement impinges upon his philosophy of art. When Tillich speaks of the realistic element necessary to religious art, he is referring to that aspect of religious style which employs the concept of estrangement and which thus points to the question side of the correlative method. *Realism is the affirmation of the ontological truth that the state of existence is the state of estrangement.* However, since the method affirms also that the question implies the answer (and *vice versa*), we may go one step further in the argument: whether in poetry or paint, the drama or novel, the realistic style involves an analysis of the questions in estranged existence to which religion offers the reply.[50] The only difference, therefore, between the artist who is consciously religious and the artist who is not is that the former tries to correlate the materials of his analysis with the theological concepts he derives from his faith; he seeks to present an amalgam of question and answer in such a way that the mutual interdependence of the two is established. Other so-called 'non-religious' artists are, by contrast, unaware of the religious answer latent within their own analysis of the human predicament, and do not view human existence and existence generally in such a way that the symbols of religion appear immediately meaningful and understandable to them. By this means a second definition may be proposed: *Realistic art is implicitly religious in that, by its depiction of the state of estrangement, it is directed towards the answer of religion.* In this respect, correlation duplicates the argument previously developed in Tillich's theory of meaning.[51]

With these remarks in mind, we turn now to Tillich's discussion of the concept of estrangement. That man is estranged constitutes the central conviction of Tillich's anthropology: 'Man as he exists is not what he essentially is and ought to be. He is estranged from his true being'.[52] But how, we may ask, does man's estrangement from his true being occur? By what process does man pass from the state of essential being

---

[49] *Ibid.*, p. 74.
[50] The degree to which the question 'implies' the answer is discussed at length in *ST*, 2: 15—18.
[51] See above p. 49.
[52] *ST*, 2: 51.

to that of existential being? What makes this transition possible in the first place, what are the motives behind it, and what are its consequences?

The primary model used by Tillich to answer these questions is the story of *Genesis* 1—3, the mythological history of Adam before and after the Fall. The first of these two stages—Adam before the Fall—can be dealt with briefly. It is distinguished by the fundamental Christian concept, *Esse que esse bonum est*, which means '"Being as being is good", or in biblical mythological form: God saw everything that he had created, and behold it was good'.[53] So here Tillich speaks of 'man's created goodness' or the 'goodness of man's created nature'.[54] Expressed in ontological terms, it is a state of 'essential being', representing man in his essential nature and in unity with God.[55] This is not, however, a stage of actual human development but rather a state of potentiality, without actualization in any place or time, and as such can be known neither directly nor indirectly. This is, to use Tillich's psychological analogy, the 'state of dreaming innocence': non-actual, non-spatial and non-temporal, without experience, responsibility and guilt.[56]

The second stage—Adam after the Fall—is the state of 'existential being' and refers to the distortion of 'essential being' in the 'actual' world, to the 'transition from essence to existence', to the fall of man in his essential nature (or created goodness) to man in existence, wherein he is subject to the ambiguities, distortions and self-destructive structures of estrangement.[57] The condition of fallen man—which Tillich describes in one of the richest sections in his theology—is one in which man is at odds with himself, the world and God. Here we find the three 'marks' of estrangement: man in the totality of his being turns away from God ('unbelief') and elevates himself as the absolute centre of his world

---

[53] 'The Theological Significance of Existentialism and Psychoanalysis', *TC:* 118.

[54] *ST*, 1: 288.

[55] *ST*, 2: 38.

[56] *ST*, 2: 38—41. 'Therefore it is inadequate to ask questions concerning Adam's state before the fall; for example, if he was mortal or immortal . . . The verb "was" presupposes actualisation in time' (*ST*, 1: 288). Elsewhere Tillich cites the growth of a child's sexual consciousness as an example of innocence and its loss. See *ST*, 2: 41.

[57] *ST*, 2: 33.

(hubris) in order that he might draw the whole of his world into himself ('concupiscence').[58] The existential situation is further characterized by the limitations of finitude: the anxiety of having to die, suffering, doubt and meaninglessness, temptation, despair and condemnation.[59] But this description of the Fall is not, Tillich underlines, the consequence of certain events which happened 'once upon a time' in the life of the first man, Adam. Neither Adam nor human history as a whole passed at a given moment from a state of essential being into a state of existential estrangement. The Fall of Adam is rather a symbol for the human situation universally, and, as such, the meaning of the myth transcends the temporal setting of Adam's fall as it is narrated in the biblical story.[60]

'Estrangement', then, is a term describing the actual ontological state of existing man, and indicates that the split between essential nature and actual existence is the basic reality of the human situation, a condition present in every living being and in every time. *To exist is to be estranged* since the actual constitution of existence implies the transition from essence to existence. So 'creation and the Fall coincide in so far as there is no point in time and space in which created goodness was actualised and had existence'.[61] Just as there was no paradise in the past, so there will be no utopia in the future because 'actualised creation and estranged existence are identical'.[62] As such, therefore, the transition is no isolated act but the universal state of man and his world: the state of estrangement is the only 'actual' state and it has never been otherwise. This is the transhistorical meaning of the Fall, that which gives it universal anthropological significance.

> ... the transition from essence to existence is a universal quality of finite being. It is not an event of the past; for it ontologically precedes everything that happens in time and space. It sets the conditions of spatial and temporal existence.[63]

---

[58] *ST*, 2: 53—63.
[59] *Ibid.*, pp. 77—90.
[60] So Tillich speaks of the phrase 'transition from essence to existence' as a 'half-way demythologisation' of the myth of the Fall (*ST*, 2: 33). It removes the 'once upon a time' element but retains a temporal element.
[61] *ST*, 2: 50.
[62] *Ibid.*
[63] *Ibid.*

This, and similar passages, seem to suggest, to use William Rowe's words, that "'to exist as a man" and "to be estranged from one's essential nature" are either *equivalent* or the second is *presupposed* by the first'.[64] The implication is that the process of actualization of essence *inevitably* results in estrangement from essential being, for potentialities cannot be fully realized and essence is distorted in existence. The actualization of that which is potential results in estrangement. To exist, therefore, is to stand out of one's essential being as in a 'fall'.

Despite such statements, however, Tillich argues also that estrangement is not simply the universal tragic destiny of all finite being: it is in addition the result of individual moral freedom. The transition from man in his essential nature to man in existence is mediated by the 'finite freedom' possessed by man alone. Man is therefore responsible for his own predicament: he is free not only because he possesses creativity and the powers of deliberation and decision, but also because he has the power of contradicting himself and his essential nature.[65] It is this final aspect of man's freedom which makes possible the transition of man as he was created to man as he actually is: 'Man is free even from his freedom; that is, he can surrender his humanity'.[66] Even in the prior state of essential being or dreaming innocence, of uncontested and undecided potentiality in which freedom and destiny are in harmony, man experienced the temptation to actualize his freedom. Thus even the state of Adam before the Fall was charged with the possibility of tension and disruption, with the 'desire to sin', or, as Tillich calls it, 'aroused freedom'.[67] In terms of the biblical account, this is illustrated by the

---

[64] W. L. Rowe, *Religious Symbols and God* (Chicago & London: The University of Chicago Press, 1968) p. 203. Cf. Tillich, 'Psychotherapy and a Christian Interpretation of Human Nature', *Review of Religion*, XIII, No. 3 (March 1949) where he writes on the Fall: 'This almost unusable word points to a universal experience of mankind, namely, to man's split within himself, to his separation from and enmity toward other beings, and to the permanent threat of losing the ground and meaning of his life. The "Fall" is not an historical event; it is the permanent and universal transition from innocence to guilt in every human being' (*Ibid.*, p. 265).

[65] Tillich also defines freedom as 'that faculty of man by which he is able to determine his being through history'. 'Freedom in the Period of Transformation', *Freedom: Its Meaning*, ed. Ruth N. Anshen (New York: Harcourt, Brace, 1940) p. 124.

[66] *ST*, 2: 36.

[67] *Ibid.*, p. 40.

divine injunction not to eat from the tree of knowledge. It presupposes a 'kind of split between creator and creature, a split which makes a command necessary, even if it is given only in order to test the obedience of the creature'.[68] But when freedom is aroused—when it becomes conscious of itself and tends to become actual—man is 'caught between the desire to actualise his freedom and the demand to preserve his dreaming innocence'.[69] Subjectively expressed, the dilemma is experienced as a double anxiety: 'the anxiety of losing himself by not actualising himself and his potentialities and the anxiety of losing himself by actualising himself and his potentialities... The anxiety of this situation is the state of temptation'.[70] Man must and does decide for self-actualization, or else he would cease to be. This decision occasions the transition from essential being and entails the fall into sin.[71]

We can see that Tillich wishes to characterize estrangement as both tragic, arising from destiny, and moral, arising from freedom. He agrees that this interpretation of the myth of the Fall of Adam, with its ontological bias, is not directly biblical since there is no explicit ontological thought in biblical religion; but, conversely, 'there is no symbol or no theological concept in it which does not have ontological implications'.[72] So it is with the story of *Genesis*. On the one hand, the myth of the Fall emphasizes the tragic universality of existence, that estrangement is a condition of existence. The tragic element which involves the whole cosmos is not dismissed in the biblical story: 'the serpent represents the dynamic trends of nature; there is the magical character of the two trees, the rise of sexual consciousness, the curse over the heredity of Adam, the body of the woman, the animals and the land'.[73] On the other hand, the *Genesis* account of Adam freely choosing

---

[68] *Ibid.*

[69] *Ibid.*

[70] *Ibid.*, p. 41.

[71] Cf. Tillich, 'The Nature of Man', *Journal of Philosophy*, XLIII, No. 25 (December 1946) p. 676. 'Theology, in dealing with man's nature as that of "finite freedom", shows that man's freedom drives him into a tragic estrangement from himself, from the other beings, and from the ultimate ground and meaning of his existence.'

[72] *ST*, 2: 13.

[73] *ST*, 2: 42. This leads to the important question of whether nature itself is implicated in the fall of man. Tillich rejects the idealistic separation of an innocent nature from guilty man, and justifies his claim to speak of

to disobey the divine prohibition not to eat of the fruit of the tree stresses 'finite freedom' both as the compulsion and agent for man's contradiction of his essential nature: it indicates that individual moral responsibility participates in the creation of the universal destiny of mankind. Existence, therefore, 'is rooted both in ethical freedom and in tragic destiny. If the one or the other side is denied, the human situation becomes incomprehensible'.[74] The transition from essence to existence is the work of finite freedom, but since it happens universally in everything finite it is a condition of existence that man is estranged. While freedom is not eliminated, it is always in bondage to destiny. This is the tragic burden of the human situation: 'of man's freedom to contradict his essential nature, and of man's fate to stand under the servitude of this contradiction'.[75] This is the reason why, Tillich concludes, all ways of self-salvation must fail. The polarity of freedom and destiny means that 'no act within the context of existential estrangement can overcome existential estrangement'.[76] He points to the failure of all legalistic, mystical, sacramental, doctrinal and emotional ways of self-salvation within the history of religion. It is a history of man's attempt to save himself and his failure to do so. All these efforts distort the way of salvation by identifying the saving power of the ultimate with

---

a 'fallen world' by recent evolutionary theories and depth psychology (*ST*, 2: 47—48). He admits, however, that Schelling's philosophy of nature was the determinative influence in the formation of this doctrine. See 'Autobiographical Reflections', *The Theology of Paul Tillich*, ed C. W. Kegley & D. W. Bretall (New York: Macmillan, 1964) p. 4.

[74] *ST*, 2: 43.

[75] 'A Reinterpretation of the Doctrine of the Incarnation', *Church Quarterly Review*, CXLVII, No. 294 (January—March, 1949) p. 141. It should be pointed out here that if, following Tillich, freedom is one of the basic elements in man's ontological structure, and if it is ontologically true that man is estranged, then the problem remains: How can the exercise of man's finite freedom responsibly decide whether to be estranged or not? In a similar vein, Reinhold Niebuhr has objected that Tillich's 'ontological speculations' have subtly shifted the emphasis in the biblical paradox of freedom and fact upon 'the fatefulness of sin rather than upon our responsibility'. 'Biblical Thought and Ontological Speculation in Tillich's Theology', *The Theology of Paul Tillich*, p. 219. Cf. Eugene H. Peters, 'Tillich's Doctrine of Essence, Existence, and the Christ', *The Journal of Religion*, XLIII, No. 4 (October 1963) pp. 298—299.

[76] *ST*, 2: 91.

human inadequacy and ambiguity, which are necessarily incapable of reuniting man and God or of healing the disruptions of man's state of estrangement.[77]

This critique of man's attempts at self-salvation does not, however, complete Tillich's account of estrangement. Correlation, we have seen, requires the juxtaposition of question and answer, and accordingly we may now deduce from an analysis of the question certain things about the nature of the answer. This does not mean that the existential question—exposed by ontological investigation and circumscribed by the split between essence and existence—is the source or guarantor of the revelatory answer formulated by theology. 'One cannot derive', Tillich writes, 'the divine self-manifestation from an analysis of the human predicament'.[78] Nevertheless, if ontology cannot demonstrate that the answer *has been given*, the mutual dependence of question and answer in the dialectic of correlation does imply that the form of the question determines the form in which the answer *would be given*. Thus, irrespective of whether the answer has been given or not, correlation can establish that the answer, should it be possible, must bring a new state of things, a New Being, relevant to and communicable in terms of the ontological state of existing man; that the answer, in other words, must provide a reply to the questions of how man's existential estrangement from his essential being can be conquered, and of how he can be saved from the evils and despair which are the consequences of this estrangement.

In this way the situation of estrangement points beyond itself to the possibility of 'salvation'. This term, originally derived from the Latin *salvus* or *salus* meaning 'healed' or 'whole', refers to the possibility of something, to a 'third', through which the cleavage between essential goodness and actual existence is overcome and healed. 'In this sense, healing means reuniting that which is estranged, giving a centre to what is split, overcoming the split between God and man, man and his world, man and himself'.[79] Thus 'salvation' refers directly both to the

---

[77] *Ibid.*, pp. 92—100.
[78] *Ibid.*, p. 14.
[79] *Ibid.*, p. 192. For Tillich's most detailed analyses of the concept 'salvation', see 'The Relation of Religion and Health: Historical Considerations and Theoretical Questions', *Review of Religion*, X, No. 4 (May 1946) pp. 348—384.

split between essential and existential being and to that through which the split is overcome. Expressed philosophically, this means 'that man's essential nature and existential nature points to his teleological nature (derived from *telos,* aim, that for which and towards which his life drives)'.[80]

From this we can see that essential being, existential being and the desire for salvation function as the three elements necessary not only to the explanation of estrangement but also to the explanation of human nature generally. And in so far as the third of these elements, the quest for salvation, is universal because the human predicament of estrangement is universal, so every individual, irrespective of his creed or culture, may once again be called 'religious' and religion itself considered as an expression of this ontological dimension of man and not merely as a special function of his spiritual life. For religion is that attitude orientated towards the reality through which final cosmic and individual healing occurs, in which reunion is achieved over against the forces of disintegration and disruption.[81] Thus, although the history of religion has already indicated that religion is not the answer to the quest for salvation, religion is the place where the question of salvation is asked and where the answer is received in revelation. 'Revelation must be received and ... the name for the reception of revelation is "religion"'.[82]

If we now attach this three-fold consideration of human nature to Tillich's aesthetics, we can see how it extends the function of his category of realism. If realism is the affirmation of the truth that existence is estranged, and if, as we have just seen, the concept of estrangement is itself bounded by the concepts of essential being and salvation, then religious art, in so far as it is realistic, will duplicate this tripartite account and include in its images those elements corresponding to what man ought to be, what he is and what he seeks or hopes for. This does not mean, however, that religious art is concerned only with the

---

[80] 'The Theological Significance of Existentialism and Psychoanalysis', *TC:* 119.
[81] Cf. *PE:* 61; *ST,* 2: 93 & 99.
[82] *Biblical Religion and the Search for Ultimate Reality* (Chicago: University of Chicago Press, 1955) p. 3.

coordination of these three aspects, with the simultaneous representation of each element in a single image, or that it is recognizably religious only when it deals with the third of these elements in which the answer of revelation is given. For each element is in itself both the presupposition and implication of the other two, and in that sense each prefigures the total correlative process wherein man asks the question that revelation answers. Put otherwise, just as these three elements are always present in man and nature[83], so they are always present in every aesthetic act by which man attributes meaning to a natural object. Thus every representation of any single element constitutes religious art, and every aesthetic act will incorporate some such representation. This, of course, is yet another variation on the theme that the realistic style is implicitly religious, except that now we have arrived at a more exact explanation of the category of realism. Realism is the picturing of any one of the three elements circumscribing the ontological condition of man and his world: of the state of essential or created goodness, of the state of actual estrangement, of the quest for salvation. On this basis we can say that the religious style may be partial or complete in its ontological account, and that its standard will increase or diminish in relation to the extent to which the relationship between these three elements is confirmed or confused.

Tillich gives various examples of the ways in which art reproduces this three-fold pattern. Of these, the representation of the state of essential being or 'dreaming innocence' is the least substantial, even though it has produced 'innumerable religious pictures'.[84] Here, Tillich tells us, is a tradition of painting which is discernible in the classical period of Greece, reaches its climax in the religious pictures of the Renaissance, and extends into the modern period with the works of Picasso's 'blue period' and the dream sequences of Henri Rousseau.[85] As

---

[83] Just as nature is implicated in the Fall, so it is implicated in Salvation. See *ST*, 2: 110—111.

[84] 'Art and Ultimate Reality', *Cross Currents*, X, No. 1 (Winter 1960) p. 8.

[85] *Ibid.*, pp. 8—9. Henri (le Douanier) Rousseau is generally associated with Expressionism. In *Der Blaue Reiter*, Kandinsky reproduced seven of his paintings in his own article 'Über die Formfrage' (pp. 74—100). Kandinsky compared Rousseau's representation of inner harmony to the art of children and his own attempt to express the 'greater absolute'.

a religious attitude 'it can be called religious humanism which sees God in man and man in God here and now, in spite of all human weakness. It expects the full realization of this unity in history and anticipates it in artistic creativity'.[86] As an artistic style, however, it is more generally known as *idealism,* since here the original unity between God and man in the states of created goodness is pictorially realized irrespective of the actuality of estrangement. This last stylistic classification is particularly important because it resolves immediately the problem of Botticelli's 'Madonna with Singing Angels'. My own suggestion, it may be remembered, was that this painting presented to Tillich an *idealization* of reality at odds with his own recent war experiences.[87] The question remained, however, of how this picture could be considered a revelation if it does not conform to the principle of realism in religious art. This question is now answered. The contrast between a reality experienced and a reality idealized is not, in aesthetic terms, a contrast between realism and non-realism since the representation of perfection, such as we find in the Botticelli, may be taken as a pictorial description of essential being, or rather as an artistic account of the first element *required by the category of realism.* As Tillich remarks, this idealistic style incorporates the 'anticipation of the highest possibilities of being' and denotes the 'remembrance of the lost, and anticipation of the regained, paradise. Seen in this light, it certainly is a medium for the experience of ultimate reality. It expresses the divine character of man and his world in his essential, undistorted, created perfection'.[88] In

---

[86] *Ibid.*

[87] See above, Ch. I, p. 7.

[88] 'Art and Ultimate Reality', p. 8. Tillich's account of 'idealist' religious art is in fact extraordinarily muddled. In 'Religion and the Visual Arts' (1956) we find a general condemnation of Renaissance art as a 'non-religious style dealing with religious contents' (p. 2). Three years later — in 'Between Utopianism and Escape from History', *Colgate Rochester Divinity School Bulletin,* XXXI, No. 2 (May 1959)—Tillich regrets the 'disrepute' into which Renaissance works of art have fallen and says that they 'must be understood in their greatness and their limits as the anticipated fulfilment of the highest human potentialities. They express our human predicament only insofar as they show images of the state of things in which this predicament is overcome' (p. 36). This is the position adopted in 'Art and Ultimate Reality' (1960): the idealistic tradition 'was despised and rejected... I myself shared this mood. The change occurred when I realized that

other words, the revelatory status of those pictures which are *not* representations of the actual conditions of estrangement is secured within the 'style of the paradise'.

In dealing next with the artistic portrayal of the state of existential being, Tillich provides us with his most comprehensive and detailed analysis—as indeed we might expect from his earlier descussion of the concept of estrangement. This aspect of religious style is concerned with the verbal or pictorial description of man's existential predicament in contrast to man's essential nature. Thus it will point to the experience of meaningless, doubt and loneliness; to the awareness of finitude, which is anxiety; to the unbelief, *hubris* and concupiscence of man; to the possibility and danger of freedom; and to the threat of non-being in all respects—from death to guilt. In his book *The Courage to Be*, Tillich presents an impressive list of artists preoccupied with this dimension of being, ranging from the medieval to the modern period: in poetry, Dante, Baudelaire, Rimbaud, Eliot and Auden; in the novel, Dostoevsky, Flaubert, Kafka, Sartre and Camus; in the theatre, Ibsen, Strindberg, Arthur Miller and Tennessee Williams; and in the visual arts, Bosch, Breughel, Grünewald, Cézanne, Van Gogh and Munch. The chief significance of this list is not that many of these artists are more generally known as expressionists—although I shall return to this point—but that *all* are here called *existentialists*.[89] This resolves the second question deferred from Chapter One: of how far Tillich's aesthetics requires and incorporates an existentialist doctrine of man.[90] 'Existential' can be defined either as an *attitude* of involvement in contrast to a merely theoretical or detached attitude, or as a fundamental

---

idealism means anticipation of the highest possibilities of being' (p. 8). A few months later, however— in 'Zur Theologie der bildenden Kunst und der Architektur' (1961)—Tillich changes his mind again and rejects the religious character of Renaissance art for precisely the same reason he gave for admitting it: 'Sie sind Visionen menschlicher Vollendung' (p. 349. See above, p. 5). Notwithstanding this muddle, I have interpreted Tillich as accepting the idealist-religious classification since otherwise we would be faced with a major contradiction of the theology of culture, which does not permit the total exclusion of any artistic style from the religious style. That said, the placing of the idealist tradition within religious art would follow the argument given on pp. 65—66.

89 *CTB:* 128—129, 136, 141—143.

90 See above, p. 7.

point of view in which man's existential situation is presented as a state of estrangement from his essential nature.[91] This second definition, Tillich continues, denotes both philosophical and *artistic* existentialism, and accordingly any philosophy, literature, poetry, drama or painting that expresses the viewpoint that man is estranged will be called 'existentialist'. 'Existential', as he writes elsewhere, 'is what characterizes our real existence in all its concreteness, in all its accidental elements, in its freedom and responsibility, in its failure, in its separation from its true and essential being'.[92] This means that the artistic representation of existential being is the 'existentialist style'; it is also means that the religious style, in so far as it incorporates the *second* element required by the category of realism, will include in its images those characteristics and symptoms of estrangement that existentialism has shown to be the actual conditions of man's predicament (*viz.*, meaninglessness, doubt and anxiety etc.).

This mention of existentialism, however, raises two further questions. To what extent does religious art, by adhering to the existentialist viewpoint, present an unnecessarily 'pessimistic' view of existence, and to what extent can Expressionism be called a form of existentialism? As to the first question, Tillich is well aware that the use of terms like 'anxiety', 'guilt' and 'despair' seems to justify this estimate.[93] His reply is that this criticism is legitimate only on the basis of an incomplete account of existentialism. In the first place, existential elements like 'despair' constitute only one part of the human predicament since the analysis of estrangement presupposes some idea of what man essentially is, of man in his created perfection. Thus 'even the most radical existentialist, if he wants to say something, necessarily falls back to some essentialist statements because without them he cannot even speak'.[94] In the second place, existential analyses determine the questioning side of the correlative method and in that sense provide the material for the question answered in revelation. Thus the existential account of human estrangement is itself directed towards the answer of salvation.

---

[91] *CTB:* 124—125.
[92] 'Philosophy and Theology', *PE:* 88.
[93] *ST,* 2: 31.
[94] 'The Theological Significance of Existentialism and Psychoanalysis', *TC:* 121.

As an example of this second point Tillich cites Picasso's 'Guernica', which he calls 'the greatest Protestant picture produced after 1900'.[95] In recording the destruction of a small Spanish town by the Fascists, Picasso has created perhaps the outstanding example of 'an artistic expression of the human predicament in our period ... The question of man in a world of guilt, anxiety, and despair is put before us with tremendous power'.[96] But if we now ask why 'Guernica' is a profoundly religious painting, Tillich's reply is that this is because of the radicalism of its question and not because it provides the answer. In this respect 'Guernica' is an implicitly religious picture: although containing no recognizably religious subject-matter or symbolism, it is a powerful expression of modern man's question concerning ultimate reality phrased in terms of his own existential situation.[97] It is, in other words, a paradigm of the way in which existentialist art, by providing a contemporary vocabulary for the question, determines the form in which that question will be answered by revelation. For these two reasons, therefore, existentialism is not an exclusive description of estrangement because it carries within itself concepts both of essential being and salvation.

Since 'Guernica' is also called an expressionist picture, we should next enquire whether the terms 'existentialist' and 'expressionist' are synonymous in Tillich's aesthetics. Although Tillich never says directly that Expressionism is artistic Existentialism, the evidence to support this claim is considerable. In his survey 'Religion and the Visual Arts', Tillich incorporates the whole expressionist tradition—notably Cézanne and Picasso—within the 'existentialist level' of art[98]; in his essay 'Art and Ultimate Reality', he talks of Expressionism showing the 'estrangement of the actual human situation from the essential unity of the human with the divine'—thus implying that it duplicates the central doctrine of Existentialism[99]; and in *The Courage To Be* he first defines Existentialism as 'the great art, literature and philosophy of the twentieth century'—a claim made elsewhere for Expressionism—then describes the expressionist disregard for the 'causal interdependence

---

[95] 'Theology, Architecture and Art', p. 55.
[96] 'Protestantism and Artistic Style', *TC:* 68—69.
[97] 'Authentic Religious Art', p. 9.
[98] *Op. cit.*, p. 3.
[99] *Op. cit.*, p. 11.

of things' and concludes with the words that in 'Existentialist art (as I like to call it) causality has lost its validity'.[100] However, the most substantial evidence for this identity is to be found by comparing Tillich's history of Existentialism in *Theology of Culture* with that of Expressionism in his earlier surveys of art. Like Expressionism, Existentialism is described as a reaction—and primarily a German reaction—against the 19th century bourgeois and industrial process of 'objectivation' (*Verdinglichung*, to use Marx's term) by which everything, including man, is transformed into an object of scientific and technical management, and in which there is and can be no apprehension of the mystery of existence.[101] Existentialism, that is to say, is a revolutionary movement opposing the capitalist destruction of individual freedom, affirming the inner and personal character of man's immediate experience, and seeking to discover on the basis of that experience an ultimate meaning of life, to encounter 'the creative realm of being which is prior to and beyond the distinction between objectivity and subjectivity'. To that extent Existentialism may also be called 'mystical': it 'does not indicate a mystical union with the transcendent Absolute; it signifies rather a venture of faith toward union with the *depths of life*, whether made by an individual or a group'.[102] This account, it need hardly be said, parallels the history of Expressionism in *Masse und Geist* and *The Religious Situation* and recalls the concepts of 'immanent mysticism' and 'belief-ful realism'.

Thus we may conclude that *Expressionism is the existentialist form of art*. This definition, however, has one further and important consequence. The term 'expressionist', like the term 'existentialist', although referring mainly to those contemporary arts in which the reality of estrangement is consciously realized and portrayed, will be applicable also to any style of any historical period in which the three stages of essential being, existential being and the quest for salvation are presented. Tillich, in other words, may now extend the notion of

---

[100] *Op. cit.*, pp. 141 & 144—145. Cf. 'Art and Ultimate Reality', p. 12; and 'Theology, Architecture and Art', p. 8.

[101] 'Existential Philosophy: Its Historical Meaning', *TC:* 93. Cf. Marx, *Der Historische Materialismus*, ed. Alfred Kröner (Leipzig, 1932) I, pp. 301 & 304.

[102] *Ibid.*, p. 107 (my emphasis). For a further discussion of the connection between Expressionism and Existentialism, see *ST*, 3: 216.

religious art as 'expressionistic' beyond the limits of the 20th century movement known as 'Expressionism', and may thus reaffirm the argument already offered by the 'category of expressiveness', namely that a style may be deemed religious irrespective of its period or tradition.[103] 'Expressionist' in this connection will designate those artistic forms in which the question of human existence in unity with the predicament of everything existing is asked, and will denote those styles in which this question is answered in the symbols of divine healing.

This last point brings us to the third element required by the category of realism, to the artistic representation of the expectation of a new and saving reality which will replace the old and estranged reality. Although the character of this quest changes from religion to religion and from culture to culture, Tillich distinguishes two major types: the non-historical and the historical expectation of the New Being. In the non-historical attitude—exemplified primarily in the mystic religions of Brahmanism and Buddhism—the New Being is a divine power 'equally near to and equally remote from each period of history', and history itself is envisaged as a 'circular, self-repeating movement'. Nothing new is therefore created by history and salvation cannot occur through it. 'The New Being in this interpretation is the negation of all beings and the affirmation of the Ground of Being alone'.[104] The artistic correlate of this attitude is that style 'in which the particularity of things is dissolved into a visual continuum'.[105] We find this in Chinese landscapes 'in which air and water symbolize the cosmic unity, and individual rocks or branches hardly dare emerge to an independent existence'; but it is more radically evident in the modern development of 'non-objective' painting, which in America was coincident with the experience of Eastern mysticism. Thus artists like Jackson Pollock 'deprive reality of its manifoldness, of the concreteness of things and persons' and 'use basic structural elements of reality like line, cubes, planes, colours, as symbols for that which transcends all reality'.[106] The

---

[103] See above, pp. 23—24.

[104] *ST*, 2: 101. Tillich's fullest account of the historical and non-historical attitudes is 'Historical and Nonhistorical Interpretations of History: A Comparison', *PE:* 16—31.

[105] 'Art and Ultimate Reality', p. 6.

[106] *Ibid.* The American Jackson Pollock is an outstanding representative of the kind of abstract painting better known in the United States and England

danger of this approach is nevertheless apparent. Just as the price paid in the non-historical expectation of New Being is the 'negation of everything that has being', so the danger of its artistic representation is that 'the attempt to express ultimate reality by annihilating reality can lead to works in which nothing at all is expressed'.[107]

Predominantly, however, Western religion and culture are concerned with the quest for salvation in the historical dimension, 'in a horizontal direction rather than the vertical one'.[108] This attitude asserts the essential goodness of being and awaits the New Being as a transformation of reality 'through a historical process which is unique, unrepeatable, irreversible'.[109] Although this belief is found in ancient Persia, Judaism, Christianity and Islam, Tillich declares that the claim of Christianity to universality is based on its conviction that 'the different forms in which the quest for the New Being has been made are fulfilled in Jesus as the Christ'.[110] This religion emphasizes the appearance of the New Being within the historical dimension in the form of the personal life of Jesus of Nazareth; but the terms it uses to symbolize this life—terms like 'Christ' and 'Messiah', which it borrowed from late Judaism—combine transhistorical and historical elements. By this means, Christianity, in its conception of the New Being appearing in Jesus the Christ, unites the horizontal direction of the historical expectation of the New Being with the vertical direction of the non-historical type; and thus it may lay claim to being the 'universal type' of the universal quest for the New Being.[111] Yet it is not universally acknowledged as such, for man's unshaken reliance upon himself, his self-saving attempts and his resignation to despair generate a self-understanding and an expectation which is contradicted by the New Being in Jesus as the Christ. The Christian concept of New Being is therefore 'paradoxi-

---

as 'Abstract Expressionism' or 'Action Painting', and in France as *art informel* or *tachisme*—the dominant artistic movement in the decade 1945—1955. At this point Tillich also refers to the Japanese artist Ashikaga, to Klee and Seurat, and to Kandinsky's 'Improvisation' (see above, p. 27 n. 62).

[107] *Ibid.*, & *ST*, 2: 101.
[108] *ST*, 2: 101.
[109] *Ibid.*
[110] *Ibid.*, p. 103.
[111] *Ibid.*

cal' in the literal sense of the word: it 'contradicts the *doxa*, the opinion which is based on the whole of ordinary human experience, including the empirical and the rational. The Christian paradox contradicts the opinion derived from man's existential predicament and all expectations imaginable on the basis of this predicament'.[112]

In view of this emphasis upon the Christian claim to universality, it is perhaps not surprising that Tillich gives no examples of the artistic representation of the quest for salvation in the Islamic, Persian and Judaic religions but concentrates exclusively upon the portrayal of Jesus as the Christ, that is, upon the expression of the *fulfilment* of the universal human expectation of a new reality. Nor should we be surprised to learn that the most successful portraits of Jesus have emerged from within the expressionist tradition—here Tillich refers to El Greco, Grünewald, Nolde, Rouault and Sutherland—and that these pictures are vastly superior to the more romantic and sentimental images of Jesus produced by a Reni or a Hoffmann, even though the latter are more often used for liturgical purposes and private devotion.[113] What is remarkable, however, is Tillich's choice of that picture which he considers to be the portrait of Jesus *par excellence*. This is the *biblical picture* of Jesus as the Christ. According to him, not only is this picture the original 'verbal' image of Jesus the Christ upon which all other subsequent images depend, but it also exhibits all the characteristics of an expressionist painting, to the extent indeed that we may speak of it as an '"expressionist" portrait ("expressionist" used in the sense of the predominant artistic style in most periods of history—rediscovered in our period)'.[114] Given what we know already about Tillich's understanding of Expressionism, the account he gives now of the expressionist character of the gospel picture is predictable. It is not a portrait in the 'naturalistic' style of art, that is, it does not seek to present a photographic-empirical description of Jesus; nor is it an 'idealistic' image of him, representing the 'painted projection of the experiences and ideals of the most religiously profound minds in the period of the Emperor Augustus'; but it is 'expressionist' to the degree that here the painter

---

[112] *Ibid.,* p. 106
[113] 'Religion and the Visual Arts', pp. 9—10.
[114] *ST,* 2: 133.

has tried to enter into the *'deepest levels* of the person with whom he deals'.

> Only then could he paint this person in such a way that his surface traits are neither reproduced as in photography (or naturalistically imitated) nor idealised according to the painter's ideal of beauty but are used to express what the painter has experienced through his partici- pation in the being of his subject. This third way is meant when we use the term "real picture" with reference to the Gospel records of Jesus as the Christ.[115]

Here, in other words, the biblical picture not only incorporates the *third* element required by the category of realism but goes beyond it: it pre- sents an image of a life through and in which the universal quest for New Being is fulfilled. To this extent we may also describe this picture as the consummation of all those pictures in which the 'teleological' nature of man—his hope for salvation—has been expressed.

A full account of Tillich's argument concerning the expressionist nature of the gospels will be given in Chapter Four. There we shall dis- cover how various important aspects of Tillich's aesthetics are brought to bear in his analysis of the biblical picture of Jesus at the Christ. Since, however, we are presently occupied more with Tillich's classification of certain categories of religious art than with his appreciation of any par- ticular religious picture, it is necessary to see now how the New Testa- ment image of Jesus determines the *entire class* of picture concerned with the portrayal of the Christ-event. In what respect, we should ask, is this image the *normative* portrait for all subsequent visual and verbal descriptions of the appearance of New Being in Jesus the Christ?

According to Tillich, the portrait presented in the New Testament depicts a two-sided event, the actuality of which is the basis of Chris- tianity.[116] This is the event 'Jesus as the Christ', one side of which is concerned with a past-historical occurrence, the other with Jesus' reception as the Christ. Expressed another way, the value of this por- trait may be said to consist in the fact that it portrays the founding of Christianity, that is, the moment when Jesus the Christ was received as the Christ. As it stands, however, this statement is misleading, for

---

[115] *Ibid.*
[116] The following account is based on my article, 'A Reply to Some Inter- pretations of Tillich's Christology', *The Heythrop Journal*, XXII, No. 2 (April, 1976) pp. 169—177. See *ST*, 2: 112—123.

Tillich is here making no suggestion that the picture chronicles the history of Christianity's origin. While, therefore, his very use of the word 'picture' may indeed presuppose some intimate relationship between the actual Christ-event and its biblical portrayal, recognition of this alone neither could nor does sanction any search for the objective facts about Jesus through scientific or historiographic analysis of those factual elements which, Tillich admits, the biblical picture contains. This is precluded by the dual character of the event itself, which entails that no uninterpreted facts relating to Jesus are discernible apart from the way in which he was originally accepted by the disciples. The biblical picture is not, then, a 'naturalistic' document, interested only in recounting the story and features of a uniquely interesting historical person; it is rather, both in presupposition and intention, a 'confessional' portrait, giving the picture of him who is the Christ, the one who has accordingly a universal significance not explicable simply in terms of his own factuality. More precisely, we should say therefore that the emphasis in the Christian religion lies not on a *fact*—the interpretation of which would be incidental to that fact's efficacy—but on an *interpretation of a fact,* that which has created and conditioned the biblical picture of the Christ. It is, so Tillich concludes, upon this picture or portrait, which is itself the product of the act of interpretation made by the first disciples in their reception of Jesus as the Christ, that faith is based; and it is to this biblical presentation of Jesus of Nazareth as the Christ, of which the Caesarea Philippi confession is the centre, that the believer aligns himself.[117]

The Christian faith is concerned, therefore, with Jesus *as* he is portrayed by the early Christian community of believers; it has no interest in any picture of Jesus other than the biblical picture of him as the Christ; it refers only to that picture created by and mediating the faith of the primitive Christian community when receiving Jesus as the Christ. If, then, the viability of the Christian position depends on the actuality of the event 'Jesus as the Christ', and if the knowledge we have of it is derived basically from its biblical source, then clearly the

---

[117] So Tillich writes that the result of historical research 'is not a picture of the so-called historical Jesus but the insight that there is no picture behind the biblical one which could be made scientifically probable' (*ST*, 2: 118). Tillich's discussion of the relation between faith and historical research will be analysed in Ch. IV.

biblical witness to the impression made by Jesus upon the first disciples is immediately endowed with a certain and quite unimpeachable epistemological significance for the believer. Put otherwise, for those not contemporaries of the event, Jesus as the Christ is encountered through the biblical picture's witness to the original encounter between Jesus and his apostles; and it is in this sense that the New Testament becomes part of the revelation it records, belonging to the substance of the event itself. As the only available account of that event in which Jesus was accepted as the Christ, the biblical picture of him in the gospels properly belongs to the receiving side of that event and witnesses to its factual side. For this reason, it is not merely that nothing could be known about the original event if it were not for its mediation through the portrait created by those who were themselves involved in the event they describe; it is rather that, apart from this transmission of the first disciples' experience of accepting Jesus as the Christ, no event would exist to be known by those not eyewitnesses of its actual occurrence. The biblical picture, to conclude, originates with an event; but for those not contemporaneous with it, this event becomes significant, that is, *becomes the event Christians assert it is,* only through the significance ascribed to it in the biblical picture.[118]

It is a short step from this last assertion to the claim that the scriptural portrait is the normative portrait for all subsequent artistic presentations of Jesus as the Christ. For the only perceptible 'fact' of the Christ-event is the interpretation made of it in the biblical picture, and without this picture no event would exist to be described in pictorial or verbal imagery. In this sense, therefore, all portraits of Jesus the Christ are, strictly speaking, *portraits of the biblical picture,* and all artistic representations of this event, irrespective of their period, manner, medium or use, are the creation of and witness to Jesus' first reception as the New Being as proclaimed in the New Testament. Thus we may say that this gospel portrait is the cause for the continuation and eventual acceptance of this particular interpretation of Jesus through and by succeeding generations of Christian believers; that in this respect alone it may be appropriately considered the foundation of Christian belief; and that it is accordingly the basis of every artistic form in which this belief has been expressed or affirmed.

---

[118] Cf. *ST*, 2: 134—135.

III. TILLICH'S CRITIQUE OF HEGEL AND MARX:
SOME PRINCIPLES OF HIS THEOLOGY OF CULTURE

We have now examined two substantial sections of Tillich's philosophy of art. We began with the cultural synthesis proposed by his theory of meaning, and we have concluded with the three major classifications of the religious-realistic style arising from his concept of estrangement—the latter analysis adding substance to the former's claim that the limits of religious art are not set by the representation of a special 'religious' sphere or function of man's spiritual life. In each case this redefinition of the scope of religious art was achieved through a redefinition of the concept of religion. In the theory of meaning religion was defined as that attitude of the spirit *presupposed* in every cultural activity, and in the account of estrangement as that *ontological* dimension of man in which the question of salvation is asked. The coincidence of these two arguments becomes even more apparent, however, when we realize that Tillich's synthesis is itself an expression of religious concern in this second sense. The theology of culture, we remember, was designed to close the gap between the sacred and secular realms in such a way that the mutual immanence between religion and culture could be established. But this gap is in turn the result of the tragic estrangement of existential being from essential being. 'The great revelation of the cleavage of the world' is that the holy and profane exist, that the Church and society are not one and the same.[119] Viewed in this light, therefore, Tillich's synthesis may be said to have a *soteriological focus:* it is directed to the answer whereby the holy ceases to be in contrast with the profane, to that situation in which both sides become one and are redeemed; it looks to the re-establishment of an original but disrupted unity and is thus concerned with the absolute demand for reconciliation and salvation.

As one might expect, this correlation of estrangement and reconciliation has important implications for the understanding of Tillich's theology of culture, the most significant of which is that it distinguishes this synthesis from all others *in which the ontological truth of estrangement is denied.* It is at this point, and largely in order to make this distinction himself, that Tillich introduces powerful critiscisms of two-

---

[119] *IH:* 226.

great predecessors in the 'way of synthesis', Hegel and Marx. Although nothing is said of their philosophies of art, it is nevertheless instructive to consider Tillich's views for two reasons. Not only does Tillich share with Hegel and Marx certain common emphases in his approach to the problem of synthesis, but, more significantly, derives from his criticisms of them certain principles of synthesis which go some way towards clarifying his own understanding of the connection between religion and culture, and, by extension, between religion and art. As we shall see, Tillich's account of each philosopher is remarkably similar. The introduction of the concept of estrangement into modern thought is the collective achievement of Hegel and Marx, the overcoming of this principle—and thus the betrayal of their original insight—the great tragedy of their mature philosophies.

This 'fateful transition' is best seen in Hegel, for if the discovery of the concept of estrangement is the achievement of the young Hegel of the *Jugendfragmenten*, its conceptual resolution is the work of the older Hegel of the *Encyclopädie* and *Philosophie des Rechts*. In the early theological fragments, Hegel describes the life-processes as possessing an original unity now disrupted, religious transcendentalism (symbolized by the nomadic Abraham) and political absolutism being the two great expressions of self-estrangement.[120] These passages conclude with Hegel's

---

[120] Cf. *Hegels theologische Jugendschriften*, ed. Herman Nohl (Tübingen: J. C. B. Mohr, 1907). E.T., *On Christianity: Early Theological Writings*, trans. T. M. Knox, with an introduction, and fragments trans. by Richard Kroner (Gloucester, Mass.: Peter Smith, 1970). Tillich analyses these essays in 'Der junge Hegel und das Schicksal Deutschlands', *Hegel und Goethe. Zwei Gedenkreden* (Tübingen: J. C. B. Mohr, 1932). *GW*, XII: 125—150. Here Tillich argues that religion and politics are the two major and inseparable preoccupations of the young Hegel. This interpretation provides an interesting alternative to that of Georg Lukács in *The Young Hegel* (London: Merlin Press, 1975). Tillich would accept that the young Hegel was a 'political revolutionary'—notably in the sense that his early writings prefigure the later Marxist concepts of 'exernalization' or 'alienation' (see below, pp. 80—82)—but would not agree that the 'belief in Hegel's "theological" early period remains a legend created and fostered by the reactionary apologists of imperialism' (Lukács, *op. cit.*, p. 16). This dichotomy is invalid since for Hegel, as for Tillich himself, the restoration of moral autonomy and political liberty goes hand in hand with religious regeneration. Cf. Heywood Thomas' comparison between Tillich and the

famous account of the reconciliation of life through love, which Tillich describes as 'one of the deepest insights into the dynamics of the love relationship'.[121] Here the 'transition from original unity through self-estrangement to reconciliation is the way of love... Love in this sense constitutes being'.[122] It is at this point, however, that the difference between the two Hegels becomes apparent. In the former we are presented with a man-centred view of human regeneration, in which the act of love is the means by which unity is recovered and separation overcome; in the latter, philosophy has superseded love and occupies the highest place—in such a way indeed that the development of philosophical thought is itself crucial for the perfection of the higher synthesis. Here the older Hegel emerges as the 'classical essentialist', his basic presupposition being that 'existence is the logically necessary actuality of essence'.[123] In the Hegelian dialectic of 'pure thought', the whole of reality is absorbed in both its essential and existential aspects, estrangement and reconciliation are bound together in the all-embracing character of the system, and the universal movement toward synthesis is itself held to be a law of necessity. Thus both the successions of history and the processes of thought are conceived as evolutions towards complete self-consciousness, and every act of human self-determination, no matter how willful or irrational, a hidden providential activity. Existence *is* essential being.

The gap is overcome not only eternally in God but also historically in man. The world is the process of the divine self-realisation. There is no gap, no ultimate incertitude, no risk, and no danger of self-loss when essence actualises itself in existence. Hegel's famous statement that everything that is, is reasonable is not an absurd optimism about the reasonableness of man. Hegel did not believe that men are reasonable and happy. But it is the statement of Hegel's belief that, in spite of everything unreasonable, the rational or essential structure of being is providentially actualised in the process of the universe. The world is

---

young Hegel in 'The Problem of defining a Theology of Culture, with reference to the Theology of Paul Tillich, *Creation, Christ & Culture*, ed. R. W. McKinney (Edinburgh: T. & T. Clark, 1976) pp. 272—287.

[121] *Perspectives in Nineteenth & Twentieth Century Protestant Thought*, p. 116.
[122] 'Estrangement and Reconciliation in Modern Thought', *The Review of Religion*, IX, No. 1 (November 1944) pp. 9—10.
[123] *ST*, 2: 26.

the self-realisation of the divine mind; existence is the expression of essence and not the fall away from it.[124]

This transition within Hegel's philosophy has had, Tillich continues, one specific historical consequence of world-significance. As we have seen, estrangement as a philosophical term was the discovery of the young Hegel; but this discovery also created the modern existentialist movement against Hegel's later doctrine of essentialism. For Tillich, it is this which above all else testifies to the singular greatness of Hegel's thought. *Hegel created the category by means of which his existentialist successors could attack the synthesis he had himself proposed.* Thus understood, Hegel is revealed as the great ally and adversary of the existentialist revolt against bourgeois society. The common point in all Existentialism is that man's actual situation is a state of estrangement from his essential nature. Hegel recognized this estrangement but believed that it had been overcome and that man was now reconciled with his true being. For all existentialists, however, this belief was Hegel's 'basic error'; and it was in order to expose it that the Existentialism of the 19th and 20th centuries arose.[125]

It is in this light, says Tillich, that Karl Marx must be approached as the great pupil and critic of Hegel. In Marx's use of the term 'alienation', and in his description of the capitalist form of property as the perfect expression of self-estrangement, whereby all relations are valued in terms of commodities, the 'experience of estrangement reached explosive power, and the demand for reconciliation reached revolutionary strength'.[126] However, by thus transferring the concept of estrange-

---

[124] *Ibid.,* pp. 26—27.
[125] *Ibid.* Cf. *TC:* 83.
[126] 'Estrangement and Reconciliation in Modern Thought', p. 14. In the following account of Marx, I have referred to five articles by Tillich in addition to those already cited:— 'Marx's View of History', *Culture in History. Essays in Honor of Paul Radin,* ed. Stanley Daimond (New York: Columbia University Press, 1960) pp. 631—641; 'The Attack of Dialectical Materialism on Christianity', *The Student World* (Geneva) XXXI, No. 2 (1938) pp. 115—125; 'The Church and Communism', *Religion in Life,* VI, No. 3 (1937) pp. 347—357; 'Between Utopianism and Escape from History', *Colgate Rochester Divinity School Bulletin,* XXXI, No. 2 (May 1959) pp. 32—40; and 'Der Mensch im Christentum und im Marxismus', *Schriftenreihe des Evangelischen Arbeitsausschusses Düsseldorf,* H. 5 (Düsseldorf: 1953). *GW,* III: 194—209.

ment from the epistemological to the practical sphere, Marx at the same time revealed his opposition to his teacher. Marx believed that Hegel had erred in imagining that the antitheses in mankind—the alienation of man from man and from himself and of class from class—had been accomodated and resolved in the logic of the universal synthesis, and that modern society was accordingly in a state of harmonious progress towards self-fulfilment. In a word, Marx considered Hegel's 'reconciliation' *unrealistic:* the overcoming of estrangement in thought does not overcome estrangement in fact, and the world is not as it ought to be. Marx's use of the dialectic of separation and identity is, by contrast, an 'extreme case of historical thinking'.[127] He does not believe in the abstract functioning of the laws of dialectic but seeks to show that their validity depends on the structure of the society in which they operate. 'As applied to Marx, "dialectical" means that he tries to reveal the driving forces in a social structure by pointing out the contradictory elements in it and describing them as necessary consequences of the structure itself. Life produces the contradictions by which it is driven onward'.[128]

This reinterpretation of the concept of estrangement is the point of departure for Marx's critique of bourgeois society. Estrangement is the corollary of this society and so true humanity is impossible under the conditions of the capitalist social order. Alienation is the fate of all groups in the industrial state, and reconciliation is most demanded where alienation is most acute, that is, in the exploited proletariat, for unlike the ruling classes they cannot camouflage their actual condition by economic power and cultural means. Thus it is the proletariat who are the 'possible reconcilers of an estranged mankind. They fight for a *real humanism,* in which, not only in theory and for the philosopher, but in practice and for everybody, life is reconciled with itself'.[129] This, then, is a dynamic and social reformulation of estrangement, providing us with an actual 'history of reconciliation' in which the course of mankind in its development towards a final perfection is described. So we find in Marx these basic ideas: first, man as he is essentially in the

---

[127] 'Marx and the Prophetic Tradition', *Radical Religion,* I, No. 4 (1935) p. 25.
[128] 'How much Truth is there in Karl Marx?' *The Christian Century,* LXV, No. 36 (September 1948) p. 906.
[129] 'Estrangement and Reconciliation in Modern Thought', p. 15.

period of 'original communism'; next, man alienated and dehumanized through capitalism; then man rebelling against his dehumanization in the age of class struggle; and finally the man of the coming 'classless society' who is again what man is essentially and ought to be. All this is embraced in the concept of estrangement as derived from Hegel, except that what Hegel achieved in the essentialist structure of his thought Marx now achieves in his notion of the fighting proletariat. For him, the restoration of the original perfection is the task of the proletarian revolution, in which the negation of all the repressive conditions of present society will create man again in his true essentiality. Thus the victory of the proletariat is, according to Marx, the requirement for this revolution which will free even the capitalist from the objective power of estrangement.

As I said at the beginning of this section, these two short accounts of Hegel and Marx provide us with further specifications of the theology of culture, and it is to these that we must now turn. Immediately two characteristics common to all three philosophers are apparent. The first is that Tillich, like Marx before him, *employs the Hegelian dialectic in his description of the dynamics of life.* The movement of life from self-identity to self-alteration and back to self-identity—the famous triad of thesis, antithesis and synthesis—is the 'basic scheme' of Hegel's dialectic. Elsewhere Tillich speaks of it as reflecting the 'trinitarian structure of life', and we have seen already how he incorporates this same pattern in his account of the process from essential being through existential being to New Being. This ternary structure is, Tillich admits, much older than Hegel's philosophy and pre-dates even Plato's use of dialectics in his dialogues; but Hegel's formulation is its classic expression and 'must be accepted as a method of describing the movements of life and history in their inner tensions, contrasts, and contradictions and in their trend toward more embracing unities'.[130]

The second common feature arises directly from the first. *Acceptance of the dialectical principle separates all three philosophers from those interpretations of history in which the universal direction of history*

---

[130] 'Marxism and Christian Socialism', *Christianity and Society* (New York) VII, No. 2 (1942) p. 17. See also *ST*, 3: 302 & 350.

is denied. For Tillich, as for Hegel and Marx, history is a dialectical process with a unique goal, history itself being essentially 'history of salvation'. This teleological conception of history Tillich expressed in his analysis of the universal quest for New Being and its fulfilment in the historical appearance of Jesus the Christ; and in that discussion, we remember, he was at pains to dissociate himself from the Buddhist circular theory of history, with its doctrine of the recurrence of the same events. In this latter respect he agrees with Hegel, who similarly discovers a providential trend in the sequences of history and in whose philosophy the universal process of self-realization of the absolute mind is the meaning of history. And the same is true of Marx. For him history is a history of class struggles, but one which leads to a classless society with which the true history of mankind begins. Here too all revolutionary catastrophes and social oppositions are directed towards a final harmony, which is the aim and end of history.

Such similarities as these are nevertheless shortlived, and from hereon the concepts of dialectic and history function more as points of disagreement than agreement. To take the concept of history first, Tillich agrees in common with all Existentialism that Hegel's interpretation is a description of logical relations but not of real processes in time, and that accordingly Hegel is wrong in thinking that the universal movement toward synthesis is a law of necessity. In conceiving history as a providential process, working behind human activity and irrespective of human irrationality, Hegel missed 'the mystery of the particulars' and thus failed to account for the unpredictability of human freedom, the element of contingency in the historical process and the accidents of leadership.[131] In saying this, of course, Tillich is at one with Marx in his attack on Hegel, and indeed reaffirms his allegiance by adopting almost wholesale the Marxist analysis of the evolution of society. He recognizes that the structure of contemporary society is determined by the capitalist economy, and that within this structure there is a necessary opposition between the owners of the means of production and those dependent on those means; he also agrees that this opposition creates the differentiation of classes, that this differentiation results in the class struggle, and that the proletariat is 'the place given by fate for resis-

---

[131] *Perspectives in Nineteenth & Twentieth Century Protestant Thought*, p. 132.

tance to the capitalist structure of society'.[132] Tillich, however, stops short precisely at the point where the Marxist synthesis is achieved, that is, *he denies that the dialectic of history moves relentlessly towards the abolition of the class society*. Marx's assumption that 'the point of complete dehumanization is the turning-point towards reconciliation cannot be verified, either empirically or rationally'; and when Marx speaks of 'vanguards' of the proletariat he must presume that they possess a 'special power' which denies 'the dogma of complete dehumanization'.[133] The inner contradiction of this hypothesis is, says Tillich, quite blatant: those who fight successfully for reconciliation against the forces of alienation must have experienced reconciliation within their own estranged situation. And the political consequence of this is devastating. Irrespective of when the age of fulfilment is expected, the actuality of estrangement will disappoint every such expectation and expose it as *utopian*. With that, only two possibilities remain: 'either a deep disappointment is evoked, and with it an often cynical alienation from every historical expectation, *or* the determination is born to hold fast to one's expectations with every means available'.[134] For Tillich, this latter possibility is the road that leads from Marxism to Stalinism.

Utopianism and its political consequences constitute Tillich's most substantial criticism of Marx. Even though Marx fought against Utopia in his socially activist philosophy, he did not escape it. Admittedly Marx did not suppose that the class situation could be changed by persuasion of the ruling classes, but he did expect that 'the economic process in unity with the revolutionary impulse of the proletarian classes would create the fulfilment of history, the classless society in which the main evils of the earlier mankind, of its "prehistory" as Marx called it, would be overcome'.[135] But why, Tillich asks, should the classless society be the end of historical dialectics? And why should the proletariat, after its victory, not succumb to the same contradictions and same differences of interest as those experienced previously by the bourgeoisie? To suppose otherwise, Tillich concludes, contradicts the basic fact of human

---

[132] 'Religious Socialism', *Political Expectation*, ed. J. Luther Adams (New York: Harper & Row, 1971) p. 49.
[133] 'Estrangement and Reconciliation in Modern Thought', p. 15.
[134] 'Christianity and Marxism', *Political Expectation*, ed. J. Luther Adams (New York: Harper & Row, 1971) p. 94.
[135] 'Marxism and Christian Socialism', p. 16.

social experience—the self-estrangement of man from himself in continuous class struggle—and thereby denies the ontological truth of the
symbol of the Fall.

It is at this point that Tillich's criticisms of Hegel and Marx conjoin.
*Neither the Hegelian nor Marxist dialectic is genuinely dialectical
because an absolute stage at the end of the dialectical process is itself
a contradiction of the dialectical principle.* Hegel and Marx offer
a cognitively or historically reparable alienation and thereby dissolve
the dialectic movement of separation and reunion in the completed
syntheses of 'absolute mind' and the 'classless society'. 'In the last
moment essence triumphs over existence, completion over infinity, and
the static over the dynamic ... The circle is closed'.[136] To use Hegel's
own term, the estrangement between essence and existence is no longer
'serious'. To be sure, both Hegel and Marx, by introducing the concepts
of estrangement and alienation into our vocabulary, testify to their own
consciousness that the structure of the world is distortion and contradiction; and each, by speaking of a final 'reconciliation', express the
fundamental truth that the estranged character of existence is *not* its
essential nature but a 'fall' from original unity; but for neither is the
Fall the universal symbol of an ontological fact, and it is for that reason
that both offer undialectical answers to the questions concerning the
overcoming of alienation. Each distorts the dialectical method into a
universal mechanism of calculable and providential processes, and each
fails to see that the qualitative distinction between essence and existence
invalidates every attempt to give a rational or materialistic explanation
of their reconciliation within historical existence. This indeed was
Kierkegaard's basic point in rejecting the Hegelian notion of 'pure
thought' as an 'invention' or 'lunatic postulate'.[137] Although reconciliation might be possible in the system of essences, this system is not the
reality in which we are living. 'Reconciliation', Tillich proclaims, 'is
a matter of anticipation and expectation, but not of reality ... Existence
is estrangement and not reconciliation'.[138]

---

[136] *IH:* 166.
[137] Kierkegaard, *Concluding Unscientific Postscript,* trans. D. F. Swenson,
with an Introduction and Notes by Walter Lowrie (Princeton: Princeton
University Press, 1941) p. 279. Quoted in *TC:* 83.
[138] *ST,* 2: 27—28.

For Tillich, therefore, *estrangement is the permanent refutation of complete or fulfilled synthesis in existence.* This immediately absolves Tillich from the charge that his own synthesis, like those of Hegel and Marx, is an exercise in self-salvation. In his interpretation of the dialectic of separation and reunion, separation is the expression of existential being and thus 'in space and time no synthesis is final' and 'no reunion is possible'.[139] Viewed from another angle, this means in turn that the claim that 'the substance of culture is religion and the form of religion is culture' is an account of religion and culture in their essential nature but not in their actual reality, or more simply that Tillich's synthesis is *one in principle but not in fact.*

> Essentially the religious and the secular are not separated realms. Rather they are within each other. But this is not the way things actually are. In actuality, the secular element tends to make itself independent and to establish a realm of its own. And in opposition to this, the religious element tends to establish itself also as a special realm. Man's predicament is determined by this situation. It is the situation of the estrangement of man from his true being. One could rightly say that the existence of religion as a special realm is the most conspicuous proof of man's fallen state.[140]

Saying that the theology of culture has a *soteriological focus* does not mean therefore that it seeks to re-establish within the area of existence the essential or original union of religion and culture—for existence does not accord with essence. What it aims to do is rather to indicate the place of religion in every cultural activity—that religion is the aspect of depth in the totality of the human spirit—and thereby to show that the contrast between the sacred and the secular is *the contrast of the estrangement of both realms in their existential but not in their essential being.* The outstanding proof of the Fall of the world is, to repeat, that a religious culture actually exists beside a secular culture, and this duality is a plain and underivable fact of existence which can never be overcome in time and space; but it nevertheless makes a substantial difference to the 'healing' of the schizophrenic position of 'double truth' if this contrast is deepened into a bridgeless gap or whether it is recognized as something which should not be, as something

---

[139] 'Reply to Interpretation and Critiscism', *The Theology of Paul Tillich*, p. 347.
[140] 'Aspects of a Religious Analysis of Culture', *TC*: 41—42.

which provides a distorted account of what these two spheres are essentially. It is this that the theology of culture is designed to do. Tillich's redefinition of the concept of religion allows us to say that in every cultural act an unconditional element is expressed and that it is therefore possible to recognize the unconscious theological character of every cultural creation. To the degree in which this is realized the conflicts between the religious and the secular are overcome in principle, and religion itself has rediscovered its true place as the dimension implicit to both Church and society but exclusive to neither. Hence the Church has no advantage over society and society no advantage over the Church. This, then, is a *theoretical reconciliation* of two spheres which are not alien to each other essentially but which are estranged in fact.

Tillich's denial of any actual historical realization of synthesis points us towards one final principle of his theology of culture. The theology of culture is the provisional expression of a final synthesis, *the complete achievement of which belongs to a dimension which is suprahistorical.* The synthesis which Hegel and Marx posited within the immanent processes of history is by Tillich projected beyond history and represented by such symbols as the 'Kingdom of God' and 'Eternal Life'.[141] According to the vision of the Book of Revelation, 'there will be no temple in the heavenly Jerusalem, for God will be all in all. There will be no secular realm, and for this very reason there will be no religious realm'.[142] This is in fact no more than another way of saying that Tillich has here taken account of the ontological truth of estrangement and from it has drawn consequences which structure his own notion of the 'transcendent' or 'transhistorical' character of final reconciliation. The answer of ontological healing is here correlated with the estranged condition of man as he exists, and for that same reason salvation cannot arise from the human situation but must originate from that which is beyond man's being and its estrangement, namely, in the transcendent fulfilment of finite being and meaning. In other words, it is this disruption of man's essential unity in existence, plus the fact that this disruption remains a reality as long as man is man, *that places Tillich's concept of final reconciliation beyond the idealist or utopian expectation of*

---

[141] See *IH:* 234 & 236; *ST,* 3: 433—452.
[142] 'Religion as a Dimension in Man's Spiritual Life', *TC:* 8.

perfection within estranged existence. He accepts with Hegel that the achievement of synthesis is the goal of life but denies that existence, as the manifestation of essential being, is its realization; he agrees with Marx that social and political forces have an unconditional significance for the development of man, but rejects the view that the proletariat is the place where the alienation of existence is overcome. Neither interpretation is dialectical since in each the contradictions of existence are brought to an end in synthesis. By contrast, Tillich's alternative is to extend the dialectic principle to the concept of reconciliation itself and thereby to indicate that the transhistorical power by which reunion is achieved is revealed in and through the forms of estrangement. By this means, reconciliation does not involve an unrealistic analysis of the structure of existence in which estrangement is denied, nor is it restricted to a second world next to or beyond the world of experience; it is evident rather as the presence of the transcendent element in the finite creativity of nature and culture, or as the fulfilment of existence *as we experience the estrangement of existence.* For this reason, Tillich defines 'providence' as the 'permanent activity of God' working through all the destructive consequences of existence, or as 'God's directing creativity' in which all existential conditions are included. Providence, he says, is '"the divine creation" which is present in every group of finite conditions and in the totality of finite conditions... It is the quality of inner directedness present in every situation'.[143]

With these last remarks we come full circle. Tillich's notion of 'providence', like his earlier theory of meaning, points to that reality present in and underlying all existential conditions, upon which the ultimate meaningfulness and significance of everything depends; or, like the concepts of 'immanent mysticism' and 'belief-ful realism', it establishes a point within reality at which reality transcends its own finitude by its manifestation of ultimate meaning and being. This is not a 'particular' interpretation of reality but indicates the universal form of reality as such, namely, that the possibility of its reconciliation is latent within the conditions of its own estrangement. The Renaissance philosopher, Nicolaus Cusanus, called this the apprehension of the *coincidentia oppositorum* ('the coincidence of opposites'), the awareness of the 'paradoxical' presence of unconditioned content within condi-

---

[143] *ST*, 1: 296.

tioned form[144]; and for Tillich it is this insight into the infinite depth of finite reality which frees the religious consciousness from the religious sphere as a sphere 'apart', and which creates an openness for an understanding of the spiritual nature of the profane. It is in following this argument that it is possible to present a religious analysis of the secular forms of culture and thereby to demonstrate that, irrespective of their secular meaning, works of art are expressions of the ultimate dimension of reality. We must now look to see how Tillich substantiates this claim in his analysis of the formal properties of art.

---

[144] *ST*, 1: 90.

CHAPTER THREE
THE CATEGORIES, PROCESS
AND FULFILMENT OF
ARTISTIC CREATION

From Tillich's use of the metaphysics of the *coincidentia oppositorum*, the following point may be derived: that the affirmation of the paradoxical immanence of the transcendent is the denial of any ostensibly naturalistic or religiously indifferent culture. This conclusion, when transposed into Tillich's aesthetics, means that, however adamant an artist may be that his work is not religious, he cannot escape the judgment that in some sense it is, although doubtless in a way unbeknown to him. So, for example, Cézanne painting an apple is an act of meaning in which the unconditionality of meaning is presupposed; and should Cézanne protest that this is not so, Tillich may then reply that secular art is defined precisely by its exclusion *from the consciousness alone* of the ultimate level of meaning entailed in every aesthetic act. And the same can be said of those 'creative expressions of despair' associated with existentialists like Kafka and Sartre. For not only is the representation of meaninglessness itself a meaningful act[1]—and so amenable to exactly the same interpretation accorded Cézanne's apple— but meaninglessness, we recall, is a symptom of estrangement, and estrangement a category of religious art. Thus, going further, even the artist's denial that his work is religious, or even his artistic portrayal of that denial, is in the end self-defeating. For this denial, once recognized as a symptom of estrangement, as a concise expression of the separation of religion and culture, may now be revealed as yet another instance of the existential condition, and may, like Picasso's 'Guernica',

---

[1] *CTB:* 139.

be deemed religious more for the radicalism of its question than for its provision of an answer.[2]

From these brief examples it becomes clear that, whatever the artist's choice of subject, no subject chosen by him can be excluded from the religious dimension—which is but another way of saying that religious art cannot be defined by its choice of subject. To this extent, Tillich's philosophy of art may be described as *pan-religious*, including as it does within its definition of religious art every conceivable style or object of artistic description, extending even to the artist's denial of religion. If 'religion is the substance of culture' (and so of art), then evidently no art can be divorced from religion, and art may thus be regarded as 'the expression (or form) of religion'. These two statements, which together constitute the central proposition of the theology of culture, are not only consistent, but, as Tillich admits, equivalent.[3] Viewed from this perspective, the claim that 'art is religious' is a tautology, the deduction of a conclusion already implicit within the definition of art. Thus X is Y because by X we mean Y.

If this prevents Tillich from ever saying that a particular artistic style is in principle non-religious—an axiom of his theory—it does not however prevent him from distinguishing between the more and the less religious. It was at this point that the 'category of realism' played its decisive role in determining the sub-divisions of religious art. The religious style, in so far as it is realistic, will be concerned with the representation of the three elements circumscribing the ontological condition of man and his world: of the state of essential being, of the state of existential being, and of the quest for that state in which the estrangement of existential from essential being is overcome, namely, for salvation. On the positive side, this three-fold classification enabled us

---

[2] Philosophy provides its own example of a religious denial of religion in Nietzsche's pronouncement that 'God is dead'. Even in this most extreme antithesis to traditional theistic belief, a 'demonic transcendence' is present; and, in that respect, Nietsche's so-called atheism may be taken as a further prophetic foreshadowing of the 20th century search of ultimatic. Cf. 'Nietzsche and the Bourgeois Spirit', *Journal of the History of Ideas* (New York), VI, No. 3 (1945) pp. 307—309; and *Perspectives in Nineteenth & Twentieth Century Protestant Thought*, pp. 197—207.

[3] 'Christian Criteria for Our Culture', *Criterion* (Yale), I, No. 1 (October 1952) p. 1.

to say that Botticelli's portrayal of the Madonna, Picasso's picture of the bombing of Guernica, and the evangelists' verbal portrait of Jesus of Nazareth are all, in their various ways, religious paintings. On the negative side, it enabled us to see why the art favoured by so many ecclesiastical magazines and churches should be placed at the lowest end of the scale. Here we find a confusion between the three elements, one in which, for example, the distorted and estranged nature of reality is glossed over and presented as a special kind of beautifying sentimental naturalism. Elsewhere Tillich describes this as religious *Kitsch*, and cites, as a final instance of it, the face of Jesus in Dali's famous 'Last Supper'. This is not poor art, based on the incompetence of the painter, but a particular form of 'deteriorized idealism'.[4]

So much by way of summary. Our next duty is to see how Tillich's claim that religion is the substance of art, already confirmed by the theory of meaning, is further substantiated by the analysis of the formal properties of art, of those elements that go to make up every artistic act. This is not to say that what follows is divorced from the theory of meaning: it is rather a transposal of the same argument into another frame of reference, according to which we may distinguish those elements within artistic structures which do or do not impart ultimate meaning to a work of art. That achieved, we have provided ourselves with the most exact method of religious-stylistic classification so far advanced. For convenience, Tillich's discussion may be split into two parts: in the first, he examines the categories of artistic creation and their inter-connexions; and, in the second, the major stylistic divisions which arise from these relations.

---

[4] 'Interrogation of Paul Tillich', *Philosophical Interrogations*, ed. Sydney and Beatrice Rome (New York: Holt, Rinehart & Winston, 1964) p. 407. Commenting on what he calls the 'ambiguity of stylistic idealism', Tillich writes: 'An ideal without realistic foundation is set up against encountered reality, which is beautified and corrected to conform with the ideal in a manner which combines sentimentality and dishonesty. This is what has marred the religious art of the last hundred years. Such art still expresses something, although not encountered reality — the low taste of a culturally empty period' (*ST*, 3: 77).

I. CONTENT, FORM AND IMPORT:
THE CATEGORIES OF ARTISTIC CREATION

Tillich begins with some general remarks about the nature of all cultural production. Culture, he says, is the self-creation of life by man, or, more exactly, the expression of that act by which man 'takes care of something, keeps it alive, and makes it grow'.[5] In the cultural act, therefore, man 'cultivates' everything he meets and creates something *new* from it, that is, something not simply identifiable with encountered reality. If we now ask what this new element consists of, the answer is provided by the earlier division between the practical and theoretical cultural sciences. This division is the consequence of the two main creative functions of man's spirit, namely, of its 'receiving' and 'reacting' capacities. Tillich calls the receptive function *theoria*. '*Theoria* is the act of looking at the encountered world in order to take something of it into the centred self as a meaningful, structured whole'.[6] As an example, he cites the meaning-creating power of language. 'As the bearer of meaning, the word liberates from bondage to the environment... Something universally valid is intended in every meaningful sentence, even if the subject spoken about is particular or transitory. Cultures live in such meanings'.[7] Aesthetic images and cognitive concepts are the instruments of *theoria*, each mirroring a fragment of a universe of meaning. Simultaneous, however, with man's grasping of reality is his shaping of it. Man here employs tools for the ordering of reality in a technical act, the products of which are such disciplines as economy, medicine, administration and education. This, the reactive function of human creativity, Tillich terms *praxis*. '*Praxis* is the whole of cultural acts of centred personalities who as members of social groups act upon each other and themselves. *Praxis* in this sense is the self-creation of life in the personal realm'.[8] Summarizing, then, we may say that what man creates in his encounter with reality—and what thereafter becomes part of reality and so the subject of further re-creation—is culture itself, culture being 'the creation of a universe of meaning in *theoria* and

---

[5] *ST*, 3: 33.
[6] *Ibid.*, p. 66.
[7] *Ibid.*, p. 73.
[8] *Ibid.*, pp. 69—70.

praxis';[9] and that, in the divisions of the *Geisteswissenschaften*, the aesthetic and cognitive creations constitute those *new* elements introduced by the receiving function of man's creativity. Artistic creativity, therefore, like all such cultural activity, presupposes the production of something new and thus the freedom to go beyond that which exists or is given. So, if 'Van Gogh paints a tree, it becomes an image of his dynamic vision of the world. He contributes to the creation of the universe of meanings by creating an image both of treehood and of the universe as reflected in the particular mirror of a tree'.[10]

It is at this point that Tillich narrows his discussion down to an account of the structure of the new creation. Every aesthetic creation, and indeed every cultural act, be it theoretical or practical, is composed of three elements: *Content* (or Subject Matter), *Form,* and *Import* (or Substance).[11] Content *(der Inhalt)* is drawn from the inexhaustible multitude of encountered objects: it denotes the external factuality of things and events, and is thus 'potentially identical with everything which can be received by the human mind in sensory images'.[12] How the artist selects his subject matter does not depend on whether it possesses qualities like good or bad, beautiful or ugly, but on the second and third elements, from which arise the principles of selection. The second element, Form *(die Form),* is that which transforms the content into the work of art: it is that which, by the use of certain materials such as sound, words, line and colour, makes the artistic product what it is. Form is accordingly the 'ontologically decisive element in every artistic creation'.[13] The third element, Import *(der Gehalt),* is that which, by its spiritual power, gives form and its content meaning or significance *(Bedeutung).*

> By content we mean something objective in its simple existence, which by form is raised up to the intellectual-cultural sphere. By substance or import, however, we understand the meaning, the spiritual substantiality,

---

[9] *Ibid.*, p. 101.
[10] *Ibid.*, p. 66.
[11] 'On the Idea of a Theology of Culture', *WR:* 165 ff. The distinction between form and import appears also in Hegel's 'Vorlesungen über die Ästhetik', *Werke* (Berlin: Duncker und Humblot, 1843), X, Part II, pp. 229 ff. Whether or not Tillich was consciously influenced by Hegel at this point remains an open question since no debt is acknowledged.
[12] 'Protestantism and Artistic Style', *TC:* 69.
[13] *Ibid.*

which alone gives form its significance. We can therefore say: *Substance or import is grasped by means of a form and given expression in a content.* Content is accidental, substance essential, and form is the mediating element.[14]

This, then, is the character of a work of art. Any artistic product that exists must have a form, and this form is itself the result of the artist's acquired or innate ability for a particular type of artistic production (for example, painting or sculpture). Every form treats of a subject (e.g., a landscape or human figure), and within and beyond both there is a meaning-import. This meaning-import may be expressive of the spiritual meaning or substance of the special style of a period, of a particular school, or of a particular period in the development of the artist himself.[15]

These three elements combine to form the artistic creation. This is not to say, however, that their combination is necessarily uniform, since, in the actual process of artistic creativity, one or other of the elements may be suppressed. Thus we find that content or subject matter is of least importance; and that form can lose its relation to content as content recedes in the face of a preponderance of import. In this way, form can acquire a quality of detachment from content, being now relative to substance alone; it can become, that is, form in a 'paradoxical sense by allowing its natural quality to be shattered by the substance'.[16] These possible variations between content, form and import enable Tillich to introduce a classification of artistic types, based on the predominance of one of the three elements in any given work of art. So there are within the visual arts 'naturalistic' styles, according to which the primary task is the representation of the objectively real; other 'impressionistic' styles in which both the content of the artistic creation and its expressive power are subservient to such formal properties as shape and light; and 'expressionistic' styles in which the artist seeks to expose the inner significance or import of his subject matter rather than to picturize its external appearance.[17]

---

[14] 'On the Idea of a Theology of Culture', *WR*: 165.

[15] 'Religion and Culture', *Asian Cultural Studies* (International Christian University, Tokyo), No. 2 (1960) p. 2.

[16] 'On the Idea of a Theology of Culture', *WR*: 166.

[17] *Ibid.*, pp. 169—170. Cf. 'Religiöser Stil und Religiöser Stoff in der bildenden Kunst', *GW*, IX: 319—320.

More elaborate classifications than these will be presented in the second section of this chapter. For the moment, it is sufficient to note the identification of the expressionist style as an import-predominant style. If we now recall Tillich's oft-repeated claim that Expressionism is the prototype of religious style, the next, and major, step in Tillich's analysis of artistic structure is foreseen. Import or substance is the 'religious element' present in every aesthetic creation: it is that which, as one of the three elements constitutive of a work of art, designates the religious element which is *a priori* part and parcel of the nature of art itself, and which, accordingly, makes art substantially, if not intentionally, religious.[18] In a word, *'Import' is another name for the unconditioned meaning intended in religion and presupposed in every artistic creation.* Thus we may say that, in every aesthetic shaping, an essential import *(Wesensgehalt)* is expressed, which is neither identifiable with the artist's representation of an object, nor with the significance he attributes to that object, but with the unconditioned ground of the significance so ascribed.

> The significance of the real as apprehended in aesthetic feeling never remains attached to a particular significance and is never to be apprehended through empirical emotional states. The unconditioned significance pulsates in and through every aesthetic experience, and every aesthetic feeling is a transcendent feeling, that is, one in which the empirical emotional agitation includes a kernel of experience pointing to the unconditional.[19]

With this specification of the unconditional meaning-import present in all aesthetic activity, new light is shed on the relations that exist between content, form and import. First, it explains why, of the three, content is of least significance. In the expression of the religious attitude, there are no objects religious in themselves. Thus art is religious —that is, revealing of import—not because its subject matter is religious but because the perception brought to expression in the aesthetic act is religious. It is conceivable, therefore, that art may be religious irrespective of its material, a fact indeed already demonstrated by the Expressionists themselves. This being so, we are led to a second point: that there can be no import without form. For form, we have seen, is precisely that by which art becomes art. Without form, therefore,

---

[18] *ST*, 3: 100.
[19] 'The Philosophy of Religion', *WR:* 67.

there would be no aesthetic creation to be religious, that is, imbued with import.

The decisive relationship in religious art, and indeed in every type of cultural creation, is therefore that between form and import; and it is in establishing the nature of this relationship that Tillich once more refers to his theory of meaning. Set within this frame, we may describe form as the mode—be it an essay, poem or painting etc.—by which the artist attributes a particular meaning or set of meanings to his subject matter. In that respect, all forms express a special encounter with reality, and all forms are forms of meaning. The bestowal of meaning, therefore, takes place through a form and in relation to reality. The theory has already stipulated, however, that such forms of meaning, when contrasted with the ultimate meaning, must be seen as having only preliminary meaning in and of themselves; that the meaningfulness of the totality of all such forms of meaning depends on the presupposition of unconditioned meaningfulness, which is the focus of the religious attitude. It is this that controls the relationship between form and import. All particular meanings are forms of meaning, and the unconditioned meaning is the import of meaning. The latter, therefore, is that which is presupposed in all forms of meaning, 'upon whose presence the ultimate meaningfulness, the significance, and the essentiality (Wesenhaftigkeit) of every act of meaning rest'.[20] Thus the unity of all forms, like every individual form, is utterly empty without the relation to the import of meaning; and to speak of an unconditioned form is a contradiction in terms.

> Even the totality of meaning need not be meaningful, but rather could disappear, like every particular meaning, in the abyss (Abgrund) of meaninglessness, if the presupposition of an unconditioned meaningfulness were not alive in every act of meaning. This unconditionality of meaning is itself, however, not a meaning, but rather is the ground of meaning. It we include in the term "forms of meaning" all particularities of individual meaning and of all separate connections of meaning and even the universal connection of meaning, then in relation to the universal connection the unconditioned meaning may be designated as the import of meaning. By the import of meaning we therefore do not mean the import attaching to the significance of a particular

---

[20] Ibid., p. 43.

consummation of meaning, but rather the meaningfulness that gives to every particular meaning its reality, significance, and essentiality.[21]

Every cultural creation, therefore, presupposes a union of form and import. 'There is', says Tillich, 'no import apart from a form, and no form without import', since form without import is meaningless, and import without form could not be the object of an act of meaning.[22] So, too, with the aesthetic creation. Here the apprehension of import without artistic form is impossible, and it is essential that the artistic form be the bearer of unconditional import. Or again, aesthetic expression is a coming into artistic form, and this form is the medium by which the import is revealed. Import is not therefore itself an artistic form, but rather the ultimate meaning or 'substantial' metaphysical power present within and beyond all such forms: it is, as it were, that which is carried within, and thereby bestows ultimacy upon, every conditional form in which the artist ascribes significance to his subject matter.

For this reason, no artistic form may stand outside the sphere of religion, for as soon as an artistic form is created it carries within itself unconditional validity. In religious art, that is to say, the holy is grasped only through artistic form; but it is not the form that is holy but the unconditional that is mediated by and through the form. Thus every form is both superficial and transitory *and* an expression of the ultimate ground of all forms. This, we need hardly say, is a variation of the argument previously introduced by the concepts of 'belief-ful realism' and 'immanent mysticism'. Here too Tillich has established that point within reality at which reality transcends its own finitude by its manifestation of ultimate meaning. For religious art, to the extent that it is orientated towards the expression of import, must utilize the forms of aesthetic perception; but in being so orientated it must transcend the finite and artistic means by which import is expressed, since the unconditioned can never be drawn directly into the sphere of the conditioned. Once again, therefore, the crucial distinction has been made between that which is expressed and the means of expression; and once more the realizations of the aesthetic act have been denoted as the *loci* of the paradoxical immanence of the transcendent. 'Nicht, weil alles Schöne von Gott stammt, ist alle Kunst religiös ... aber weil alle Kunst einen

---

[21] *Ibid.*, pp. 57—58.
[22] *Ibid.*, p. 53.

Gehalt, eine Stellung zum Unbedingten zum Ausdruck bringt, darum ist sie religiös'.[23]

These connexions between form and import, while deciding for the religious quality of all art, similarly decide for the religious quality of all culture. For no matter how various the cultural forms of meaning, be they of scientific, aesthetic, legal or social structure, these forms are necessarily expressive of import, that is, of the religious element upon which the ultimate meaningfulness of every cultural act depends, theoretical as well as practical. Thus in every apprehension of the conditioned forms of culture the ultimate attitude or relation to the Unconditioned is presupposed. 'There is', says Tillich, 'no period in human history in which, hiddenly or openly, there was no such substance underlying cultural forms. In all cultural realms, an ultimate meaning in this sense is expressed'.[24] Conversely, import without form would be import divorced from the cultural means of expression, and so meaningless. Accordingly, every religious act must be a cultural act, namely, framed in terms of the cultural forms and so dependent on that process by which the human spirit encounters being through meaning. *'In the cultural act, therefore, the religious is substantial; in the religious act the cultural is formal'*.[25]

Thus we arrive at yet another formulation of the theology of culture, the mutual immanence of culture and religion being here described as a synthesis of form and import. From this, however, two important consequences follow. The first is that the construction of this synthesis is *only possible from the standpoint of import*. Form, as we have just seen, although deciding for the cultural character of all religion, cannot, like import, decide for the religious character of all culture. The realization of the theology of culture must therefore proceed from the side of import, even though import only attains cultural existence in form.[26] Import, as the only unconditional and immediate spiritual substance constitutive of all cultural creation, is thus revealed as the only element through which a permanent and universal unity of the cultural functions can be achieved.

---

[23] 'Religiöser Stil und Religiöser Stoff in der bildenden Kunst', *GW*, IX: 318.
[24] 'Christian Criteria for Our Culture', p. 1.
[25] 'The Philosophy of Religion', *WR:* 60.
[26] 'On the Idea of a Theology of Culture', *WR:* 164.

If the intuition of the forms of meaning filled with import is the presupposition of the theology of culture, a second consequence follows. It is that the theologian of culture, unlike the artist and other representatives of the *Geisteswissenschaften, is not directly productive with regard to culture;* that he is not concerned, in other words, with the creation of the conditioned artistic form, but with the apprehension of the unconditioned import in that form.[27] Tillich makes much of this difference, and assigns to the theologian of culture three main tasks, these tasks corresponding to the three-fold character of the cultural sciences as described in the previous chapter.[28] When dealing with art, these duties may be stated as follows: first, to establish the categories that govern aesthetic creation (namely, content, form and import); second, to record the variations between the categories as they are actualized in the individual works of art, and thereafter to systematize these variations in the construction of a typology of artistic styles (e.g., Naturalism, Impressionism and Expressionism); and third, to produce an ideal outline of an artistic style penetrated by religion, that is, to work as the architect of synthesis by indicating the direction in which a truly religious artistic style, and by implication a truly religious system of culture, may be realized. But under no circumstances can he produce this style himself. His duty is to indicate the presence or (relative) absence of import in the actual cultural expressions, and to work towards the cultural-religious ideal of synthesis.

Herein lies the limitation of the task of systematization assigned to the theologian of culture: but his universal significance also originates here. Far removed from every restriction to a special sphere, he can give expression from the standpoint of substance to the all-embracing unity of the cultural functions and demonstrate the relations that lead from one phenomenon of culture to another, through the substantial unity of the substance finding expression in them; he can thereby help, from the viewpoint of substance, to bring about the unity of culture in the same way that the philosopher helps from the viewpoint of pure forms and categories.[29]

It is an error to suppose, therefore, that the tasks of the theologian of culture, in aesthetics or any other branch of the cultural sciences,

---

[27] *Ibid.,* p. 167.
[28] See above, p. 43.
[29] 'On the Idea of a Theology of Culture', *WR:* 167—168.

are merely analytical. Analysis is certainly required in the formation of concepts like form and import, in determining the degree to which the different cultural creations are expressive of religious import; but, beyond these things, the culture-theologian undertakes the synthetic task of setting forth a normative and systematic outline of a religiously imbued culture and artistic style; that is, of a culture and a style both of which reveal import through form, and both of which thereby give a religious quality to every material or subject with which they deal.

It is in this direction that Tillich now proceeds. He begins with an analysis and explanation of the actual variations of the aesthetic categories and their stylistic consequences, and from that constructs a detailed, if hypothetical, image of art in the state of synthesis. This image may be better described as an image of the ideal fulfilment of the aesthetic expression of import through form, in comparison with which we may judge the real and existing styles of such expression. Here, then, we are provided with a further criterion for the classification of religious art, based on the degree to which the aesthetic function succeeds or fails in its expression of import. This in turn explains why the following discussion is dominated by the importance Tillich attaches to those forces or elements which either hinder or abet the artistic power of expressiveness.

II. AUTONOMY, HETERONOMY, AND THEONOMY: THE PROCESS AND FULFILMENT OF ARTISTIC CREATION

Tillich maintains that there are certain elements, necessary to the process of artistic creation, which determine the approximation of an artistic style to its synthetic ideal. The elements are *the structural elements of reason,* which, under the conditions of estrangement and as testimony to the finitude of reason, move against each other and thus initiate a series of self-destructive conflicts within human rationality itself. These elements are denoted by the terms 'autonomous reason', 'heteronomous reason', and 'theonomous reason'.[30] Since in every relation

---

[30] *ST,* 1: 92—94. The concepts of autonomy and heteronomy appear in Kant's *Grundlegung zur Metaphysik der Sitten* (1785). Here Kant speaks of the autonomy of the will as 'the supreme principle of morality' *(das alleinige Prinzip der Moral),* and of heteronomy of the will as 'the source

of the mind to reality a conflict between these three occurs, irrespective of whether the mind is receiving its world *(theoria)* or reacting to it *(praxis)*, this condition is constitutive of every act by which the artist imputes meaning to his subject matter. *It is the interaction of these elements that decides for the variation of the aesthetic categories.* Because, however, any content or subject matter is in principle amenable to form, we may disregard it for the moment and focus on the decisive categories of form and import. In the act of meaning which is the aesthetic act, one may concentrate attention upon the forms of meaning or upon the import of meaning. For Tillich, the former involves the exercise of autonomous reason, the latter the exercise of theonomous reason:—'The more the form, the greater the autonomy; the more the substance or import, the greater the theonomy'.[31] The exercise of heteronomous reason results in two further variations: either the attempt to grasp import apart from form, or, more usually, the limitation of the unconditioned import to certain particular and conditioned forms.[32] With these associations, another typology can be devised which is concerned, first, with the ascription of meaning in accordance with the autonomous, heteronomous and theonomous attitudes, and, second, with the classification of styles according to the creations of such attitudes, namely, with autonomous, heteronomous and theonomous art.

1) Autonomy *(Selbstgesetzlichkeit)* denotes the *nomos* ("law") of *autos* ("self"). It does not refer to the freedom of the individual to be a law to himself but to 'the obedience of the individual to the law of reason, which he finds in himself as a rational being'.[33] Autonomous reason, therefore, resists the danger of being conditioned by a particular

---

of all spurious principles of morality'. *Kant's gesammelte Schriften*, Bd. IV (Berlin: George Reimer, 1903) pp. 440—441. E.T., T. K. Abbott, *Kant's Critique of Practical Reason and Other Works on the Theory of Ethics* (London, 1909) p. 122. For a general account of their Kantian usage, see Friedrich Delekat, 'Autonomie und Heteronomie des Willens', *Immanuel Kant* (Heidelberg: Quelle & Meyer, 1966) pp. 283—291. Cf. also Luther Adams, 'What Kind of Religion has a Place in Higher Education?' *Journal of Bible and Religion*, XIII (1945) pp. 185—192. Here Adams discusses some of the 18th and 19th century sources for the concepts of autonomy, heteronomy, and theonomy.

[31] 'On the Idea of a Theology of Culture', *WR:* 164.
[32] *Ibid.*, p. 164; and 'The Philosophy of Religion', *WR:* 75 & 78.
[33] *ST*, 1: 93.

time, place or environment, but considers these as the material which reason has to grasp or shape according to the structural laws of *theoria* and *praxis*. Autonomous reason is thus independent reason: not in the sense of expressing individual arbitrariness but in terms of its refusal to obey any authority (secular or divine) which goes against reason's own essential structure. Applying this concept to the relation between religion and culture, we may call an autonomous culture 'the attempt to create the forms of personal and social life without any reference to something ultimate and unconditional, following only the demands of theoretical and practical rationality'.[34]

2) The suppression of autonomy is heteronomy *(Fremdesgesetzlichkeit)*. Throughout history, Tillich tells us, there have arisen heteronomous authorities challenging the independence of autonomous reason and demanding that it subject itself, in one or all of its functions, to a law *(nomos)* that is strange *(heteros)* or superior to its own structure. Heteronomy 'issues commands from "outside" on how reason should grasp and shape reality'.[35] The struggle that ensues, however, is not a fight between reason and non-reason but a dangerous and tragic conflict within reason itself. The heteronomous powers do not challenge the independent actualization of reason in the name of something completely alien to reason but in the name of the 'depth of reason', which, they claim, autonomy has disregarded. Heteronomy is thus a reaction against an autonomy which has lost its depth and become empty and powerless. 'The basis of a genuine heteronomy is the claim to speak in the name of the ground of being and therefore in an unconditional and ultimate way'[36]; and this it does in myth and cult, which it regards as the direct and intentional expressions of the depth of reason. In terms of the relation between religion and culture, we may conclude that an heteronomous culture is one which 'subjects the forms and laws of thinking and acting to authoritative criteria of an ecclesiastical religion or a political quasi-religion, even at the price of destroying the structures of rationality'.[37]

---

[34] 'Religion and Secular Culture', *PE:* 57.
[35] *ST,* 1: 93.
[36] *Ibid.,* p. 94.
[37] 'Religion and Secular Culture', *PE:* 57.

3) In this way, then, autonomy and heteronomy move against each other and try to destroy each other: a process which tends towards the destruction of reason itself. According to Tillich, the resolution of this situation lies in the recognition that both autonomy and heteronomy are rooted in theonomy, and that 'each goes astray when their theonomous unity is broken'.[38] Theonomy *(Gottesgesetzlichkeit)* does not mean the imposition of a divine law by authority but rather 'autonomous reason united with its own depth. In a theonomous situation reason actualizes itself in obedience to its structural laws and in the power of its own inexhaustible ground'.[39] That God *(theos)* is the law *(nomos)* is the condition of the theonomous situation; but under the conditions of estrangement no such situation can exist but only approximations to it. Only revelation, says Tillich, can overcome the conflict between autonomy and heteronomy by re-establishing their essential unity, and indeed the quest for salvation is synonymous with the quest for theonomy which arises from within these conflicts of reason. This quest, however, is particularly urgent today because autonomy, having become dominant under the guidance of technical reason and having thereby rendered life shallow and meaningless without the 'dimension of depth', has now been challenged by powerful heteronomies of a quasi-political character. These heteronomies have entered the vacuum created by an autonomy lacking the depth of reason. Thus empty autonomy and destructive heteronomy determine the nature of our times and its quest for theonomy. Viewed in terms of the relation of religion and culture,

---

[38] *ST*, 1: 94.
[39] *Ibid.* Under the heading 'Theonomie' in the famous second edition of *Die Religion in Geschichte und Gegenwart*, ed. Hermann Gunkel *et al.*, (Tübingen: Mohr, 1931), Tillich writes: 'Theonomie, ursprünglich Gottesgesetzlichkeit im Gegensatz zu Selbstgesetzlichkeit oder Autonomie, hat in der gegenwärtigen Diskussion einen bestimmteren Sinn bekommen. Sie wird scharf abgegrenzt gegen Heteronomie, d. h. gegen die Zerbrechung der selbstgesetzlichen Formen menschlichen Denkens und Handelns durch ein dem Geiste fremdes und äußerliches Gesetz. Theonomie ist im Gegensatz zu Heteronomie Erfüllung der selbstgesetzlichen Formen mit transzendentem Gehalt. Sie entsteht nicht durch Verzicht auf Autonomie etwa im Sinne des katholischen Autoritätsgedankens, sondern nur durch Vertiefung der Autonomie in sich selbst bis zu dem Punkt, wo sie über sich hinausweist. Das Transzendieren der autonomen Formen in Kultur und Gesellschaft, ihr Geprägtsein von einem sie tragenden und zugleich durchbrechenden (nicht zerbrechenden) Prinzip: das ist Theonomie' (Bd. V, pp. 1128—1129).

we may say that a theonomous culture 'expresses in its creations an ultimate concern and a transcending meaning not as something strange but as its own spiritual ground'.[40] A theonomous culture denies that man is the source and measure of religion and culture or that man must be subjected to an alien and superior law; rather, it asserts 'that the superior law is, at the same time, the innermost law of man himself, rooted in the divine ground which is man's own ground: the law of life transcends man, although it is, at the same time, his own'.[41] For Tillich, therefore, theonomy is an expression of the synthesis to be sought between religion and culture, the most precise statement of which is that 'religion is the substance of culture and culture the form of religion'.[42]

As a first step in relating the concepts of autonomy, heteronomy and theonomy to the classification of artistic styles, it is important to notice that to each concept Tillich appends a history. As cultural types, constantly acting and interacting in dialectical fashion, each may be used in the interpretation of a particular historical epoch. The shallowness of an autonomous and secularized culture creates a vacuum of despair which preludes the advent of a theonomous period, in which empty cultural forms are reunited with the dimension of depth. Theonomy, however, tends to degenerate into an oppressive heteronomy, which in turn provokes an autonomous reaction. Thus the circle begins anew.[43] So, for example, Clement and Origen created a Christian

---

[40] 'Religion and Secular Culture', *PE:* 57.
[41] *Ibid.*
[42] *Ibid.*
[43] In this analysis of the dialectical interaction of autonomy, heteronomy and theonomy, I have followed Tillich's account in *ST*, 3. Here the quest for theonomy arises out of the conflict between autonomy and heteronomy, this conflict being described as the key to any theological understanding of cultural-historical development (*Ibid.*, p. 94). It is important to note, however, that this interpretation differs considerably from earlier accounts, notably those given in 'The Philosophy of Religion' (1925) and *Das System der Wissenschaften* (1923). Here it is the dialectical interaction of autonomy and theonomy that is decisive, heteronomy being a product of it. So Tillich writes:—
Der Kampf von Theonomie und Autonomie ist die tiefste Triebkraft des schöpferischen Geistprozesses; er ist der dialektische Stachel der Geschichte, der sie nie zur Ruhe kommen läßt. In jeder Lage aber wirken beide zugleich. Die Theonomie, die Richtung aller Formen auf das Unbedingte, kann sich nur in Formen verwirklichen, die unter dem Gesetz der Form stehen, also

theonomy which later came under the heteronomous influence of
Athanasius and Augustine; the theonomy of the early and high Middle
Ages ended in the heteronomy of the Inquisition; the Renaissance,
despite the theonomous character of its beginnings, became increasingly
autonomous, notably with Erasmus and Galileo; the Reformation
quickly deteriorated into the heteronomy of Protestant orthodoxy and
then finally succumbed to the almost complete victory of autonomy in
the 18th and 19th centuries. The final subjection of our civilization to
the technical pattern of thought and action shows 'the character of an
extremely emptied and secularized autonomy in an advanced stage of
disintegration'.[44] These examples, Tillich concludes, indicate once again
that the quest for theonomous reunion arises out of the conflict between
autonomous and heteronomous reason.

Although we may regret its lack of historical detail, this account of
the cultural development of autonomy, heteronomy and theonomy is not
without importance. For if we compare this history with, say, the
history of art in *Masse und Geist*, a significant pattern emerges. Early
Gothic painting, with its suppression of individual characteristics in
favour of the pervasive 'supernatural idea', belongs to the theonomous
high Middle Ages, which Tillich dates between A.D. 1200—1300; late

---

die Tendenz zur Autonomie haben, und die Autonomie kann sich nicht auf
Formen richten, ohne den Gehalt zu erfassen, den sie ausdrücken, also ohne
theonomes Element. — Ein Konflikt tritt ein, sobald die Theonomie Formen
heiligt und aufrecht erhält, die dem Bewußtsein der Gültigkeit wider-
sprechen, und die Autonomie Symbole rationalisiert, begründend oder be-
kämpfend, deren Sinn es lediglich ist, Ausdruck des Gehaltes zu sein. Wo
das geschieht, wird die Theonomie heteronom: Sie schafft eine Sonder-
funktion neben den übrigen, die Religion, die vermöge der ihr innewohnen-
den Unbedingtheit die übrigen vergewaltigt und unterdrückt, und die
Autonomie wird profan: Sie schafft die Kultur als Inbegriff außerreligiöser
Sinnerfüllung. Es entstehen die großen, unlösbaren *Konflikte zwischen
Religion und Kultur*, zwischen kirchlicher und profaner Metaphysik, Ethik
usw. Aber dieser Zustand ist innerlich unwahr; er macht aus der notwen-
digen Spannung der Sinnelemente zwei selbständige Sinnfunktionen und
führt zur Zerstörung beider. Die Religion gibt bedingten, dem autonomen
Prozeß unterworfenen Ausdrucksformen unbedingte Geltung, und die
Kultur holt die Symbole des Unbedingten in die Sphäre der Rationalität
herab und nimmt ihnen Sinn und Wesen. (*Das System der Wissenschaften*,
GW, I: 272—273).
[44] 'Religion and Secular Culture', *PE*: 58.

Gothic and early Renaissance art, conveniently bracketed together and dated between A.D. 1300—1450, is, by its use of three-dimensional space and emphasis upon the individual, representative of the autonomous period of the late Middle Ages; Impressionism, described as the style of the late 19th century bourgeoisie, belongs to a period of thoroughgoing autonomy, in which nature is subordinated to an artistic 'technology'; and Expressionism, by its revelation of the 'new mysticism', recalls its early Gothic predecessor and belongs to the dawn of a new theonomous age. Expressionism is thus coincident with a period and culture 'striving toward theonomy, toward a culture which presents the depth and seriousness of ultimate meaning, of spiritual substance, in all its utterances'.[45]

By linking these two histories together we can see more clearly what Tillich means when he says that concepts like autonomy and theonomy, as cultural types indicative of certain cultural attitudes, may provide us with the key to our interpretation of a variety of styles previously thought unconnected. For example, once we take Impressionism as the representative of a disintegrating bourgeois autonomy, this helps us to explain the otherwise 'puzzling experience' of Expressionism. Expressionism, we may now say, is not the wanton destruction of the earlier naturalism in art and literature but the visionary repudiation by artistic means of bourgeois idealism, the 'rebellion of the vital and unconscious side of man's personality against the moral and intellectual tyranny of consciousness'.[46] In other words, what might otherwise be taken as the fanatical and iconoclastic tendencies of the Expressionists are here considered the symptoms of a theonomous revolt, as indications of the prophetic and passionate opposition by a group of artists to a culture so secularized that it has lost its ultimate reference.

The most interesting feature of this method for deciphering styles is that it may be used also in the interpretation of specific artists. In his contribution to the symposium *The Christian Answer* (1945), Tillich

---

[45] 'Christian Criteria for Our Culture', p. 3. The historical dating is given in Tillich's *A History of Christian Thought* (New York & Evanston: Harper & Row, 1968) p. 135.
[46] *Ibid.*, p. 58.

examines the disintegrative influence of bourgeois society on the modern concept of personality, and cites, by way of example, the work of Giotto, Titian and Rembrandt. Together these three painters indicate the gradual supersession of theonomy by autonomy, the loss of the personality determined by his relation to transcendent reality, and the emergence of the naturalistic personality formed by the developing mechanisms of trade and technical rationality. Thus with Giotto, and particularly noticeable in his portraits of St. Francis, we find clear expression of the theonomous ideal dominating the high Middle Ages: 'Giotto's Francis is the expression of a divine power by which man is possessed and elevated beyond his individual character and personal experiences'. Here 'every individual participates in a communal movement created by loyalty to a transcendent reality. It is an all-embracing community in which every individual, both peasant and prince, is borne forward by the same spiritual reality'. With Titian, however, we enter a different world: the world of the autonomous Renaissance in its final flowering, of the outstanding but isolated individual as the representative of general humanity. In Titian's art we encounter 'individual expressions of humanity as such, representatives of the greatness, beauty, and power of man. The transcendent reality to which Giotto subjects all individuals, their actions and emotions, has disappeared'. Nevertheless, Tillich continues, it is only with Rembrandt that we witness the emergence of the truly 'unique individual', that is, the 'personality of the early bourgeois spirit'. To study Rembandt's portraits is to be confronted by characters 'who are like self-enclosed worlds—strong, lonely, tragic but unbroken, carrying the marks of their unique histories in every line of their faces, expressing the ideals of personality of a humanistic Protestantism'. This personality stands by itself, 'independent alike of transcendent grace and of humanity'. Thereafter, however, with the replacement of humanistic reason by technical intelligence, things go from bad to worse, and personality becomes at once 'the ruler and the servant of Leviathan'. Thus the greatness of Rembrandt's canvases gives way to the art of the triumphant bourgeoisie, and the Impressionists complete the 'dominant trend toward a mechanized world'. In this sphere of *l'art pour l'art* 'aesthetics becomes an end in itself and man's alienation from himself is forgotten through pure aesthetic enjoyment'. By this route, we arrive at that stage in the development of our civilization—the late 19th century—which is utterly autonomous and secular, but which provides at the same time the frame for the revolutionary opposition of Expressionism against the mechanization of man.[47]

Some years later, in 1956, Tillich provided an interesting footnote to this article of 1945. From Rembrandt to the Expressionists, there is, he says, 'no important religious art'. This is the 'Great Gap' in the history of religious style, lasting from the middle of the 17th century to about the year 1900.[48] From this sweeping generalization, the following may be deduced: that religious style is coincident with the theonomous attitude represented by the Gothic and Expressionist artists; and that its decline is concurrent with the fully developed autonomous culture represented by the Impressionists. Seen from this vantage-points, the oscillation between the more and the less religious styles is synonymous with that between the theonomous and autonomous movements of reason. Nor should we be surprised by this. For if, as we have seen, 'theonomy' designates an attitude of the mind orientated towards the religious element of 'import', then the religious attitude, whether expressed artistically or not, will be theonomous *a priori*. Any other attitude—whether it be autonomous or, as we shall discover presently, heteronomous—which tends to detract from the theonomous attitude will thus produce a correspondingly low level of religious art. Summarizing, then, we may say that, in the dialectical relationship that exists between autonomy, heteronomy and theonomy, religious style is determined by its approximation to the theonomous ideal, that is, to the synthetic state in which artistic forms are expressive of import; and that the forces disposed to operate against such an approximation are designated by the terms 'autonomy' and 'heteronomy'.[49]

---

[47] *The Christian Answer*, ed. Henry P. Van Dusen (New York: Scribner, 1945). Reprinted in Tillich, *The World Situation* (Philadelphia: Fortress Press, 1965) pp. 11, 14 & 33.

[48] 'Theology, Architecture, and Art', p. 55.

[49] In 'Religiöser Stil und Religiöser Stoff in der bildenden Kunst', Tillich provides the following analogy for the relation of import and form in religious style:—

Wenn wir uns den Gehalt als die Sonne, die Form als die Planetenbahn vorstellen, so gibt es für jede Kulturform eine Sonnennähe und eine Sonnenferne gegenüber dem Gehalt. Ist es die Macht der Sonne, die sich in der Sonnennähe offenbart, so ist es die Eigenkraft der Planetenbewegung, die in der Sonnenferne zum Ausdruck kommt; und doch ist es die Sonne, die beides, die Nähe und die Ferne, trägt. So gibt es Stile, in denen die Herr-

For Tillich, however, autonomy, heteronomy and theonomy are more than convenient tags for artistic or cultural classification. For just as these three elements of reason decide for the variegation of human rationality within culture, by which the autonomous, heteronomous and theonomous forms of culture are created, so they also govern the dialectical movement of reason and its creations within the aesthetic act. More precisely, *the variety of artistic forms is decided by the dialectical activity of autonomous, heteronomous and theonomous reason under the law of theoria.* If aesthetic creativity begins with the receptive act of looking at reality in order to attribute meaning to reality, then these three elements of reason circumscribe the possible ways in which meaning may be so attributed and reality so perceived. Thus, as the creations of such activity, it is appropriate to speak of autonomous art, heteronomous art, and theonomous art in the determination of artistic styles.

1) *Autonomous art.* Art, says Tillich, stands directly under the sovereignty of autonomy.[50] The artist, in the act of creating something new, cannot be constrained to adopt any style or interpretation of reality which does not emerge from his own receptive encounter with reality. This is the first characteristic of autonomous art, and from it Tillich derives a criterion of judgment appropriate to every artistic style: *the principle of honesty.* Honest art is 'authentic' art, namely, the product of the creative and autonomous act of the individual artist in relation to his world and tradition and excluding beautification or imitation. The principle of honesty does not claim that authentic art is necessarily great or profound, but it does affirm that such art 'must be freshly and honestly conceived and executed'.[51] The crude art of children and untrained adults often has this quality, even though their insights may be inadequate. By the same token, however, honest and authentic art differs radically from all prescriptive or academic art, no matter how excellent its craftsmanship or noble its purpose. 'For such prescriptive

---

schaft des Gehaltes über die Form ebenso scharf hervorsticht wie die anderen die Eigenbewegung der Form; und doch ist beides, der gehaltsbeherrschte und der formenbeherrschte Stil, als Stil ein Ausdruck des Gehaltes. Diese eigentümliche Dialektik ermöglicht es nun, von einem religiösen Stil im engeren Sinne zu reden (*Ibid.*, p. 319).

[50] *Das System der Wissenschaften, GW,* I: 279.
[51] 'Authentic Religious Art', *Art Institute of Chicago* (Chicago, 1954) p. 8.

art is produced according to some formula and lacks the *sine qua non* of authentic art, that is, fresh imaginative creativity'.[52] Dishonest or 'unauthentic' art is therefore either a beautified and unrealistic image of reality or simply imitative—imitative of some older style (e.g. the Gothic), or of some renowned artist or established school, or even of the artist's own past performance. Conversely, authentic art, irrespective of its style or historical context, is always an affirmation of creative imagination and artistic integrity, and a denial of any retreat into an empty formalism, traditional conventionalism, or 'dishonest saccharine prettiness'.[53]

If this first characteristic of autonomous art allows us to judge between authentic and unauthentic styles, its second occasions its own condemnation as 'empty and without power of life and creativity'.[54] Autonomous art is directed to the conditioned and artistic forms of meaning and their fulfilment and *not* to their unconditioned meaning: it stops short at the representation of finite reality and its relationships, and asserts that man, as the bearer of universal reason, is the source and measure of culture and religion—that indeed he is his own law to which every representation of reality must be subordinated. Autonomous art, in a word, is *secular art: it denies that aesthetic apprehension depends upon a fundamental metaphysical attitude towards reality, that the artistic form is the bearer of unconditional import.* When the autonomous artist receives and describes nature according to the aesthetic function of *theoria*, he replaces 'mystical' nature by rational nature, eliminates the transcendental references so favoured by the Gothic stylists, and studies

---

[52] *Ibid.*
[53] *Ibid.*, p. 9. In his 'Aspects of a Religious Analysis of Culture', Tillich writes:—
   One principle which must be emphasized again and again in religious art is the principle of artistic honesty. There is no sacred artistic style in Protestant, in contrast, for example, to Greek-Orthodox doctrine. An artistic style is honest only if it expresses the real situation of the artist and the cultural period to which he belongs. We can participate in the artistic styles of the past in so far as they were honestly expressing the encounter which they had with God, man, and world. But we cannot honestly imitate them and produce for the cult of the Church works which are not the result of a creating ecstasy, but which are learned reproductions of creative ecstasies of the past (*TC:* 48).
[54] 'The Philosophy of Religion', *WR:* 77.

it in its objective form alone, subject to exact scientific discipline and technical control—considers it in fact as a naturalist or impressionist. Are we to say, then, that autonomous art is *unbelief-ful art?* Strictly speaking, of course, every creative act is, following the theory of meaning, 'belief-ful' in so far as it presupposes the unconditional meaning; but the attitude of autonomous art, and of every typically autonomous culture, remains nevertheless unbelief-ful: its *intention* is to determine the meaning of things within the system of finite meanings, to concern itself with objects in their immediacy and conditioned form, and not to penetrate through to their ultimate meaning or import. Indeed, so preoccupied is autonomy with the world that even when it speaks of God it talks of him as 'a synthesis of immanental forms'.[55] With this deliberate exclusion by autonomy of the religious dimension, and having thus 'lost its ultimate reference, its centre of meaning, its spiritual substance', autonomy beggars itself, is unable to sustain its own system of finite meanings, and by inward necessity reaches that point at which 'it cannot create a single content of life'.[56] Under the oppressive weight of the laws of rationality and the humanistic principles of self-sufficiency, life itself disintegrates into legalism and antinomianism, and man himself is finally reduced to a machine or unit of labour. With the assumption that man and his world represent the universe of meaning, a new emptiness of meaning is produced and the experience of conscious or unconscious despair is created. 'When the Unconditional', says Tillich, 'is grasped only as the unconditional validity of logical, ethical or aesthetic form, life is destroyed'.[57]

Here, therefore, is the inherent 'tragedy' of the autonomous artist exposed. Although motivated originally by the laudable ambition to secure for himself the freedom necessary for genuine arstistic creativity, he has been led to rely more and more upon himself and his own valuation of his world, and to experience in that correlation first the fulfilment of meaning and then the despair of it. Autonomous art, accordingly, although often impressive in itself, has developed dangerous

---

[55] *Ibid.*
[56] 'Christian Criteria for Our Culture', *PE:* 58; and 'The Conquest of the Concept of Religion in the Philosophy of Religion', *WR:* 152.
[57] 'The Conquest of the Concept of Religion in the Philosophy of Religion', *WR:* 152.

consequences, not by accident but by its very nature as part of the eviscerating process towards a 'metaphysics of a finitude which postulates its own absoluteness'.[58] Under the forces of secularization and naturalistic reduction, it eliminates the ultimate meaning and spiritual centre from its representations of reality, and thereby contributes to its own fate of dissolution in the mediocre and stultifying artistic conventions of the bourgeois and technological society.

2) *Heteronomous art.* Heteronomous art is the product of the authoritarian determination of artistic style by the secular or religious powers. Whenever an artist is compelled to adopt a particular artistic form as the expression of his encounter with reality, and thus wherever creative freedom is subverted, the artistic result is heteronomous. Although secular examples abound—the use of art for propaganda purposes is one—Tillich concentrates almost exclusively on the religious domain. *Heteronomous art is the suppression of autonomous art in the name of religion.* Nor is Tillich entirely dismissive of this style, for, criticisms apart, it remains a *type* of genuine religious art.

There are two reasons for this. In the first place, heteronomous art springs from the counter-attitude to the *hubris* of autonomous art: it is aware that an autonomous culture and art cuts the ties of a civilization with its ultimate ground and aim, and that, in the measure to which autonomy succeeds, a civilization will become self-complacent and spiritually empty; to this extent, it is an attempt to reorientate autonomous artistic forms towards the expression of unconditional meaning or import. And, in the second place, heteronomous art employs, albeit distortedly, a further principle for the determination of religious style. This is the *principle of consecration.*

The principle of consecration is concerned with the use of cultural forms in the aesthetic life of the churches, and states that the churches are *justified* in their request 'that the religious art they accept express what they confess'.[59] Consecrated religious art is therefore a confession of faith expressed in aesthetic terms, or rather the representation by each church of the meaning of its life in artistic forms. This explains why the Eastern, Roman and Protestant churches often express the same symbols (e.g., the Christ picture or the passion story) in different

---

[58] *RS:* 87.
[59] *ST,* 3: 211. Cf. *ST,* 3: 267—268.

ways: the difference in the treatment of the symbols reflects a difference in the particular historical and theological traditions. So we may distinguish between Grünewald's 'Crucifixion' and the radically different image of the Christ found in Eastern mosaics: the one expresses the experience of the pre-Reformation groups to which Grünewald belonged, the other an aspect of Orthodox christology, in which as an infant in Mary's lap Jesus is already the ruler of the universe. Accordingly, 'it is understandable that such a picture as that of Grünewald would be censured by the authorities of the Eastern church, the church of the resurrection and not of the crucifixion'.[60] Taken together, however, all these multifarious artistic presentations of Christian belief constitute the 'constructing' function of the churches in the aesthetic sphere of cultural creation. Here the whole range of artistic expression—the poetic, the musical, the visual—is mobilized for the aesthetic representation of the confessions of faith. Since this is a conscious activity on the part of the churches, it is to be sharply distinguished from the intentionally non-religious and autonomous concerns of the secular arts.

In two senses, therefore, may we consider heteronomous art as a legitimate form of religious art: first, because it protests against the self-sufficiency and secular humanism of autonomy; and second, because it affirms its own unconditional reference in the manner of its confessional-artistic form. Herein lies the ecclesiastical recognition that the aesthetic realm is more than a beautifying addition to devotional life, and that art may function as an expression of faith and thus as a powerful means of influence, stabilization and transformation.[61]

The importance attached to art by the churches also explains their frequent and successful attempts to place those who produce religious art under ecclesiastical control. Nowhere is this better exhibited than in the *misuse* of the principle of consecration. For what was originally designed as a means of distinguishing between the consecrated and autonomous artistic forms is now used for the suppression of autonomous cultural creativity altogether. By ecclesiastical dictate, and as a symptom of the churches' own self-accredited inviolability, the consecrated artistic forms are elevated to unconditionedness and exempted from autonomous criticism and re-evaluation. More exactly, then, heteronomous religious

---

[60] *Ibid.*
[61] *Ibid.*

art is the result of the subordination of the principle of honesty to the authoritarian determination of artistic style, by which the consecrated forms of artistic expression may claim absolute validity and may thus be defended against every new stylistic development in the name of the creed they confess. Much primitive art has this character—the statues of gods, fetishes, dance masks, and so on[62]—but the same phenomenon is apparent in Roman church music, Protestant hymnic poetry, and, most glaring of all, in Greek Orthodox iconography: 'the icons, the sacred pictures, are not simply pictures but have in themselves, by their very nature, sacramental character. Therefore the church is justified in telling the artist definite rules according to which a sacred picture must be made'.[63] What results, however, is idolatry and almost total artistic stagnation. For contrary to the whole *ethos* of the theology of culture, a specific religious sphere has now been created—be it ordained by a book, a person, an institution or doctrine—whose authority is such that the artist need be concerned only with the imitation of the traditional symbols, without regard to their possible irrelevance to the contemporary situation. So Tillich comments that, in the history of religious art, the principle of consecration predominates almost exclusively in the periods of artistic unfruitfulness.[64]

Heteronomous religious art reflects, therefore, a demonically distorted union of religious and culture, in which the truth that the unconditional import grounds aesthetic meaning and significance has been transformed and perverted into the idolatrous untruth that the unconditional import is all this in an objective sense: that God, in other words, is a world alongside the world, delineable in terms of certain prescribed representations of reality. 'Faith is no longer directedness toward the Unconditional through conditioned forms, rather it is directedness toward conditioned forms viewed as unconditional'.[65] Heteronomous religious art fails to respect legitimately autonomous forms and is more a subordination of culture to religion than an organic union of the two, for it is 'the attempt of a religion to dominate autonomous cultural creativity from the outside . . .'[66] What began as the

[62] 'Das Dämonische', *GW*, VI: 42—71. E.T., *IH: 77—122*.
[63] 'Theology, Architecture, and Art', p. 7.
[64] 'Zur Theologie der bildenden Kunst und der Architektur', *GW*, IX: 353.
[65] 'The Philosophy of Religion', *WR:* 78.
[66] 'Author's Introduction', *PE:* xii.

counter-attitude to the *hubris* of autonomy has finished as the *hubris* of religion.

Pausing here for a moment, it is not difficult to see how this opposition between autonomous and heteronomous art induces the schizophrenic attitude which is symptomatic of the opposition of religion and culture generally. The principle of honesty, it would seem, militates against the principle of consecration, and *vice versa,* just as the victory of heteronomy is the defeat of autonomy, and *vice versa.* Must artistic freedom be limited therefore in order to be built into the life of the churches? And if this is rejected, how can the artist be prevented from replacing the religious dimension by self-creative acts of his own? This predicament, ever recurring, drives artists and church members alike into deep moral conflict and brings about a division of the consciousness between two kinds of truth, each of which lays illegitimate claim to absolute validity. For the failure of autonomy is that, in destroying the heteronomous idolatry, it loses contact with the divine import of meaning and becomes formalistic and shallow, without power of life and creativity; and the failure of heteronomy is that, without the autonomous attitude and by attributing ultimate significance to the confessional-artistic forms, it becomes artistically and spiritually impossible: it likewise loses its power of creativity and becomes a demonic means of power and suppression, until it too breaks down.[67] Both, therefore, are unable to solve the fundamental theological problem of 'the relation of the absolute, which is assumed in the idea of God, and of the relative, which belongs to human religion'.[68] Without a permanent solution, however, the unity of the life of the mind will be totally disrupted, and, says Tillich, theology itself will degenerate into a secular-rational discipline.[69]

3) *Theonomous art.* In the artistic dimension, theonomous art provides this solution. For theonomous art is the aesthetic expression of the theology of culture; or, to use Tillich's earlier terminology, it is the artistic realization of the metaphysics of 'belief-ful realism' and 'immanent mysticism', in which a synthesis is attained between an autonomous interpretation of reality and a religious transcending of reality.

---

[67] 'The Philosophy of Religion', *WR:* 78. Cf. *Das System der Wissenschaften, GW,* I: 272.
[68] *IH:* 25.
[69] *Das System der Wissenschaften, GW,* I: 150—151.

This definition, although correct, is nevertheless misleading. As we have seen before, every expression of the synthesis is an expression of an ideal and not a reality; and so it is with the concept of theonomous art. If this concept resolves the division between autonomous and heteronomous art, it does so in principle but not in fact, while the division itself remains as testimony to the Fall of the world. Tillich's account of theonomous art is therefore a hypothetical account of art in the fulfilled synthesis. 'Perfected theonomy', as he remarks, 'is the perfected Kingdom of God, that is, it is a symbol and not a reality'; and it is this insight, he continues, into what ought to be but is not which 'brings a quality of waiting, of "not yet" ... into all our cultural creativity'.[70] That apart, however, the ideal may still function as the yard-stick in distinguishing between the more and the less religious styles. For if in reality—namely, in the imperfect and estranged state of existence—we are dealing no longer with the perfected synthesis in which no division between autonomous and heteronomous styles can be drawn, we are nevertheless concerned with the nearest artistic approximations to that idealized state, with those artistic styles which, consciously or not and with greater or lesser degrees of success, reveal their ultimate import and their theonomous character in the manner by which they represent phenomena in artistic forms.

How this state may be achieved, or even approached, may be described in terms of the coordination of the two principles governing autonomous and heteronomous art, namely, the principles of honesty and consecration. As regards the first principle, theonomous art denies that the exercise of autonomous freedom is a refutation of the religious attitude since this would negate its own powers of creativity. Theonomous art, on the contrary, recognizes the unconditional validity of the law of autonomous reason, accepts that 'theonomy is itself destroyed where this law is rejected in the name of the holy', and thereby subjects itself to that principle of creative honesty which controls the whole realm of individual and social aesthetic creativity. Thus the first characteristic of theonomous art is that it acknowledges autonomy as an attribute of the creative process. There is, says Tillich, no theonomous art 'where a new style of artistic creation is suppressed in the name of

---

[70] 'The Philosophy of Religion', *WR:* 81; and 'Religion and Secular Culture', *PE:* 60.

assumedly eternal forms of expressiveness ... Religion cannot force any style upon the autonomous development of the arts'.[71]

From this last remark, it is clear that the concept of theonomous art is at the same time a criticism of the heteronomous-ecclesiastical control of art by means of the principle of consecration. According to this principle, to repeat, secular art exhibits an autonomous orientation, and religious art a consecrated orientation: in the former, the consciousness is directed towards the conditioned-artistic forms of meaning, and, in the latter, towards the unconditioned import of meaning expressed in consecrated-artistic forms. This sharp juxtaposition, however, is inappropriate and, under the terms of theonomy, contrary to the nature of authentic religious art. For while it is true that the artistic consciousness cannot direct itself towards the unconditioned import except through the medium of artistic forms and through the creative function of *theoria,* theonomous art does not have in mind thereby *specific* artistic forms consecrated as expressions of the ultimate, but rather the *totality* of every actual and possible artistic form subject to the autonomous and creative act. Theonomous art, in other words, *consecrates every conditioned artistic form to which the principle of honesty applies as the possible vehicle for the revelation of unconditioned import.* This leads to a second characteristic of theonomous art, already familiar to us from previous chapters: that the theonomous works of cultural artistic creation may express the ultimacy of meaning even in the most limited or 'neutral' vehicles of meaning—a chair or flower, for example—even though perhaps not consecrated by a church.[72]

Strictly speaking, therefore, theonomous art, unlike its autonomous and heteronomous counterparts, cannot carry the subtitles of either 'secular' or 'religious' since it signifies the *disappearance* of artistic creativity as an aspect of life apart from the religious dimension; since, indeed, it denotes that artistic mode of expression in which the unconditionality of existence is apparent in *every* representation of reality, even those apparently antipathetic to religion. Thus portrayals of fear, anxiety or even the loss of God may be included in explicit or implicit artistic expressions of the religious attitude, that is, as descriptions of actual existential states through which the ultimate import may be

---

[71] *ST,* 3: 267 & 214.
[72] *Ibid.,* p. 266.

revealed. In this respect, the metaphysic of theonomy duplicates the metaphysic of expressiveness, namely, that the unconditioned meaning is perceptible through the finite and estranged forms of conditioned meaning; and here too the division between religion and secular culture is overcome since theonomy, by its extension of the principle of consecration, renders any 'theological aesthetic' impossible.[73] Theology, it is true, can show what artistic attitudes most nearly correspond to the metaphysical attitude of theonomy; but it cannot itself create the material, separate and identifiable as religious subject matter, necessary for that attitude to be theonomous. Once again it is the perception of ultimacy that consecrates the material, and not the material the perception. Such considerations and identities as these allow Tillich not only to re-establish the use of estrangement in religious styles, but also to re-identify the category of expressiveness as the theonomous category, and thus as the governing principle of such styles.

> From the point of view of theonomy, one can say that the expressionistic element is most able to express the self-transcendence of life in the vertical line. It breaks away from the horizontal movement and shows the Spiritual Presence in symbols of broken finitude. This is the reason why most of the great religious art in all periods has been determined by the expressionist element in its stylistic expression. When the naturalistic and idealistic elements are predominant, the finite is either accepted in its finitude (though not copied) or is seen in its essential potentialities but not in its disruption and salvation. Naturalism, when predominant, produces acceptance, idealism, anticipation, and expressionism the breakthrough into the vertical. *Thus expressionism is the genuinely theonomous element.*[74]

From these consequences of coordinating the principles of honesty and consecration, we are brought to the third and final characteristic of theonomous art: that it both precedes, follows and contains the contrasting elements of autonomy and heteronomy against which it struggles.[75] This is the most comprehensive definition so far presented by Tillich of the cultural-religious synthesis denoted by theonomous art; and behind it stands the familiar and dialectical scheme by which Tillich describes the 'trinitarian' movement of life and history, namely, of essential being, existential being, and the quest for salvation. With this

---

[73] *Das System der Wissenschaften, GW,* I: 280.
[74] *ST,* 3: 274 (my emphasis).

in mind, we may interpret theonomous art in the following way: first, as art in the state of essential being and thus *prior* to the condition of estrangement as exemplified in the division between autonomous and heteronomous art; and second, as art in the state of reunion and thus *posterior* to that division. Theonomous art, accordingly, *is both the original union and final reconciliation of autonomous and heteronomous art: it is both the presupposition of their separation and that to which their estrangement points.* Thereby theonomous art indicates that moment at which both the autonomous evaluation of culture and the heteronomous evaluation of religion share in their directedness towards the Unconditional—that indeed both evaluations are theonomous in principle if not in fact—and so transcends the otherwise divisive tendencies of autonomy and heteronomy.

This last account of theonomous art helps us to explain Tillich's otherwise confusing attempt to distinguish the *aim* of the aesthetic function. While all would agree, he says, that Truth is the ultimate aim of the cognitive function—'the desire to bridge the gap between subject and object'[76]—it is hard to determine the aim of the aesthetic function. The most common term used to describe it is 'beauty', largely because of its associations with the Greek combination of the beautiful and the good. This word, however, is now redundant 'because of its connections with the decadent phase of the classical style—beautifying naturalism'. Tillich's own choice of term is, significantly enough, 'expressive power' or 'expressiveness' (*Ausdrucksmächtigkeit*). *Thus the aim of the aesthetic function is to express.*[77] But to express what? Tillich replies that the aim of the aesthetic function, whether in poetry, the visual arts or in music, is to open up or reveal an otherwise hidden level or 'quality of a piece of the universe (and implicitly of the universe itself)'.[78] *This is is the dimension of the depth of reality.* 'Das expressive Element ... bringt etwas Verborgenes im Begegnenden ans Licht, es bringt eine Tiefe in den Dingen an die Oberfläche'.[79] Tillich concludes by saying that only those styles which, in their representation of objects, express this depth-dimension can be considered religious styles: 'Sie allein können den *Ge-*

---

[75] *Ibid.*, p. 267.
[76] *Ibid.*, p. 68.
[77] *Ibid.*
[78] *Ibid.*
[79] 'Zur Theologie der bildenden Kunst und der Architektur', *GW*, IX: 348.

halt eines spezifisch religiösen Symbols in religiös angemessener Weise ausdrücken'.[80] Thus it emerges that the artistic expression of reality's depth is a theonomous activity; and that the aim of the aesthetic and receiving function of man's spirit is, in artistic creativity, to produce a theonomous-expressive style. Only this style is 'transparent' to ultimate meaning, thereby transforming the media of expression into 'vessels of a spiritual content'.[81]

When Tillich talks therefore of the expressive aim, he is not, as might be suspected, contradicting himself by supposing that every artist intends to be religious: he is speaking rather of the *teleological nature* of the aesthetic function, realized under the conditions of synthesis and pointed to by both the essential and existential natures of artistic creativity. This is the ideal and fulfilled state of theonomous art, in which a final reconciliation is achieved over against the divisive forces of autonomy and heteronomy. Here exposed is the *soteriological focus of artistic expressiveness*, according to which the aesthetic aim may be translated in terms of the theonomous quest for salvation.

This, of course, is no new idea. We met it before in Tillich's theory of meaning, where the unconditionality and fulfilment of meaning is presupposed in every meaningful act, and then again in his correlative use of estrangement, where the possibility of salvation is latent within the ontological state of man and his world. In each case, both the artist's attribution of meaning to, and his description of, estranged reality pointed beyond themselves and looked to the re-establishment of an original but disrupted perfection. In the present instance, however, the claim that theonomous art is the goal of all artistic activity does not depend on the nature of the meaning being ascribed by the artist, or on the ontological status of the object being so treated, but on the relationship existing between the interpreting subject and his object in the aesthetic act.

To make this point clearer, we should recall that the law governing the relation of the artist to his object is the law of *theoria*, according to which the mind, in the exercise of its freedom to create, first 'receives' reality and then 'transcends' it by constructing images from it that are not identical with reality. Thus the freedom of 'receiving rationality'

---

[80] *Ibid.*, p. 349.
[81] 'Author's Introduction', *PE:* xii.

is essential for all aesthetic creation and thereby contributes to the self-creation of life under the dimension of the spirit. Inasmuch, however, as it is *reason in the artist* which is attentive to the meaning of things, and which enables him to participate in the creation of the universe of meanings, reason itself is subject to the conditions of finite reality, is beset by the self-destructive conflicts natural to its existential state, and looks to their reconciliation in salvation. These conflicts, indicative of the finitude of reason, are designated by the struggle between autonomous and heteronomous reason, and the hope of salvation by the quest for theonomy. Just, therefore, as theonomous reason arises *out* of the conflicts of reason and not in opposition to them, so too theonomous art emerges from the struggle between autonomous and heteronomous art, between the exercise of artistic freedom and its suppression. Theonomous art may thus be considered the fulfilment of art because it is the re-establishment of art in its essential being, and because it alone embraces the truth of autonomous and heteronomous art while avoiding their errors: it rejects both a divine law imposed by outside authority and a self-sufficient creativity divorced from its depth.

It is Tillich's fundamental contention, therefore, that artistic creativity no more escapes the universal transition or 'fall' of man from an essential to existential state than does any other aspect of his life; and that art, too, requires salvation, here symbolized in the concept of theonomous art. Theonomous art, we should say, *is the expression of the unconditional power of reconciliation manifest in the process by which the artist receives and shapes his material.* The law of *theoria* remains as the principle of all artistic activity: this activity is therefore theonomous; but the meaning of this law does not lie within itself since it is also the vehicle for the apprehension of that which breaks through every law and artistic form: this activity is also *theo*nomous. Tillich's thesis that theonomous art is the goal of artistic creativity is, in other words, inherent within the very nature of the relationship that the artist, to be an artist, must have to reality, namely, in the movement of the artistic mind towards its object as defined by the operation of autonomous, heteronomous and theonomous reason. Put otherwise, we may say that theonomous art is the expression of the paradoxical immanence of the transcendent as revealed in the way the artist perceives his object; that it is the concept of the salvation of artistic creativity entailed within the nature of the creative act. To be sure, theonomous art remains an idealization of art because of the existential estrangement underlying all aesthetic creation, which explains why it is an ideal only fragmentarily realized by the artist; but the existential defeat of theonomous art is always limited by the fact that, in the act by which the mind creates something new, all artistic creation is essentially theonomous or substantially religious in the degree to which it too looks to the reunion of the estranged.

As a last remark, it is worth repeating that, from the viewpoint just described, it is not the case that some artistic styles and not others are expressive-religious styles. Art, both in presupposition, structure and direction, is 'immer gehaltlich', which means that all artistic acts and their creations are expressive of a certain attitude to reality which is the religious attitude, and this irrespective of the subject matter chosen by the artist and no matter how strong or weak his artistic form. The artist cannot escape religion even if he rejects religion, since religion involves the apprehension of ultimate import through conditioned form. While it is true, therefore, that a style is created by the autonomous act of the individual artist in combination with other historical factors,[82] nevertheless this religious perception into the nature of reality is necessary to the concept fo style itself. More exactly, every style contains an implicit metaphysic; and to that extent the sphere of religion, in so far as it is expressed in cultural styles, embraces the whole of autonomous cultural creation.

This conclusion has two consequences. The first is that a morphology of cultural and artistic styles worked out from the religious point of view becomes a necessary task; the second, that every artistic style of every historical epoch may be regarded as a document testifying to the religious life of that period. It is, says Tillich, the duty of the analytic historian to decipher these documents and as far as possible to relive the meanings embodied in them. When that happens a whole past culture comes alive again, since in many instances these documents are the only evidence we have of its existence. And yet, even if that were not the case, analysis of artistic styles remains the most direct and expressive means of discovering the past beliefs of an artist, school or civilization. That is why it is impossible to write a History of Religion without first investigating the sources provided by the visual arts, and *Sinnes der Kunstwerke).*[84]

---

[82] See above, p. 20.

without first attempting to discover the various ways in which people from different historical periods regarded themselves and their position in the universe. This means, Tillich concludes, that without a Theology of Culture there can be no proper appreciation of the History of Culture; and that without a Theology of Art, no understanding of the final meaning of individual works of art *(kein Verstehen des letzten Sinnes der Kunstwerke)*.[83]

---

[83] 'Zur Theologie der bildenden Kunst und der Architektur', *GW*, IX: 347.

CHAPTER FOUR

REVELATION, SYMBOLS, AND THE
CERTAINTY OF FAITH

The final section of Tillich's philosophy of art begins with two questions: What type of knowledge is given to us in religious art? And what artistic form or 'language' is appropriate for the communication of this knowledge? I use the word 'type' in the first question because Tillich maintains that we are here dealing with a special knowledge and a special language, distinguishable from the ordinary processes of cognition and discourse. What follows, therefore, may be taken as an account of the epistemological distinctiveness of religious art. This distinctiveness Tillich describes in his concepts of revelation and religious symbolism.

To begin with, however, a few preliminary remarks are required. Both our opening questions may be introduced by the perennial problem of whether an artistic style, or indeed the arts in general, is concerned with the subjectivity of the creating artist or with the objectivity of the reality encountered by him. For Tillich, this problem is rooted in the split between subject and object, which is the precondition of all knowledge and which 'presupposes the self-world structure as the basic articulation of being'.[1] Following the Platonic tradition, Tillich contends that 'knowledge' is a 'form of union', in which knower and known, subject and object, are united in the cognitive act: 'The subject "grasps" the object, adapts it to itself, and, at the same time, adapts itself to the object'.[2] But this union is peculiar in that it is a union mediated through

---

[1] *ST*, 1: 183.
[2] *Ibid.*, p. 105.

detachment and separation. Cognitive distance is, in other words, the presupposition of cognitive union: 'In order to know, one must "look" at a thing, and, in order to look at a thing, one must be "at a distance"'.[3] The demand to make this cognitive relation intelligible—the strangeness of subject and object, and, in spite of it, their cognitive union—poses the basic problem of knowledge. In that form of knowledge called 'understanding', these elements are balanced and their unity preserved; but their separation, and the tendency to concentrate on satisfying the demands of one element to the relative neglect of the other, appear in all theories of knowledge, and help explain the diversity of traditions in the history of philosophy.[4]

In similar fashion, the history of artistic style can be interpreted in terms of the separation of, and preference for, subject and object. Tillich rejects therefore the claim of the Kantian school (classical as well as Neo-Kantian) that in artistic intuition and its images a reunion of subject and object, which otherwise could not be reached, is possible—a claim which, he says, explains why 'sophisticated cultures tend to replace the religious by the aesthetic function'.[5] But the artistic image is no less 'ambiguous' in this regard than the cognitive concept: 'the subject tries to bridge the gap by receiving the object in words, concepts, and images, but never achieves this aim. There is reception, grasp, and expression, but the gap remains and the subject remains within itself'.[6] In the aesthetic function of *theoria*, the gap between the knowing subject and the object to be known thus exists as the gap between the expressing subject and the object to be expressed; and here too a concentration on one or the other is indicated in the varieties of artistic style. For examples of these varieties, we need look no further than those already given by Tillich in earlier chapters. Naturalism presents a picture of objective reality in its surface appearance, and results in a questionable imitation of nature; Idealism refers to the contrary artistic impulse, in

---

[3] *Ibid.*

[4] *Ibid.*, p. 106.

[5] *ST*, 3: 69.

[6] *Ibid.*, p. 77. Tillich adds that 'the opposite happens in the self-creation of life by the functions of *praxis,* including their technical element. In them it is the object that is to be transformed according to concepts and images, and it is the object which causes the ambiguous character of cultural self-creation' *(Ibid.).*

which the artist imputes qualities to the object which have no foundation in fact, thereby replacing encountered reality by beautified or sentimentalized images of it; Impressionism, preoccupied with the momentary impressions of external nature, subordinates the object to the technical expertise of the subject, and disregards the content and meaning of artistic creations for the sake of their form; and even Expressionism, we remember, involves a radical disruption of the naturally given appearance of objects by the subject. Other, more extreme, examples can be given: of styles in which objects are manipulated for specific purposes, such as polemics or propaganda; or of styles in which the receptive function is deliberately perverted in order to distort or contradict the reality which it is supposed to receive.[7] Irrespective therefore of these stylistic variations, it is a permanent feature of aesthetic activity that, in contributing to the creation of the universe of meanings, it should separate the meaning from the reality to which it refers. In this sense, the precondition of the split between subject and object cannot be avoided. Every act of receiving objects by the mind, whether in the cognitive or aesthetic functions of *theoria*, opens up a gap between the object received and the meaning created in its reception by the subject.[8]

What distinguishes religious art may now be stated. In religious art the aesthetic function, although of necessity determined by the division between subject and object, operates for the expression of that which overcomes and transcends that division, of that which is *the ontological prius of both subject and object*. If we ask, therefore, whether religious art expresses the subject or the object, the answer is that it expresses neither the one nor the other, rather the theonomous union of the two. Thus, in this instance, it is impossible to enumerate the varieties of religious style, based on the possible oscillations between subject and object, because here we are concerned with the manifestation of that *point of identity* without which neither the separation nor interaction of subject and object could be thought. Going further, religious art is rooted in an interpretation of reality which identifies reality neither with 'objective being', in the sense applied in imitative or naturalistic styles, nor with 'subjective being', in the sense applied in Idealism and

---

[7] Cf. *Ibid.*, p. 74.
[8] *Ibid.*, pp. 73—74.

Impressionism. Religious art brings to expression a level of reality in which the contrast between subject and object does not arise and in which the distinction between knowing and known is not actual.

It is at this point that Tillich's theories of meaning and being coincide. The ultimate meaning to which the artistic consciousness submits itself in the spiritual-aesthetic act is at the same time that level of reality to which the whole subject-object structure of being is subordinate. In other words, the 'import' of meaning is here identified as a 'realm' or 'quality' of being, which is both prior to and beyond the subject-object distinction upon which every act of meaning rests. What is expressed in religious art is therefore the artist's immediate experience of that meaning-reality which constitutes the unity of meaning and being, where that which is 'known' is the presupposition both of the meaning being attributed by the artist and of the ontological structure in which that meaning was created. This is the knowledge of revelation. We speak of 'revelation', accordingly, wherever the unconditioned import breaks through the conditioned forms of meaning, and wherever that which transcends the subject-object structure of being is manifest in that structure.[9] In short, with the concept of revelation we arrive once more at the principal assumption of the theology of culture, namely, at the theonomous and expressive apprehension of the paradoxical immanence of the transcendent, in which the creations of culture serve as the media for the revelation of that which is the ultimate of meaning and being.

I. RELIGIOUS ART AS REVELATION

One of the most important features of Tillich's analysis of religious art is that he regards *both what the artist is portraying and the portrait he creates as revelations*. This first emerges in his discussion of 'original' and 'dependent' revelations, his example being the relation of the event 'Jesus as the Christ' to its portrayal in the New Testament. An original revelation, he says, is one 'which occurs in a constellation that did not exist before'.[10] Thus Peter's confession at Caesarea Philippi was original

---

[9] 'The Philosophy of Religion', *WR:* 105.
[10] *ST,* 1: 140.

in that both sides of it—the objective side (the manifestation of the revelation, the actual appearance of New Being in the man Jesus) and the subjective side (the reception of the revelation in Peter's acceptance of Jesus as the Christ)—are 'joined for the first time. Both sides are original'.[11] However, in a dependent revelation, namely in one which is received by following generations of Christains through the medium of the biblical picture, the focus is upon 'the Jesus who *had* been received as the Christ by Peter and the other apostles'.[12] Tillich concludes from this that there is a continuity of revelation and a continuous revelation, since in the original revelation the fact and the reception of the revelation are the two correlated elements, whereas, in the dependent revelation, these formerly distinct elements conjoin to form the 'giving side, while the receiving side changes as new individuals and groups enter the same correlation of revelation'.[13]

The biblical picture, therefore, by combining the objective and subjective sides of the original revelation of Jesus as the Christ, functions as the objective side of a dependent revelation; and this, moreover, *is the status of all religious pictures, biblical or otherwise, verbal or visual.* In other words, the character of a religious picture is synonymous with the fact that it incorporates the artist's own witness to, and response towards, a revealing event, whatever that event may be. The work of art, that is, here becomes the 'giving' side of a dependent revelatory occurrence because the original revelation—the artist's own experience of revelation, be it through the medium of a natural object, historical event, group or person—is itself only present to those who subsequently receive it as a revelation *through the medium of the artist's own pictorial re-presentation of it.* In this sense, then, a religious work of art is both a document of revelation and revelatory: the artist

---

[11] *Ibid.,* This corresponds to the two-sided character of the Christ-event. See above, Ch. II, pp. 73—74.

[12] *Ibid.* (my emphasis).

[13] *Ibid.* For further discussions of the revelatory character of the biblical picture of Jesus, see Leon J. Putnam, 'Tillich, Revelation, and Miracle', *Theology and Life,* IX (Winter, 1966) pp. 363—368; and Avery R. Dulles, 'Paul Tillich and the Bible', *Paul Tillich in Catholic Thought,* ed. T. A. O'Meara and C. D. Weisser (London: Darton, Longman & Todd, 1965) pp. 109—132.

is involved in the revelation he describes, while his description may act as the medium of revelation for others.[14]

Now since, as we have seen, revelation entails a special and extra-ordinary type of knowledge, this knowledge is applicable to a religious picture in its function as the objective side of a dependent revelation. Thus both the knowledge given to the painter and the knowledge given to us through his painting contradict that of ordinary cognition, neither being bound to the epistemological subject-object distinction implied in all normal cognitive acts. Tillich reinforces this point when he examines two of the so-called 'marks' of revelation. These are 'ecstasy' and 'miracle', and they denote respectively the subjective and objective sides of revelation. Ecstasy is not over-excitement or enthusiasm: it is that state of mind 'in which reason is beyond itself, that is, beyond its subject-object structure'.[15] But ecstasy, Tillich insists, is not irrational or antirational: it rather 'transcends the basic condition of finite rationality, the subject-object structure'.[16] In this respect, the ecstatic state is similar to demonic possession, since in both 'the ordinary subject-object structure of the mind is put out of action'.[17] Demonic possession, how-ever, destroys the rational structure of the mind, whereas ecstasy affirms and elevates it, even though transcending it. The same is true of the objective side of revelation, called 'miracle'. A miracle does not desig-nate a supernatural happening which contradicts the laws of nature, but neither is it identifiable with the natural structure of events. A miracle is a 'sign-event' which 'produces astonishment': it is 'unusual' and 'shaking'.[18] Just, therefore, as ecstasy does not destroy the rational structure of the mind by which it is received, so the 'sign-event' does not destroy the rational structure of the reality in which it appears, even though it cannot be simply equated with that structure. Indeed, such is the correlation between ecstasy and miracle, it is possible to

---

[14] I say 'may act as the medium of revelation' to indicate the contingency of a revelation's reception. That a revelation is given does not entail that it is received. See *ST*, 2: 115—116.

[15] *ST*, 1: 124. According to Tillich, the etymological root of the term 'ecstasy'—"standing outside one's self"—points to the extraordinary state of mind in which the mind transcends its ordinary situation *(Ibid.).*

[16] *Ibid.*

[17] *Ibid.*, p. 127.

[18] *Ibid.*, pp. 128 & 130.

interchange these concepts. 'One can say that ecstasy is the miracle of the mind and that miracle is the ecstasy of reality'.[19]

Following these remarks, we may conclude that a religious picture is a composite of miracle and ecstasy. In the original revelation, the artist receives the miracle in an ecstatic state of mind; but in the dependent revelation, which is the religious picture, these two elements combine to form the 'sign-event' or miracle which is received in ecstasy by those for whom that picture is a revelation. *We cannot therefore receive what religious art reveals apart from the situation of revelation.* We cannot determine, for example, what is revealed either by analysis of what the painter is describing, or by analysis of the artistic form of his description, or even by analysis of how we ourselves view the picture created. For all these relations are, in their various ways, governed by the concepts of miracle and ecstasy, and so fall within that sphere of knowledge which contradicts the whole realm of scientific or practical knowledge. 'Knowledge of revelation', so Tillich concludes, 'can be received only in the situation of revelation, and it can be communicated —in contrast to ordinary knowledge—only to those who participate in this situation'.[20]

What, then, is revealed by religious art in the situation of revelation? Earlier Tillich described it as a particular *dimension of reality*, one which, as the *prius* of subject and object, cannot be determined by the schema of rationality which otherwise governs the cognitive relation of the finite mind to all aspects of its environment and world. But quite what this means is still hard to see. So far Tillich has given us no further account of this dimension, has not explained how anything, let alone something, can be the *prius* of subject and object, or indeed how knowledge of such a reality is even possible. These questions are answered when he turns to the last 'mark' of revelation, 'mystery'.

A revelation, Tillich writes, 'is a special and extraordinary manifestation which removes the veil from something which is hidden in as special and extraordinary way. This hiddenness is often called "mystery" ...'[21] The distinguishing feature of mystery is that it 'cannot

---

[19] *Ibid.*, p. 130.
[20] *Ibid.*, p. 143.
[21] *Ibid.*, p. 120.

lose its mysteriousness even when it is revealed'.[22] Initially, the reasons given for this view of mystery follow the argument employed with the concepts of miracle and ecstasy. 'Mystery characterizes a dimension which "precedes" the subject-object relationship'.[23] As such, it is incapable of description or analysis in terms of the subject-object dimension to which both the processes of practical and theoretical enquiry, and the forms of normal discourse, are bound. This does not imply that the revelation of mystery is without cognitive elements: it means rather that the revelation of the essentially mysterious entails 'the manifestation of something within the context of ordinary experience which transcends the ordinary context of experience'.[24] Even when revealed, mystery cannot, therefore, be reduced to the level of the normal cognitive approach, for (to use Marcel's distinction) while a 'problem' is in principle solvable, a 'mystery' is that which is in principle concealed.[25]

The crucial point of this discussion is reached, however, when Tillich goes on to say that the genuine mystery appears only when

> reason is driven beyond itself to its "ground and abyss", to that which "precedes" reason, to the fact that "being is and non-being is not" (Parmenides), to the original fact *(Ur-Tatsache)* that there is *something* and not *nothing.*[26]

Two points are involved here, the one negative, the other positive; and they refer respectively to the 'abyss' and 'ground' of being and reason just mentioned. The negative or abysmal side of the mystery is revealed by the '"stigma" of finitude ... which appears in all things and in the whole of reality', and by the '"shock" which grasps the mind when it

---

[22] *Ibid.*, p. 121.

[23] *Ibid.*

[24] *Ibid.* Here, too, Tillich argues that the derivation of the word 'mystery' —from *muein,* "closing the eyes" or "closing the mouth"— corroborates this understanding of the term *(Ibid.,* pp. 120—121).

[25] See Gabriel Marcel, *The Philosophy of Existence* (Chicago: Henry Regnery, 1952). For an analysis of Marcel's understanding of 'mystery', see John B. O'Malley, *The Fellowship of Being* (The Hague: Martinus Nijhoff, 1966) pp. 16—17, 24—59; and for a more general discussion of the concept, I. T. Ramsey, *Models and Mystery* (London: Oxford University Press, 1964).

[26] *ST,* 1: 122.

encounters the threat of non-being'.[27] Now according to Tillich, finitude is 'being, limited by non-being'[28]—a 'dialectical' definition which requires that the problem of finitude, posed by the basic ontological question of why there should be something and not nothing, must be approached in terms of this inescapable dialectical relation between being and non-being.[29] Non-being, that is to say, is not the absolute negation of being, but the negation of being *within* being, appearing as the 'not yet' and the 'no more' of being. 'It confronts that which is with a definite end *(finis)*'.[30] With this in mind, Tillich can proceed next to a metaphorical description of being. Being, he says,

> is the *power* of being! Power, however, presupposes even in the metaphorical use of the word, something over which it proves its power . . . What can that be which tries to negate being and is negated by it? There is only one answer possible: That which is conquered by the power of being is non-being.[31]

'Non-being', then, is that 'quality of being by which everything that participates in being is negated'; and 'being' is the power of being which overcomes non-being.[32] Non-being is related to being in the sense of resistance to it, while the ontological question raised by looking into the 'abyss' of possible nothingness can be answered only in terms of being. For this reason, the 'abyss' of being points dialectically to the 'ground' of being, which is the positive side of the 'mystery of being', to that which resolves the question of the continual ontological threatenedness of the finite situation. Consequently, the 'mystery of being' made manifest in the situation of revelation is called the 'power of

---

[27] *Ibid.*

[28] The term 'being' in this context does not designate our physical existence in time and space, but 'the whole of human reality, the structure, the meaning, and the aim of existence. All this is threatened; it can be lost or saved' *(Ibid.,* p. 17).

[29] For his dialectical understanding of non-being, Tillich appeals to the Greek philosophic concept of *me on,* to Augustine's notion of 'sin', to the Judaeo-Christian doctrine of man's creatureliness, and to the work of the modern existentialists, Heidegger and Sartre *(Ibid.,* pp. 209—210).

[30] *ST,* 1: 210.

[31] *Love, Power, and Justice* (New York: Oxford University Press, 1960) p. 37 (my emphasis). Cf. *Christianity and the Problem of Existence* (Washington, D.C.: Henderson Services, 1951) pp. 30—31 (mimeographed).

[32] *Ibid.,* p. 38.

being', or the 'ground of our being', because it is that which ultimately determines our being or non-being by infinitely resisting the threat of non-being.[33]

However, from the viewpoint of determining what Tillich means by 'knowledge of revelation', the most important feature of his analysis of mystery is that he regards the revelation of it—the appearance of the 'power of being', conquering non-being—as the revelation of God as 'being-itself'. *Thus knowledge of revelation is essentially knowledge of God or being-itself.* The concept of 'being-itself', Tillich continues, 'points to the power inherent in everything, the power of resisting non-being. Therefore, instead of saying that God is first of all being-itself, it is possible to say that he is the power of being in everything and above everything, the infinite power of being'.[34] The same point is made in Tillich's use of his famous phrase, 'ultimate concern'. 'Revelation is the manifestation of what concerns us ultimately'; and 'our ultimate concern is that which determines our being or non-being'.[35] 'God', therefore, is the *name* for that which concerns man ultimately, being applicable only to the mystery revealed as the infinite power of being, being-itself. Elsewhere Tillich is even more emphatic. The element of 'power', so understood, is the

> basis of Godhead, that which makes God God. It is the root of his majesty, the unapproachable intensity of his being, the inexhaustible

---

[33] *ST*, 1: 122—123. It should be mentioned here that Tillich's dialectical interpretation of 'ground' and 'abyss' (partially indicated by the German words, *Grund* and *Abgrund*) has puzzled many scholars. For example, J. Heywood Thomas, in 'Some Comments on Tillich's Doctrine of Creation', *The Scottish Journal of Theology*, XIV, No. 2 (June 1961), argues that Tillich has made the '"nothing" out of which we come a something with fatal power', so that 'we are once more faced with Dualism' (p. 118). On the other hand, Kenneth Hamilton, in *The System and the Gospel* (London: S.C.M. Press, 1963), rejects this view, and cites Tillich's words that 'Non-being belongs to being, it cannot be separated from it' (p. 194). Despite this, however, Heywood Thomas' point is a fair one. For if the only power of non-being is its resistance to being, then there is a dualism if both being and non-being are taken as co-eternal—which Tillich appears to imply.

[34] *ST*, 1: 261.

[35] *Ibid.*, pp. 123 & 17.

ground of being in which everything has its origin. It is the power of being infinitely resisting non-being, giving the power of being to everything that is.[36]

Revelation, therefore, is the appearance of our 'ultimate concern', being-itself as the 'power of being' in which everything exists, actual in the creative process in all its forms. Put differently, it is the manifestation of that which is the necessary infinite 'quality' implied in and constitutive of the finite structure of reality, participating in all that 'is', and creating that in which it participates.[37] All the metaphors used by Tillich in his analysis of the meaning of God are interpreted with this connotation of 'power'. So, for example, God is the 'ground of being' or 'depth of existence', that which is the supporting power of being in every conditioned actuality, its very root of being.[38] This means that 'everything finite participates in being-itself and in its infinity. Otherwise it would not have the power of being. It would be swallowed by non-being, or it never would have emerged out of non-being'.[39] God is also the 'abyss of being', that which cannot be 'exhausted by any creation or by any totality of them...'[40] This, in turn, implies that the 'being of God cannot be understood as the existence of a being alongside or above others'.[41] God, in other words, as the 'power of being', is not subject to the finite destiny not to be, but is above every being and the totality of being threatened by non-being.[42] As these remarks suggest, God thus

---

[36] *Ibid.*, p. 278.

[37] Cf. 'The Protestant Principle and the Proletarian Situation', *PE:* 163.

[38] See the sermon, 'The Depth of Existence', *The Shaking of the Foundations* (London: Penguin Books, 1966) pp. 59—70.

[39] *ST*, 1: 263.

[40] *Ibid.*, p. 88.

[41] *Ibid.*, p. 261.

[42] The view that God does not exist as a being accounts for the charge of atheism sometimes made against Tillich. In fact, he acknowledges that 'it is as atheistic to affirm the existence of God as it is to deny it (*Ibid.*, p. 263), and means by this that both the assertions 'God exists' and 'God does not exist' are atheistic because both accept the premise that God *could* exist. It is then that the premise is judged in a positive or negative way. For Tillich, the *possibility* of God's existence or non-existence is inconceivable because the notion of existence itself is incompatible with the concept 'God'. John Hick, in 'The Idea of Necessary Being', *The Princeton Seminary Bulletin*, LIV, No. 2 (November 1960) pp. 11—21, argues that

has a positive and negative relation to everything existing, primarily indicated by the terms 'ground' and 'abyss'. Positively, all that has being is sustained by the power of being that is God. Negatively, all that exists lacks the absoluteness of God's infinite power, so that, to this extent, his unconditionality stands over against the relativity of the whole structure of being. According to Tillich, therefore, the true meaning of the relationship is that God is the power of being in all that is, acting as its creative 'ground', but at the same time transcending every finite being infinitely as the 'abyss' of being.[43]

If we now relate what has been said so far about the nature of revelation to the function of a religious picture as the objective side of a dependent revelation, the following may be deduced: that both the dependent picture and the original event to which it refers serve to reveal that which transcends them infinitely—namely, God as being-itself, overcoming the ontological threat of non-being—and that both thereby disclose that which concerns us ultimately. More specifically, the revelatory character of a work of art is identical with the fact that it contains *the ecstatic response of the artist grasped by the mystery of being in an original miracle*. It is in this sense alone that we may speak of 'inspiration', although Tillich is careful to avoid any supernaturalistic idea of the divine imparting information. Inspiration, he tells us, is the 'name for the cognitive quality of the ecstatic experience'.[44] The inspiration of an artist thus consists in his reception and creative witness to a 'sign-event', through which that past event is continued and made available to those not contemporaries of it.

Irrespective therefore of whether we are speaking of an original event or a dependent representation of it, what is revealed in miracle

---

this is another formulation of the distinction between the necessary being of God and the contingent being of man. Cf. Sidney Hook, 'The Atheism of Paul Tillich', *Religious Experience and Truth*, ed. S. Hook (New York: New York University Press, 1961) pp. 59—64.

[43] In seeking to express this two-fold relation in terms of man's religious experience of it, Tillich adopts Rudolf Otto's terminology, and speaks accordingly of the encounter with the 'Holy' as *tremendum* and *fascinosum*. These terms signify 'the experience of "the ultimate" in the double sense of that which is the abyss and that which is the ground of man's being' (*ST*, 1: 239). See also 'Die Kategorie des "Heiligen" bei Rudolf Otto', *Theologische Blätter* (Leipzig), II, No. 1 (January 1923) pp. 11—12.

[44] *ST*, 1: 127.

and received in ecstasy is strict mystery, that which cannot be subject to an attitude or language bound to the subject-object scheme. In both cases, what is encountered is an actual revelatory happening, one which opens up a dimension of knowledge, relative only to man's ultimate concern and to the double relation of everything finite to being-itself. More exactly, religious art is a medium through which the mystery of being, being-itself, manifests its creative and abysmal relation to us and to the structure of being as a whole. In calling this relation 'creative', we remember that Tillich is pointing to the fact that everything participates in the infinite ground of being; and that, in calling it 'abysmal', he is pointing to the fact that all things are infinitely transcended by their creative ground. As we shall now see, it is this double characteristic of God—the mystery which appears in revelation as ground and abyss—which accounts for the important contrast between knowledge of revelation and ordinary knowledge, and thus for the epistemological distinctiveness of religious art.

We begin with the *abysmal* side of God, since it is this which, Tillich maintains, makes revelation mysterious.[45] In holding that revelation is the communication of that which is in principle inaccessible to the cognitive consciousness, Tillich is re-emphasizing the infinite qualitative distinction between the unconditioned and the conditioned, or rather the radical abysmal character of God as the 'power of being', as that which infinitely transcends both the finite structure of being grounded in him, and that split between subject and object which is the precondition of all knowledge subject to that structure. Being-itself does not participate in non-being, and thus is 'beyond' or 'before' the contrast of subject-object which characterizes the finitude of man's cognitive reason. God, in other words, as the abyss of being, is not an 'object' of knowledge among other objects, for that which is man's ultimate concern cannot be found 'within the entire catalogue of finite objects which are conditioned by each other'.[46] This particular distinction between the unconditioned (or unconditional) and the conditioned is better expressed

---

[45] *Ibid.*, p. 173. Strictly speaking, of course, a separate discussion of the 'abysmal' over against the 'creative' notion of God is impossible, given the dialectical relation between them; but, for the purpose of clarifying their significance in the present context, such a division is unavoidable.

[46] *Ibid.*, p. 238.

if we recall briefly the German translation of 'ultimate concern'. In the German edition of *Systematic Theology,* ultimate concern is *was uns unbedingt angeht,* 'what concerns us unconditionally'.[47] In his 'Religionsphilosophie' of 1925, faith is defined as *die Richtung auf das Unbedingte,* as 'directedness toward the Unconditional'.[48] In both works, the meaning of the German word for 'unconditional' *(unbedingt)* explicitly excludes all sense of the limitation of *das Unbedingte* by being made into a 'thing' *(Ding).* God, accordingly, is not the 'object' of faith, if by that is meant that faith's concern is with a concrete object established in the temporal order. That which is man's ultimate concern is in no way dependent on man or on any finite being or concern, for the unconditioned cannot be equated either with a single form or with the totality of all forms of conditioned reality. As Tillich insists: 'Only that which is unconditional can be the expression of unconditional concern. A conditioned God is no God'.[49]

In this discussion of God as the *abyss of being,* all objective thinking is thus ruled out, for, as that term signifies, what is under consideration is not an object which can be found alongside, above, or simply within 'things'. The notion of 'abyss' is rooted in an understanding of God which does not identify him with 'objective' being in any of these senses; and it was this, we remember, which provided Tillich with the substance of his case against the 'blasphemous' arguments for the existence of God, namely, that 'a God about whose existence or nonexistence you can argue is a thing beside others within the universe of existing things'.[50] These conclusions do not, of course, prevent Tillich from realizing that, logically speaking, everything toward which the cognitive act is directed *is* considered an object, whether it be God, inanimate matter, the self or a mathematical definition. 'In the logical sense everything about which a predication is made is, by this very fact, an object'.[51] In this respect, then, the theologian cannot escape making God an object, just as he cannot avoid a tendency to use objectifying

---

[47] *Systematische Theologie,* Bd. I, trans. Renate Albrecht *et al.* (Stuttgart: Evangelisches Verlagswerk, 1956) p. 19.
[48] *GW,* I: 331. See below, Ch. I, p. 38.
[49] *ST,* 1: 275.
[50] 'Religion as a Dimension in Man's Spiritual Life', *TC:* 5.
[51] *ST,* 1: 191.

concepts when speaking of him. But, Tillich continues, the basic point
to be grasped here is that this continual danger of 'logical objectifi-
cation' is never merely logical: 'it carries ontological presuppositions
and implications'.[52]

> If God *is* brought into the subject-object structure of being, he
> ceases to be the ground of being and becomes one being among others
> (first of all, a being beside the subject who looks at him as an object).
> He ceases to be the God who is really God.[53]

Notwithstanding the fact, therefore, that everything which becomes real
within the cognitive realm enters the subject-object correlation, theology
must always reaffirm the abysmal character of God—the divine
transcendence over the subject-object structure of reality—and, in so
doing, 'remember that in speaking of God it makes an object of that
which precedes the subject-object structure and that, therefore, it must
include in its speaking of God the acknowledgment that it cannot make
God an object'.[54]

We can now draw more specific conclusion about the type of knowledge to be gained through religious art. The religious artistic creation
is, in every case, a composite of revelations, being both a document of
revelation and a revelation, witnessing to that of which it is a part. What
it reveals is God in his attribute of absolute concealment. Moreover,
every situation in which revelation occurs is unique in that here alone
the normal cognitive correspondence of subject and object is affirmed
and denied simultaneously: it is affirmed because man is a centred self
to whom every relation involves an object; and it is denied because God,
as the abyss of being, can never become an object of man's knowledge. In
calling a work of art 'religious', we are therefore imputing to it a meaning
which cannot be evaluated in terms of, or drawn into, the subject-object
correlation because it is a meaning relative only to that which infinitely
transcends that correlation and is not an element within it. The *a priori*
of valuation implied in such a designation is that the particular work
in question manifests the abysmal character of God. Thus, no law and
no category can be applied to it which is taken from an approach to
finite being, since the structure of the content of revelation infinitely

---

[52] *Ibid.*
[53] *Ibid.* (my emphasis).
[54] *Ibid.*

transcends the whole subject-object structure of reality. This is why the actual meaning ascribed by the artist to the original 'sign-event', and by us to the artist's representation of it, must issue in a redefinition of the normal cognitive connection between subject and object, between the knower and the known. *The revelation of ultimate import is the revelation of the abyss of meaning.*[55] Meaning, that is to say, is here constituted in a dimension which, by virtue of that to which it refers, has left behind the totality of finite meaning-relations, and which, in the categorical understanding of the word, contains no 'relation' at all. This important conclusion establishes Tillich's contrast between knowledge of revelation and ordinary knowledge. Revelation is the disclosure of that which remains hidden despite being revealed: it is the manifestation to the consciousness of that 'mysterious' side of God which, by his infinite power of being, transcends absolutely the whole finite structure of being and meaning grounded in him. Such, then, is the disjunction between revelation's mystery and existent being that there can be no justification of the content of *any* revelation on the basis a knowledge or meaning which is itself dependent on the finite form of reality. In the present case, however, this is so not because of the finitude of reason, because of the conflicts that occur in every activity of the mind, both theoretical and practical: it is because it is in the nature of the knowledge given and received in the situation of revelation that there can be no demonstration or verification of revelation except to and for those in that situation. Revelation, accordingly, involves a particular knowledge, unavailable and unattainable outside *a particular disposition of the human subject*—the 'religious' disposition—evinced in his acceptance of revelation as the appearance of the abyss of being within the natural order of being.

This same conclusion is met in Tillich's discussion of the *creative* aspect of God. Here, however, we find a different form of argumentation. The division accounting for the epistemological character of religious art—the division between knowledge of revelation and ordinary revelation—is not, in this instance, sustained by the *negation* of any identity between the finite subject and infinite 'object' in revelation, but by its *affirmation*. Tillich does not, of course, intend by this to impugn the radical transcendence of God as the abyss of being: he is referring

---

[55] 'The Philosophy of Religion', *WR:* 58.

instead to its dialectical counterpart, namely, to the creative side of God as the 'ground of being', implied in and constitutive of all existent being, and by which reality resists non-being. The affirmation of an identity between the human subject and the divine 'object' of religious knowledge depends, therefore, upon that immanent quality of God as the *depth of existence* in which all things finite participate.

The way in which this emphasis upon the creative aspect of God determines the epistemological status of religious art can be seen best if we turn again to Tillich's use of the expression 'ultimate concern'. Up to this point, the term has been employed chiefly to characterize the 'objective' side of religion, that to which faith is directed, namely, the unconditional and 'abysmal' nature of God as being-itself or the infinite power of being. And yet the meaning of the phrase varies in Tillich's theology, since he uses it also to delineate the 'subjective' side of religion: the act of faith itself. So, for example, Tillich speaks of ultimate concern as the 'infinite passion ... passion for the infinite' experienced by each and every individual in the totality of his personality.[56] It is hardly surprising, therefore, that this use of 'ultimate concern' has been thought highly ambiguous. Does the phrase apply to an attitude of concern or to the object of that attitude? Does it refer to the individual's own acceptance of revelation in faith, or to the content of that received by faith through revelation?[57] For our purposes, however, the significant point to be made here is that, elsewhere in his work, Tillich does resolve this difficulty by explicitly *identifying* the attitude of ultimate concern with its object. 'The ultimate of the act of faith and the ultimate that is meant in the act of faith are one and the same'.[58] Expressed in abstract language, this entails '... the disappearance of the ordinary subject-object scheme in the experience of the ultimate, the unconditional'.[59] Thus the term 'ultimate concern' unites the subjective and the objective side of the act of faith—the *fides qua creditur* (the faith through which one believes) and the *fides*

---

[56] *DF:* 9.
[57] See John Hick, *Philosophy of Religion* (Englewood Cliffs, N.J.: Prentice-Hall, 1963) p. 68. Cf. his 'Article Review' of the *Systematic Theology*, Vols. 1 & 2, in the *Scottish Journal of Theology*, XII, No. 3 (September 1959) pp. 288—289.
[58] *DF:* 11.
[59] *Ibid.*

quae creditur (the faith which is believed). The first is the classical term for the centered act of the personality, the ultimate concern. The second is the classical term for that toward which this act is directed, the ultimate itself, expressed in symbols of the divine. This distinction is very important, but not ultimately so, for the one side cannot be without the other. There is no faith without a content toward which it is directed.[60]

In Tillich's view, therefore, ultimate concern provides the place in which the subject-object dichotomy is removed. It is for this reason that he refuses to speak of 'knowledge' here, since that 'finally presupposes the separation of subject and object, and implies an isolated theoretical act...'[61] Ultimate concern is not, accordingly, an expression of the attitude of one reality *toward* another, because the ultimate, being-itself as the *prius* of our own being, can be no object for us as subjects. Consequently, there can be no self-affirmation of a finite being, and no interaction between the human subject and any object, in which the ground of being and its power of conquering non-being is not effective. With this in mind, Tillich replaces the word 'knowledge' by the word 'awareness', a 'neutral' term which may be defined as 'mystical' because the experience it denotes is comparable to the mystic's experience of the identity of subject and object in relation to God.[62] Ultimate concern is thus the awareness of the ultimate itself, the *esse ipsum*, which precedes all differences between subject and object, or, to use St. Augustine's terminology, of the *veritas ipsa*, the 'truth-itself'.[63] Faith, therefore, as the state of being ultimately concerned, is not a matter of objective knowledge, of empirical research or rational information, but is the immediate awareness of the presence of the unconditional element in ourselves and our world, the basis of religious experience. It is rooted in a 'mystical *a priori*', which is 'an awareness of something that transcends the cleavage between subject and object'.[64]

Following this analysis of ultimate concern, we may say that, for Tillich, the content of that which is received in the situation of revela-

---

[60] *Ibid.*, p. 10.
[61] 'The Two Types of Philosophy of Religion', *TC*: 23.
[62] *Ibid.*
[63] See Tillich, 'The Problem of Theological Method', *The Journal of Religion*, XXVII, No. 1 (January 1947) p. 23.
[64] *ST*, 1: 12.

tion is identical with the structure of him who receives it: identical, that is, in the sense that *what is received is the necessary quality implied in the being of the recipient.* The implication of this understanding of revelation as the appearance of God as the *depth* of being is, then, that faith receives and accepts that which *excludes,* by its creative power, any observer who is not himself conditioned by it in his whole being. The finitude of the human subject implies non-being, but is in fact more than non-being: it carries within itself the power of being; and this power of being issues from its participation in God as being-itself, the creative ground of being. Indeed, the meaning that faith attaches to revelations *as* revelations implies this ontological relation. The revelatory significance perceived in, and ascribed to, certain elements of reality by faith entails faith's awareness that by them is manifested that infinite power of being which is its own depth or ground of being.

If somebody says, then, that a particular picture is religious—that it is directed toward the unconditional—he is testifying to his own attitude of faith in relation to that picture, or rather to his apprehension of that which is the focus of his ultimate concern. Here, through the medium of the picture, appears something that is identical with him even though it transcends him absolutely: something from which he is estranged by the finitude of his own existence, but from which he cannot be separated by virtue of his own limited power of being. It is, therefore, tautologically true to say that religious art is revelatory art; that it witnesses to the manifestation of the creative attribute of God; and that, moreover, it possesses a unique cognitive value for those who receive it as revelation. For knowledge of revelation involves no 'knowledge' at all—if by that term one is referring to the capacity of the human subject to know the divine 'object' as distinct from himself—since in revelation 'God remains the subject, even if he becomes a logical object'.[65] In the situation of revelation, to repeat, the knowing subject is ontologically determined by that which is the logical object of his concern. It is this relation that distinguishes again the epistemological character

---

[65] *Ibid.,* p. 191. An affinity with Karl Barth's theology is evident here. Thus Barth writes: 'The Subject of Revelation is the Subject that remains indissolubly Subject'. *The Doctrine of the Word of God,* trans. G. T. Thomson (Edinburgh: T. & T. Clark, 1949) Vol. I, Part 1, p. 438. For an analysis of Barth's position, see James Brown, *Subject and Object in Modern Theology* (London: S.C.M. Press, 1955) pp. 140—167.

of religious art. In the normal process of aesthetic activity under the law of *theoria,* the act of knowing or expressing proceeds on the basis of the knower's initial and necessary detachment from the object to be known; but in religious aesthetic activity, that which is known is the *prius* of the knower, the necessary presupposition of every being, and so, of every thought. 'God can never be reached if he is the *object* of a question, and not its *basis*'.[66] In religious art, therefore, what is communicated to faith is implied in, and precedes, every relation between subject and object, and thus involves no knowledge which it itself dependent on that correlation. *The revelation of ultimate import is the revelation of the ontological ground of all meaningfulness.*[67] Thus the perception of ultimate meaning in art is simultaneous with the immediate and personal awareness that art reveals that quality of 'ultimacy' implicit in the structure of existence as a whole, namely, the infinite power of being which precedes and governs all practical and theoretical distinctions between subject and object. This meaning is not, accordingly, either derived from, or accessible in terms of, the cognitive relation of subject and object entailed in all other cultural acts of meaning.

In summary, the significance attributed to a work of art as 'revelation' originates with the perception that through that work appears God in his double characteristic of abyss and ground. The *giving* of this meaning proceeds from the *receptive* act of faith in the situation of revelation: it is an act, in other words, of ultimate concern, relative only to the reception of that which, by its power of being as being-itself, transcends and determines the subject-object scheme implied in all aesthetic acts and in all normal cognitive judgments. The epistemological distinctiveness of religious art thus depends on two things: first, that what is received by faith through religious art is no 'object', but the ultimate, the absolutely hidden, that which cannot be approached by any form of knowledge appropriate to known or knowable reality; and second, that what does manifest itself through religious art is known,

---

[66] 'The Two Types of Philosophy of Religion', *TC:* 13. It follows from this that God is also 'the presupposition of the question of God' *(Ibid.)*—an insight into the relation of our mind to the Absolute which is, Tillich adds, the essential truth contained in the so-called 'ontological argument'. The question of God *can* be asked because there is an unconditional element implicit within the very act of asking any question (*ST,* 1: 227—231).
[67] 'The Philosophy of Religion', *WR:* 58.

not by detached observation or evaluation, but by each individual's 'awareness' of his identity with that which is the 'subject' of his own finitude, governing the being or non-being of his own existence.[68] On both counts, therefore, the knowledge communicated to us through religious art is incapable of being subject to, or drawn into, the subject-object structure of ordinary knowledge. To suppose otherwise is to confuse the one dimension of knowledge with the other.

II. RELIGIOUS ART AS RELIGIOUS SYMBOL

Tillich's theory of being, as he presents it in his concept of revelation, leaves us in much the same dilemma as did his earlier theory of meaning. The theory of meaning, we remember, stipulated that, since all aesthetic acts are acts of meaning, and since every act of meaning presupposes ultimate meaning, *all* artistic styles are therefore religious styles, irrespective of what they describe or intend. Thereafter, the problem was of distinguishing between the more and the less religious arts. In the theory of being, we meet much the same difficulty. If the idea of God as the power of being includes all reality, then everything that artistically expresses reality (i.e., *every* artistic form) will express God, whether it intends to do so or not. Similarly, if the being of the artist requires the being of God as its creative ground, then God is as necessary to the aesthetic act as the artist himself. How, then, are we to differentiate between artistic styles in their approximation to the theonomous-religious ideal? Nor is that the only problem. If all art is, in these senses, religious art, then to what extent is Tillich justified in distinguishing between the epistemological character of, say, Impressionism, which is determined by the subject-object structure, and religious art, which is not?

---

[68] With Tillich's translation of 'revelation' in this way, one is able to understand faith in terms of the ultimate itself, namely as man's concern about that which is revealed as the ultimate, and to understand the ultimate in terms of faith, namely as that about which man is ultimately concerned in the situation of revelation. This double possibility—which, Tillich maintains, preserves the ultimacy of the ultimate but which allows for a conception of the ultimate from the viewpoint of man's awareness of it in the depth of his being—constitutes for him a third and superior position 'beyond naturalism and supranaturalism' (*ST*, 2: 5—9).

Tillich answers these questions in his theory of religious symbolism, in itself one of the most complex and pervasive features of his theology.[69] This theory reinforces the contrast drawn between knowledge of revelation and ordinary knowledge, but it does so by concentrating not so much upon the character of that which is revealed as upon the character of that which reveals it. In other words, the religious symbol is the particular *form of expression* required of the media of revelation for their expression of the ultimate of being, being-itself. It is this that provides us with the means once more of constructing a heirarchy of religious styles, based on the extent to which that form is present or absent. In common therefore with the theory of meaning, the theory of being maintains that it is the artistic form itself that can deny its own innate or essential power of expressing that which concerns us ultimately: it possesses, as it were, the capacity to make itself less 'transparent' to ultimacy by making itself less symbolic. However, that this *is* and *will* be the case is the tragic fate of artistic form under the conditions of estrangement, since there an ontological separation exists between what is and what ought to be. Thus, once again, the classification of the more and the less religious styles depends on their approximation to the perfected and synthetic state: only those styles will be judged religious

---

[69] For further details on Tillich's discussion of religious symbolism, see the following articles:— R. F. Aldwinckle, 'Tillich's Theory of Religious Symbolism', *Canadian Journal of Theology*, X, No. 2 (April 1964) pp. 110—117; W. P. Alston, 'Tillich's Conception of a Religious Symbol', *Religious Experience and Truth*, ed. S. Hook, pp. 12—26; Bowman L. Clarke, 'God and the Symbolic in Tillich', *Anglican Theological Review*, XLIII, No. 3 (July 1961) pp. 302—311; John Y. Fenton, 'Being-itself and Religious Symbolism', *The Journal of Religion*, XLV, No. 2 (April 1965) pp. 73—86; Lewis S. Ford, 'The Three Strands of Tillich's Theory of Religious Symbols', *The Journal of Religion*, XLVI, No. 1 (January 1966) pp. 104—130; H. D. McDonald, 'The Symbolic Theology of Paul Tillich', *Scottish Journal of Theology*, XVII, No. 4 (December 1964) pp. 414—430; Michael Simpson, 'Paul Tillich: Symbolism and Objectivity', *The Heythrop Journal*, VIII, No. 3 (July 1967) pp. 293—309; and, both by Paul L. Holmer, 'Paul Tillich and the Language about God', *Journal of Religious Thought*, XXII, No. 1 (January 1965—66) pp. 35—50, and 'Paul Tillich: Language and Meaning', *Journal of Religious Thought*, XXII, No. 2 (April 1965—66) pp. 85—106. For a full-length analysis, see W. L. Rowe, *Religious Symbols and God* (Chicago and London: The University of Chicago Press, 1968).

that reveal the ultimate of being in the manner appropriate to its revelation. This is the artistic religious and symbolic form, which is the required form of theonomous art. In its perfect realization, therefore, even the religious symbol is an ideal and not a reality.

As a preliminary indication of how his argument proceeds, Tillich tells us that, because every person and thing necessarily participate in the infinite power of being, 'there is no reality, thing, or event which cannot become a bearer of the mystery of being and enter a revelatory correlation'.[70] This is the *ontological warrant* for Tillich's earlier extension of the principle of consecration to cover every artistic form as the possible expression of the ultimate, and, indeed, for the theology of culture as a whole. He adds, however, that 'nothing has become the bearer of revelation by its outstanding qualities...'[71] Thus, while all objects have in principle an equal ontological status because all participate in being-itself, no element of reality can serve as the medium of revelation unless it manifests to the consciousness the mystery of being. No natural thing or process subject to the structure of being can become, therefore, a vehicle of revelation through what it is *in itself,* but only through its manifestation of that which is both implicit within and distinct from it as the 'ground' and 'abyss' of its own being and meaning. It is not, for example, the historical significance or personal greatness of the medium's individual characteristics that make it revelatory. This stipulation, in Tillich's view, avoids the danger of a 'natural theology' in revelation.

> Revelation through natural mediums is not natural revelation. "Natural revelation", if distinguished from revelation through nature, is a contradiction in terms, for if it is natural knowledge it is not revelation, and if it is revelation it makes nature ecstatic and miraculous... Natural theology and, even more definitely, natural revelation are misnomers for the negative side of the revelation of the mystery, for an interpretation of the shock and stigma of non-being.[72]

---

[70] *ST*, 1: 131.
[71] *Ibid.*
[72] *Ibid.*, p. 133. Cf. 'Natural and Revealed Religion', *Christendom*, I, No. 1 (Autumn 1935) pp. 159—170. However, for an alternative opinion, see Lewis S. Ford, 'Tillich's Implicit Natural Theology', *Scottish Journal of Theology*, XXIV, No. 3 (August 1971) pp. 257—270.

It is precisely this same affirmation and negation of the object's own concrete qualities which stand at the centre of Tillich's theory of religious symbolism. According to him, the form of the religious symbol is such that it simultaneously *affirms* the necessity of using material taken from finite reality in order to give content to the cognitive function in revelation, and *negates* the normal cognitive use of those finite materials by expressing that which both 'transcends' and 'precedes' the structure of being to which these materials properly belong. Here, the negation of the functional importance of the object's specific characteristics in determining the significance attributed to it *as* a medium of revelation evolves from the necessary denial that such characteristics are in any way attributes of what that object reveals. Tillich's doctrine of religious symbolism is designed, in other words, to avoid the danger of subjecting the ultimate mystery of being to the subject-object structure of being from which all the media of revelation are drawn; and it is for this reason that the theory also requires that *no picture can be regarded as a vehicle of revelation simply on the basis of a critical evaluation of the object it is representing.* If the contrary is the case, then the meaning of such a picture as a medium of revelation becomes self-contradictory, since, being now dependent on what is capable of analysis or description, it is no longer related to our ultimate concern, being-itself. In this way, then, Tillich's notion of 'religious symbol' further upholds the distinction between the dimensions of revelatory knowledge and ordinary knowledge. For it implies that the veracity of a 'religious' picture is not governed by any analysis of the correspondence between the meaning therein ascribed to an object and that object's own factual-historical mode of being; and this is in direct contrast to the process of knowing normally presupposed in talk of pictures and their validity. We shall return to this point presently.

In all the various accounts Tillich has given of his theory of religious symbolism, he contrasts religious symbols with symbols generally. The function of symbols may be summarized briefly in four propositions:—

1. Symbols are figurative, that is, they point beyond themselves to something for which they stand: they are 'self-transcendent'.

2. Symbols participate in the reality of that which they symbolize.

3. Symbols cannot be replaced arbitrarily or according to expediency: they grow and die, but are not invented or abolished.

4. Symbols open up levels of being and levels of the soul which only symbols can open: they disclose dimensions of reality which cannot be experienced except through symbols.[73]

The religious symbol, while possessing all these characteristics of symbol, has, however, its own special features. Religious symbols point to the deepest level of being which is not *a* level but the creative 'ground' in all levels: they are representations of that which is man's ultimate concern.

> They must express an object that by its very nature transcends everything in the world that is split into subjectivity and objectivity. A real symbol points to an object which never can become an object. Religious symbols represent the transcendent immanent. They do not make God a part of the empirical world.[74]

The distinctive function of religious symbols is therefore to point to the ultimate level of reality, being-itself. That 'God is being-itself' is the only direct, non-symbolic affirmation open to theology, and is implicit in every religious thought about God.[75] For if, Tillich, argues, the question, 'Is there a nonsymbolic statement about the referent of religious symbols?' cannot be answered affirmatively, then 'the necessity of symbolic language for religion could not be proved and the whole argu-

---

[73] Tillich has written six major essays on religious symbolism:— 1) 'Das religiöse Symbol', *Blätter für deutsche Philosophie* (Berlin), I, No. 4 (January 1928) pp. 277—299. This has been translated and revised in *Religious Experience and Truth*, ed. S. Hook, pp. 301—321; 2) 'Religious Symbols and Our Knowledge of God', *Christian Scholar*, XXXVIII, No. 3 (September 1955) pp. 189—197, and reprinted as 'The Nature of Religious Language' in *TC*: 53—67; 3) 'Theology and Symbolism', *Religious Symbolism*, ed. F. Ernest Johnson (New York: Harper & Bros., 1955) pp. 107—116; 4) 'Existential Analyses and Religious Symbols', *Contemporary Problems in Religion*, ed. H. A. Basilius (Detroit: Wayne University Press, 1956) pp. 35—55, and reprinted in *Four Existentialist Theologians*, ed. Will Herberg (Garden City: Doubleday Anchor Books, No. 141, 1958) pp. 277—291; 5) 'The Meaning and Justification of Religious Symbols', *Religious Experience and Truth*, ed. S. Hook, pp. 3—12; 6) 'God as being and the Knowledge of God', *ST*, 1: 264—268. The present summary is based on Tillich's own in 'The Word of God', *Language: An Enquiry into its Meaning and Function*, ed. Ruth N. Anshen (New York: Harper & Bros., 1957) pp. 122—133.

[74] 'The Religious Symbol', p. 303.

[75] *ST*, 1: 264—265.

ment would lead into a vicious circle'.[76] A religious symbol is, in other words, symbolic because it represents that which is unconditionally beyond its own conceptual sphere, the ultimate reality implied in the religious act; and that 'God is being-itself' is not symbolic because, as the fundamental and most abstract ontological concept, it points to no higher mode of being beyond itself. 'It means what it says directly and properly; if we speak of the actuality of God we first assert that he is not God if he is not being-itself. Other assertions about God can be made theologically only on this basis'.[77]

Thus every statement about being-itself—other than the statement that God *is* being-itself—is symbolic. 'To speak unsymbolically about being-itself is untrue'.[78] The pivotal point of Tillich's argument here is

---

[76] 'The Meaning and Justification of Religious Symbols', p. 6. The question of the non-symbolic status of the assertion 'God is being-itself' is one of the most perplexing issues in Tillich's theology, if only because he appears to have reversed his position at least twice. His nonsymbolic doctrine, advocated primarily in *ST*, 1, differs from his earlier, pan-symbolist view that 'all knowledge of God has a symbolic character' ('The Religious Symbol', p. 316). This change, says Tillich, followed upon Wilbur Urban's criticism that 'in order to speak of symbolic knowledge one must delimit the symbolic realm by an unsymbolic statement' ('Reply to Interpretation and Criticism', *The Theology of Paul Tillich*, ed. Kegley and Bretall, p. 334). However, in *ST*, 2: 9, Tillich maintains that the only nonsymbolic statement is 'the statement that everything we say about God is symbolic. Such a statement is an assertion about God which itself is not symbolic'. Yet this position is not only closer to that criticized by Urban —namely, that no positive, literal characterization can be made of God as the unconditioned—it is also self-contradictory. The statement that 'everything we say about God is symbolic' should, on its own terms, be symbolic and not the literal assertion Tillich wishes to affirm. For our present purposes, to accept the view that 'God is being-itself' is a literal identity statement has, to use William Rowe's words, the important consequence 'that the ontological status of God and the ontological status of being-itself are not two different questions but one and the same' (*op. cit.*, pp. 30—31). This has been my own underlying position in the analysis of 'revelation'. Cf. Wilbur M. Urban, 'Tillich's Theory of the Religious Symbol', *Journal of Liberal Religion*, II, No. 2 (Summer 1940) pp. 34—36; and Lewis S. Ford, 'Tillich's One Non-symbolic Statement: *A Propos* of a Recent Study by Rowe', *Journal of the American Academy of Religion*, XXXVIII, No. 2 (June 1970) pp. 176—182.

[77] *ST*, 1: 265.

[78] *CTB:* 175.

that the ultimate level of reality to which religious symbols refer is not subject to the finite structure of reality and its limitations. God, as being-itself, is the ground of the ontological structure of being without being determined by this structure himself. 'Therefore, if anything beyond this bare assertion is said about God, it no longer is a direct and proper statement, no longer a concept. It is indirect, and it points to something beyond itself. In a word, it is symbolic'.[79] A statement is symbolic, that is, in so far as it uses a segment of finite experience to say something about God; but since God, as the transcendent absolute, being-itself, is a reality beyond the subject-object structure of being, no element of being therein discovered can be literally applied to him. Accordingly, no literal assertion concerning the laws and structure of nature, the biological and psychological character of man, or the facts and processes of history can be identified with religious symbols. Conversely, religious symbols are immune to the criticisms of non-symbolic language, since they are not circumscribed by any law, process or fact concerning man and his world. Such criticisms are not only confusions of literal and symbolic language, but are, since language expresses reality, confusions also of the dimensions of reality to which those different kinds of language refer.

As a basic characteristic of all religious symbols, this non-literal form is evident in each of the various types of religious symbol. Briefly put, Tillich distinguishes between two classes of religious symbol, the 'primary' and the 'secondary', the former pointing directly to the referent of religious symbolism, being-itself, the latter supporting or re-symbolizing the primary.[80] To the extent, therefore, that a religious picture is a medium of revelation, manifesting to us the mystery of being, it also functions *as a primary religious symbol*. This class of religious symbol Tillich further subdivides into two levels: 'the transcendent level, the level which goes *beyond* the empirical reality we encounter, and the immanent level, the level which we find *within* the encounter with reality'.[81] Primary-transcendent religious symbols consist in the central symbol of a 'highest' being to whom certain qualities are attributed (*viz.*, personality, power, love, justice, etc.), and encompass

---

[79] *ST*, 1: 265.
[80] 'The Meaning and Justification of Religious Symbols', p. 8.
[81] 'The Nature of Religious Language', *TC:* 61.

also those symbols characterizing the divine actions (*viz.*, creation, providence, judgment, etc.). Primary-immanent religious symbols, on the other hand, live in the realm of 'appearances of the divine in time and space', and so include all events, things or people through which the unconditioned transcendent has been manifested.[82] Thus, while this second type involves primarily those historical personalities who have become the object of the religious act (e.g., the Christ or the Buddha), it extends to *every* element of reality which has occasioned an awareness of the ultimate, whether it be, for example, the sacramental materials of the Lord's Supper or even a Crucifix.[83]

Following these classifications, we can be still more specific about the symbolic status of religious art. *All religious artistic forms are primary-immanent religious symbols.* This is so because they, in common with all the finite media of revelation, are vehicles through which the mystery of being, being-itself, appears within the natural order of being. Thus both the 'miracle' first received by the artist and his subsequent artistic representation of that event, as the 'giving' sides of original and dependent revelations respectively, belong in this category, it being a level of religious symbolism appropriate only to the 'manifestation of the divine in things and events, in persons and communities, in words and documents'.[84] Significantly enough, this suggests in turn that, as symbols of this type, these two revelations conform to the non-literal structure of religious symbols generally; and that, accordingly, *neither has a place in the rational world of concrete objects.* In the case of an original revelation, this point is underlined when Tillich, speaking of those historical personalities that have become primary-immanent symbols, both affirms their 'objectivity' and negates their 'rational objectivity'.[85] His acceptance of the necessary facticity of the figures regarded as media of revelation is, in other terms, contrasted here with his denial that any practical or theoretical process could establish their historical reality *as* media of revelation. This signifies 'that those objects that possess a holy character are not empirical, even if they can only be conceived as existing in the empirical

---

[82] *Ibid.*, p. 63.
[83] *Ibid.*, pp. 64—65.
[84] *DF:* 48.
[85] 'The Religious Symbol', p. 316.

order'.[86] The personalities, that is, that have become the focus of a religious act are empirical to the extent that they belong to the subject-object structure of being; but they are not empirical in that the meaning attributed to them in that act cannot be validated within the subject-object schema of rationality.[87] This being so, then religious art, by claiming to be similarly based on an actual revelation, claims also to portray a 'holy reality', the original nature of which precludes any judgment of its truth *as* a revelation on the basis of a critical assessment of its factual-historical mode of being, of its placing within the objective world. For the theory of religious symbolism indicates that while such primary-immanent symbols have historical elements—in that the peculiarity of these symbols 'depends precisely upon their historical reality, their reality in the objective sense'[88]—*they do not mediate any literal truth about themselves from which their meaning as symbols may be deduced.* If the meaning of any element of reality as a primary-immanent religious symbol depends on its revelation of the ultimate to the human consciousness, then the criterion of its truth as a symbol cannot be a non-symbolic comparison between its own individual qualities and the ultimate reality to which it refers. This is because the reality thus pointed to by the religious symbol transcends infinitely the structure of being to which every finite segment of reality, and every epistemological distinction between subject and object, are bound. It is, so Tillich remarks,

> The first step in the deterioration of religion when it identifies symbols with the world of finite interrelations which furnishes the material of the symbols—which are the material and not that which is signified. That which is signified lies beyond the symbolic material. This is the first and last thing we must say about religious symbolism.[89]

---

[86] *Ibid.*
[87] A view, we remember, which accords with Tillich's analysis of 'miracle'. See above, pp. 129—130.
[88] 'The Religious Symbol', p. 316. Tillich adds that it would be 'entirely contradictory to the religious consciousness if one characterized these personalities, or what they did and what happened to them, as symbols... The use of symbolism with regard to this world in which the holy is supposed to be really present would involve a denial of its presence and hence the destruction of its existence' *(Ibid.).*
[89] 'Theology and Symbolism', p. 116.

Since, therefore, no thing, person or event which manifests the absolutely hidden can be equated with the mystery it reveals, so the truth of the object received by the artist as a primary-immanent religious symbol cannot be determined by any evaluation of the literal correspondence between the quality or character of its finite material and the revelatory significance the artist ascribes to it in his ecstatic reception of it.[90] The importance of this symbol depends on its expression of the ultimate *in* its unconditionedness; but this requirement is not met if the conditioned reality which here serves as the vehicle of revelation is elevated to the dignity of the unconditioned. That which is perceived by the artist in the situation of revelation manifests itself through the medium; but the medium is the agent and not the source of the manifestation. Hence revelation is not the communication of knowledge concerning the ultimate based on any analysis of the properties of the medium. To suppose otherwise is 'idolatry', the substitution of the unconditioned by the conditioned, the attribution of divine predicates to a finite reality.[91]

This same pattern of argument is evident when we turn from the original to the dependent revelation, namely, to religious art itself. Religious art functions as a primary-immanent religious symbol in that through it is conveyed the original response and witness of an artist to a revelation of the ultimate. For those not contemporaries of that original event, the artist's apprehension of the ultimate of being through the medium of a finite object is here made available through the medium of an artistic form, the 'language' of which is the artistic expression of the state of revelatory ecstasy originally experienced by the artist himself. Thus it is correct to say that the particular category of symbolism to which religious art belongs is, like the original event to which it refers, distinguished by the fact that it embraces simultaneously

---

[90] Although not directly linked to his doctrine of religious symbolism, this point is implicit in Tillich's contention that the revelation witnessed to by the biblical picture is the *final* revelation, namely, the revelation which contains the medium's *own* rejection of all ultimate claims for itself. See *ST*, 1: 147—153.

[91] This explains what Tillich means by the 'risk of faith'. This risk is the tendency within faith to identify the religious symbol with the ultimate it reveals; it has nothing to do, therefore, with the risk of accepting uncertain historical information. See *ST*, 2: 134 & *TC*: 60—61.

finite and transcendent aspects: that it acts for the manifestation of the unconditioned within the order of conditioned being, for the immanence of the transcendent. But to this we should add that, since the ultimate stands by its very nature beyond the subject-object structure of being, the meaning of every statement about the unconditioned is in principle different from the meaning of every statement about the conditioned. From this we must further conclude, therefore, that the distinctive feature of religious art is that, in seeking to portray an event belonging to the class of primary-immanent symbols, it includes at the same time images or assertions about the concrete form of that event's objective existence which are fundamentally incompatible with those expressive of that event's meaning as a religious symbol, namely, with those relative to the perception of the ultimate in it—this incompatibility stemming from the different dimensions of reality to which each group of images or assertions refers.

In this way we can see that religious art, as a revelation testifying to a revelation, contains the same symbolic structure and has the same epistemological status as the original revelation it is signifying. So, in like fashion, the truth of a religious picture's statements regarding an artist's witness to a 'miracle' or 'sign-event' cannot be guaranteed by any evaluation of whether his own representation of the actual concrete-historical form of that event is true or not. The truth of a religious symbol, Tillich maintains, 'has nothing to do with the validity of factual statements concerning the symbolic material. However problematic the symbolic material in its literal meaning may be, its symbolic character and its validity as a symbol are not determined by it'.[92] It is, accordingly,

---

[92] 'The Meaning and Justification of Religious Symbols', p. 11. Elsewhere Tillich writes: 'The truth of a religious symbol has nothing to do with the truth of the empirical assertions involved in it, be they physical, psychological, or historical' (ST, 1: 266). Remarks like this go some way towards explaining Tillich's attitude to 'demythologization'. For him, myths are symbols of faith expressed in terms of events in time and space. The truth of myths depends, therefore, on their adequacy in expressing the revelations to which they point, and is not determined by the literal truth of their empirical references. He thus agrees with Bultmann in the 'deliteralization' of myths, but denies that one can 'demythologize' (i.e., do away with myths altogether) since 'there are no substitutes for the use of symbols and myths: they are the language of faith' (DF: 51). So Tillich argues: 'Myth is more

a disastrous misunderstanding of the function of religious art as a primary-immanent religious symbol to identify the validity of the meaning it attributes to objects or events with the objective accuracy of its pictures of them. Even the historian, viewing such pictures, cannot therefore falsify the portrait of an ecstatic response to a revelation: he may be able speak of it with scientific precision as a report about an assumed revelation, but he cannot speak of it as a witness to an actual revelation, and hence can contribute nothing to the knowledge of revelation mediated by it.

At this point we can return to our basic question: How does Tillich's theory of being enable us to distinguish between religious styles? The answer is that the distance between the more and the less religious styles is the distance between symbolic and literal truth, which is the same as saying that such stylistic differences depend on the possible relations between the various media of revelation and what is revealed by them. As we have seen, God, as being-itself, can appear through any object; but these objects have, besides their status as the possible bearers of ultimacy, another status, namely, that they belong to the finite structure of being with which God is *not* identified. Thus it is apparent that religious style always has something to 'overcome' when it uses such objects: 'den Eigengehalt des Stoffes, der ja nicht religiös ist und erst durch Negierung seiner profanen Beziehungen ins Religiöse erhoben werden muß'.[93] This is the process of religious symbolism; and where it is absent we find a corresponding drop in an artist's capacity to express revelation. Moreover, it is equally evident that those styles which concentrate less on the historical or natural value of things are most

---

than a primitive worldview with which Bultmann wrongly equates it; it is the necessary and adequate expression of revelation. In this I agree with Barth, who for some questionable terminological reason calls it "Sage" (Saga)'. 'The Present Theological Situation in the Light of the Continental Development', *Theology Today*, VI, No. 3 (October 1949) p. 306. Cf. *Perspectives on Nineteenth and Twentieth Century Protestant Thought*, pp. 227—228. On this difference between Tillich and Bultmann, see Klaus Rosenthal, 'Myth and Symbol', *Scottish Journal of Theology*, XVIII, No. 4 December 1965) pp. 431—432; and Robert H. Ayers, ' "Myth" in Theological Discourse: A Profusion of Confusion', *Anglican Theological Review*, XLVIII, No. 2 (April 1966) pp. 204—211.

[93] 'Religiöser Stil und religiöser Stoff in der bildenden Kunst', *GW*, IX: 321.

suitable for the expression of that which transcends the objective world as our ultimate concern.

This provides us with fresh insight into the earlier classification of autonomous, heteronomous and theonomous art. Autonomous art admits of no religious symbolic form because it recognizes no revelation: it is directed ·rather to the creation of forms and to the determination of meaning within the subject-object system of finite meanings. Heteronomous art, on the other hand, knows of revelation but gives to the media of revelation the absoluteness of revelation itself: it identifies the material of the symbolic with what it signifies. Both styles emerge therefore as *forms of literalism,* the one by limiting meaning to the finite forms of meaning, the other by limiting revelation to certain exclusive bearers of revelation. Neither can speak of revelation as the unconditioned import of meaning 'breaking through' the form of meaning. Theonomous art, however, transcends both in its religious-symbolic expression of divine immanence. Since revelation is here defined as the self-manifestation of the ground or depth of being, it cannot contradict our being and the autonomous or 'honest' affirmation of creative freedom; but this same definition implies that what freedom creates is not identical with what appears through the artistic creation: that the artistic form, although thus 'consecrated' as a holy object, is not the holy itself but transparent to it. In this way, theonomous art exposes its religious-symbolic structure in its affirmation and negation of artistic forms as the media of revelation. For this reason, theonomous art is the only proper artistic expression of the apprehension of ultimacy, and thus the only proper artistic style which, in the correlation of dependent revelations, may be considered revelatory—revelatory, that is, not from the viewpoint of its aesthetic form but from the viewpoint of its power of expressing some aspect of that which transcends us ultimately *in* and *through* its aesthetic form.

As a final point, it is worth noting that what applies to theonomous art applies also to the whole class of so-called 'expressive' arts—the expressive element denoting, we recall, the theonomous element in a work of art, and signifying the 'breakthrough into the eternal'.[94] What, then, is meant by an 'expressive picture'? An expressive picture, we may

---

[94] See above, pp. 118—119.

say, *is always symbolic and never literal*. It is symbolic because it manifests to receiving faith an original revelation through the medium of its images; and it is not literal because it is true only in so far as it incorporates the original meaning of the revelatory situation to which it refers, not because it provides objective, verifiable information about the nature of that situation. The significance of expressive art lies, in other words, in the meaning it attributes to a thing, but concerning which it can make no definite, critically evaluable judgments. This does not entail, however, that the non-literal form of an expressive picture either impugns the reality of its material or that it can never provide a description of the material's characteristics; it is rather designed to show that the truth of the importance it ascribes to an object *as* a medium of revelation is unrelated to any literal-scientific verification of the 'objective truth' of its assertions about that object. No such tests can confirm or deny anything of relevance to the religious truth revealed in such a picture. This is so because the pictorial presentation and consequent acceptance of this object as a 'miracle' raises the object, whatever it be, to a dimension in which its actuality as a medium derives from the apprehension of its relation to the unconditioned transcendent—that is, from a perception of faith—and not from any analysis of its empirical-historical form. Expressive pictures, as primary-immanent religious symbols, are in this respect independent of any empirical criticisms of their own empirical statements about, or re-presentations of, revelatory events. They speak of objects but not objectively, of history but not historiographically. They do this because the meaning faith therein attaches to an object is relative only to faith's awareness through it of that which precedes and transcends the subject-object level of rationality, to which all such 'ordinary' forms of knowledge belong.[95]

---

[95] Expressed differently, the revelation of the 'mystery' of being, God as being-itself, precludes any view of it formulated on the basis of the preparatory acts of man. This theory of knowledge, says Tillich, parallels the Pauline-Lutheran doctrine of justification by grace through faith alone—a claim he develops in two early articles: 'Rechtfertigung und Zweifel', *Vorträge der theologischen Konferenz zu Gießen*, 39 (Gießen: Alfred Topelmann, 1924) pp. 19—32; and 'Die Idee der Offenbarung', *Zeitschrift für Theologie und Kirche* (Tübingen), VIII, No. 6 (1927), pp. 403—412.

III. THE CERTAINTY OF FAITH AND THE BIBLICAL PICTURE
OF JESUS AS THE CHRIST

Tillich's scepticism about the degree of verifiable information to be derived from religious pictures does not therefore involve any parallel depreciation of their function *as* pictures of genuine revelatory events. Indeed, it is an important feature of Tillich's aesthetics that he is not purely negative at this point. For while insisting that ordinary knowledge cannot impugn the value of such pictures, he is jest as presistent in arguing that they refer to something that happened objectively—to the real appearance of a 'miracle' and its 'ecstatic' reception by the artist—and that through them what did happen is made presently actual for us. The validity of such pictures thus rests upon their correspondence with the reality of those events of which they are the result; and to this extent all religious pictures are *a posteriori* interpretations about particular occurrences *in* their ultimate existential meaning as revelations of God as being-itself.

The juxtaposition of these negative and positive elements brings us to the final set of problems with which Tillich's philosophy of art is concerned. If religious pictures provide no objective information about the revelatory events to which they refer, then how, we may ask, can Tillich claim that they are nevertheless pictures of *specific* occurrences of a particular type (to which the terms 'miracle' and 'ecstasy' are appropriate), that a real correlation exists between them and the actual events on which they are based, and that they are not in consequence products of the artistic imagination? The reason why Tillich maintains that religious art is independent of the processes of ordinary knowledge is, I think, clear enough. What is not so clear, however, is how he can affirm, in the light of that independence, the reality of that which is being portrayed. Tillich has spoken of the validity of religious pictures; but what kind of validity is it that can be dissociated from the validity born of the subject-object form of knowing?

These problems become even more acute when we return to the most important of all religious pictures, the 'expressionist portrait of Jesus as the Christ'. This portrait, we recall, is the creative product of the 'ecstatic' (or receiving) side of an original revelation, and functions as the 'miracle' (or giving) side of a dependent revelation. Thus it either refers to, or acts as, a finite medium of revelation. That being the case, we may further conclude that the biblical picture belongs to the primary-immanent category of religious symbols and that it conforms to the non-literal structure of religious symbolism generally. From this it also follows that no amount of historical research can falsify or validate this portrait because this portrait's truth is not determined by the objective and literal accuracy of its biographical detail. The possible scientific discovery of the actual manner and content of Jesus' earthly existence can therefore neither confirm nor disconfirm the validity of faith's acceptance of him as the Christ in its biblical picture.[96] But that said, Tillich next insists that this picture is a 'real picture' of an actual event, in which Jesus the Christ is 'both an historical *fact* and a *subject* of believing reception'.[97] This, he emphasizes, excludes the view that the biblical portrait is either the product of man's imagination or the creation of existentialist thought or experience: 'The New Testament image of Jesus as the Christ is certainly not an "abstraction", but a portrait of a reality which is presupposed and interpreted'.[98] But how, we must ask again, can Tillich make such a claim in the absence of any historical test? If no correspondence need be established between the historical information provided by the biblical picture and the actual life of the man it interprets as the Christ, then how can faith justify its assertion that the figure there described *was* the New Being, and that accordingly the title 'Christ' was appropriate to the historical man called 'Jesus'? In this connection, Harnack's famous question to Karl Barth is still relevant. If one refuses to study the Jesus of the gospels by means of historical methods, how can one arrive at anything but a dreamed-up Christ in place of the real one?[99] As we shall see, what Tillich says now in reply applies to the whole class of religious pictures.

---

[96] Hence Tillich's repudiation of the so-called 'quest for the historical Jesus' (*ST*, 2: 116—123). For further details of Tillich's position, see my articles, 'A Reply to Some Interpretations of Tillich's Christology', *The Heythrop Journal*, XXII, No. 2 (April 1976) pp. 169—177; and 'Can the Historian Invalidate Gospel Statements? Some Notes on Dialectical Theology', *The Downside Review*, XVII, No. 2 (January 1977) pp. 11—18.

[97] *ST*, 2: 113.

[98] 'Interrogation of Paul Tillich', *Philosophical Interrogations*, ed. S. & B. Rome (New York: Holt, Rinehart and Winston, 1964) p. 365.

[99] Karl Barth, 'Ein Briefwechsel mit Adolf von Harnack', *Theologische Fragen und Antworten* (Zollikon/Zürich: Evangelischer Verlag, 1957) p. 9.

He begins by saying that there is a final sense in which faith, by its own power and without recourse to any kind of historical test, can 'guarantee the existence of Jesus of Nazareth and at least the essentials in the biblical picture'.[100] Tillich admits that this remark is ambiguous, so he proceeds to define more precisely what it is that faith can guarantee. That which is assured by faith is 'only its own foundation, namely, the appearance of that reality which has created the faith'.[101] This reality is identified with the New Being 'who conquers existential estrangement and thereby makes faith possible. This alone faith is able to guarantee—and that because its own existence is identical with the presence of the New Being'.[102] Faith, then, is the 'immediate (not mediated by conclusions) evidence of the New Being within and under the conditions of existence'[103]; and, as such, it cannot be investigated or determined by the methods of historical enquiry. Referring to the Augustinian-Cartesian refutation of radical scepticism—which 'pointed to the immediacy of a self-consciousness which guaranteed itself by its participation in being'—Tillich stresses similarly that it is faithful participation, and not historical argument, which 'guarantees the reality of the event upon which Christianity is based'.[104]

It would appear that the argument employed here revolves round the familiar two-fold structure of the event 'Jesus as the Christ', namely, its 'factual' and 'receptive' character. Jesus as the Christ is the bearer of the new reality, the New Being, and he is received as such by faith. These are the two components that make the Christ-event the event it is. For Tillich, however, the concept of New Being is itself intelligible only in so far as it includes the actuality of a 'personal' life in all its concreteness. This is so because, it is held, the ambiguities of existence can only be overcome by the participation of the bearer of the New Being *in* existence. Existential ambiguity—which ontological analysis has shown characterizes the conditions under the 'old eon' or 'old reality'—can only be conquered in the earthly existence of the personal life of him who is the bearer of the New Being in the totality of his own

---

[100] *ST*, 2: 131.
[101] *Ibid.*
[102] *Ibid.*
[103] *Ibid.*
[104] *Ibid.*

being.[105] It follows, therefore, that faith necessarily receives the 'personal' reality of the New Being when it accepts and receives 'Jesus as the Christ'. Consequently, to say that a man has faith entails that he has received that which *has* overcome existence *in* existence. In this sense, so the argument runs, faith does guarantee the historical basis of Christianity, for it guarantees that 'someone' conquered existence. But it does not ensure, Tillich adds significantly, that Jesus of Nazareth is that 'someone'. While faith, in other words, may be able to affirm in this way 'a personal life in which the New Being has conquered the old being', it does not 'guarantee his name to be Jesus of Nazareth. Historical doubt concerning the existence and the life of someone with this name cannot be overruled. He might have had another name'.[106] This, Tillich agrees, is the historically absurd but logically necessary conclusion resulting from the contingent and preliminary character of historical assertions and techniques. The 'Jesus' element in the event 'Jesus as the Christ' indicates only the personal and factual foundation of that event: it is not, however, to be equated with the particular details concerning, or the particular incidents surrounding, the life of him who is called 'Jesus of Nazareth'. Following this distinction, Tillich recognizes the logical possibility of an historian concluding that the man, Jesus of Nazareth, never lived; but he also admits that faith, even though it could not legitimately deny this conclusion on critical grounds, can nevertheless guarantee the appearance of the New Being in an historical and personal form *irrespective* of it.

> Faith cannot even guarantee the name "Jesus" in respect to him who was the Christ. It must leave that to the incertitudes of our historical knowledge. But faith does guarantee the factual transformation of reality in that personal life which the New Testament expresses in its picture of Jesus as the Christ.[107]

As David Kelsey has remarked succinctly, in this argument 'the fact *named* by Jesus of Nazareth turns out to be different from the fact *pointed to* by Jesus of Nazareth'.[108] In other words, whereas the fact

---

[105] See *ST*, 2: 112 & 138—139.
[106] *Ibid.*, p. 131.
[107] *Ibid.*, p. 123.
[108] Kelsey, *The Fabric of Paul Tillich's Theology* (New Haven & London: Yale University Press, 1967) p. 93.

'named' is subject to critical examination—it being one of those details in the biblical narrative which could conceivably be false—the fact to which the name refers, the actuality of a personal life through which New Being entered existence and transformed it, is subject only to faith's apprehension of it. Since the relation between faith and the factual element which it interprets within the Christ-event is such that the interpretation does not acquire validity by understanding precisely the way in which this fact occurred, so the statement that 'Jesus is the bearer of New Being' does *not* assert an identity between the fact called 'Jesus' and the fact referred to by that name. For Tillich, the denial that the Christ received and proclaimed by faith *was* Jesus of Nazareth is historically ridiculous; but the logical possibility that this was not his name is nevertheless an important exemplification of the principle that the truth of faith neither can nor does depend on the literal-historical truth of *any* detail of its picture of the Christ, even to the point of its naming of him. Faith cannot guarantee the empirical accuracy of the biblical portrait of Jesus as the Christ since faith's nature is such that it does not contain detailed historical information about the precise manner in which the event occurred. But faith does involve a certainty about the actual meaning of the event on which it is based and to which it responds: it does, that is to say, include certitude about its own foundation on the 'Christ'-event, and can thus assert the reality of a personal life in the past which, by its manifestation of New Being, conquered the estranged condition of old being. Essentially the same point of view is, we should add, suggested in Tillich's otherwise perplexing description of the Crucifixion and Resurrection as symbols based on facts.[109] Faith cannot ensure the accuracy of its biblical stories concerning the particular Crucifixion and Resurrection of a man 'Jesus of Nazareth'; but it can, for all that, guarantee the subjection to, and conquest of, existence by him who is called the 'Christ'—of which these biblical stories are the respective symbolic representations. This crucial distinction follows the line of argument already drawn by the theory of religious symbolism, namely, that the truth of the meaning ascribed by faith to the being of the Christ is independent of the literal truth of any aspect of faith's own account of his life in the biblical picture. According to it, faith

---

[109] See *ST*, 2: 176—182.

cannot guarantee that the Christ was named 'Jesus', that he in fact died on a cross at Golgotha or rose again on the third day; but it can nevertheless guarantee that he whom the picture calls 'Jesus' *was* the Christ, and that he therefore *did* surrender himself to the finite consequences of existence (the symbol of the Cross), and *did* overcome the death of existential estrangement (the symbol of the Resurrection).

It is therefore the *a priori* of faith that these conditions were fulfilled by him whom faith receives and proclaims as the bearer of New Being. More exactly, faith's reception of the Christ entails its correlation with the 'giving' side of a revelatory event in which the disruptions of existence were simultaneously experienced and healed in one individual human life. Faith is the subjective response to that objective happening which fulfils those requirements necessary for the transformation of the situation of old being: its own existence is, in other terms, identical with the existence of New Being within the area of estrangement. For Tillich, these are analytically true statements concerning the nature of faith; and it is on the basis of them that faith can continue to assert the presence of New Being in the person portrayed by the New Testament, irrespective of his original name or circumstances. '*Whatever* his name, the New Being was and is actual in this man'.[110] And yet, though photographable, no photograph exists of this event, for neither faith itself nor the probabilities of research can provide such a photograph. It is for this reason that historical science, while it may be able to bring to the fore certain critical doubts about the life of someone named 'Jesus of Nazareth', cannot thereby violate faith's dependence on the actual appearance of New Being in the person presented by the biblical picture.

> Faith can say that something of ultimate concern has happened in history because the question of the ultimate in being and meaning is involved ... Faith can say that the reality which is manifest in the New Testament picture of Jesus as the Christ has saving power for those who are grasped by it, no matter how much or how little can be traced to the historical figure who is called Jesus of Nazareth. Faith can ascertain its own foundation, the Mosaic law, or Jesus as the Christ, Mohammed the prophet, or Buddha the illuminated. But faith cannot ascertain the historical conditions which made it possible for these men to become matters of ultimate concern for large sections of humanity.

---

[110] *ST*, 2: 131 (my emphasis).

Faith includes certitude about its own foundation—for example, an event in history which has transformed history—for the faithful. But faith does not include historical knowledge about the way in which this event took place.[111]

Tillich's brief discourse on the name 'Jesus of Nazareth' is perhaps the most extreme consequence of his earlier distinction between ordinary and revelatory knowledge, here represented in the division between historical research and faith. Here he makes clear that the non-literal form of the biblical picture—which allows even the logical possibility that Jesus might have had another name—does not invalidate the ultimate existential significance faith attributes to the being of the person called 'Jesus'. Since the truth of faith's interpretation of Jesus as the Christ is independent of all critical judgments which either are or could be made by the historian, the truth of such empirical conclusions is irrelevant to the meaning of the reality perceived by faith in and through the picture. This, then, is an instance of Tillich's contrast between the contingency of the picture's factual-historical statements about the concrete form of Jesus' existence and the certainty of its assertions expressive of faith's perception of the ultimate in him. Following it, one cannot infer from the conceivable inaccuracy of 'Jesus' as the actual name the possible inappropriateness of the title 'Christ' to the personal reality referred to by that name.

This completes the first stage of Tillich's argument concerning the certainty of faith and the biblical picture. But what of the certainty of faith in relation to religious pictures generally? Given the variety in content of these pictures, we cannot say of them, as we can of the gospel portrait, that faith is here preoccupied with guaranteeing the real transformation of existence in a particular life denoted by the name 'Jesus'; but we can say that faith is here similarly concerned to show that such pictures, irrespective of the diversity of their subject matter, are in all cases products of actual and original revelatory occurrences in which the artist participated; and that they are not, accordingly, creations of the artist's imagination but of his ecstatic response to something that was *given*. And this faith can do in precisely the same way that it secured the validity of the biblical image of Jesus the Christ. Faith can, that is, certify *by its own existence in relation to a picture*

---

[111] *DF:* 88—89.

that that picture is based on, and signifies, an actual event in which the mystery of being was revealed. How so? Because 'revelation' refers neither to ecstasy nor miracle alone, but to those occurrences in which the two are held 'in strict interdependence' and 'cannot be separated'[112]; because, in other words, it is the *a priori* of faith that it be correlated with the miracle that occasioned it and to which it responds. Such, then, is the constitution of revelatory events that the fact of faith in relation to a picture is the 'immediate (not mediated by conclusions) evidence' for the actual manifestation of revelation through the medium of that picture, and thus for its status as the 'giving' side of a dependent revelation.

As we shall see presently, this position is further clarified and extended in the second stage of Tillich's argument, where he introduces us to his important concept of the *analogia imaginis*. However, before dealing with this concept, it is worth pausing here for a moment to indicate that a special problem arises from Tillich's preceding discussion of the gospel portrait, one which, indeed, the *analogia imaginis* is specifically designed to resolve. The nature of the problem originates from the clear circularity of the position there advanced by our author. Faith, we have seen, cannot ensure the exactitude of the biblical picture's narrative of the historical conditions under which the New Being appeared in Jesus the Christ, not even that 'Jesus' was his name; but it can guarantee an actual correlation between the meaning faith attaches to the person called 'Jesus of Nazareth' in its picture and the meaning faith first attributed to him in the original event 'Jesus as the Christ'. Faith, in other words, recognizes Jesus to be the bearer of New Being through the medium of the biblical portrait; but it interprets him in this way only on the basis of that initial interpretation made by the first disciples which is incorporated within that portrait. Present faith thus involves a knowledge of Jesus dependent on faith's original knowledge of him as the Christ: it relies on the personal reminiscence of those for whom the man named 'Jesus' acquired the meaning of Christ.

This, I think, clearly shows the circularity of the argument Tillich is employing here. The event 'Jesus as the Christ' becomes a reality for present faith through faith's expression, in pictorial form, of its own original experience of this reality. What faith perceives now arises from

---

[112] *ST*, 1: 123—124.

what faith perceived then. With this, our problem becomes apparent. If Jesus as the Christ is known by faith only through the apostolic memory-impression which created faith's portrait, and if the truth of this portrait's empirical statements about Jesus' life is irrelevant to the truth of those claims it also makes about his ultimate significance as the Christ, then how is it possible for Tillich to assert a continuity between a figure of the past in which the New Being in fact appeared and the gospel presentation of Jesus as that person? How can this be sustained if no concrete characteristics of the Christ's actual existence, or if no single detail of the conditions under which he lived and worked, can be historically verified by faith? As George Tavard remarks,

> It is not enough to state that the original fact is the Apostles' interpretation of Jesus. For how can we accept an interpretation if we do not know what is to be interpreted? How can we share the Apostles' interpretation if we choose to doubt the identity of whom and what they interpreted?[113]

This problem, indeed, may be said to stem from Tillich's juxtaposition of two, seemingly incompatible, arguments. On the one hand, he subscribes to the view that the kerygmatic interpretation of Jesus as the Christ is unintelligible apart from some appreciation of the way the earthly man called 'Jesus' transformed existence in the totality of his being. More must be asserted than the mere *Dass* of his factuality.[114] So, for example, the title 'Christ' is appropriate to the name 'Jesus' only if he to whom the name refers did actually exhibit a life which contradicted the 'marks' of estrangement at every point (*viz.*, unbelief, *hubris*, and concupiscence).[115] And yet, on the other hand, Tillich also maintains that the validity of this kerygmatic interpretation cannot be guaranteed by the 'historical truth' of those biblical stories which are said to

---

[113] George H. Tavard, *Paul Tillich and the Christian Message* (New York: Charles Scribner's Sons, 1962) p. 109.

[114] It is here that the christologies of Bultmann and Tillich are most distinguishable. See my article, 'Paul Tillich's Critique of Bultmann's Christology', *The Heythrop Journal* XX, No. 3 (July 1979) pp. 279—289.

[115] See *ST*, 2: 144—146. Tillich lists other characteristics of the earthly Jesus which are overcome by Jesus the Christ: he is anxious before death and appears strange and homeless in his world; he is subject to temptation, guilt and insecurity; he experiences loneliness, uncertainty in judgment, the risks of error and the limits of power; above all, he feels abandoned by God. *ST*, 2: 138—156.

'confirm' the absence of such 'marks' in the man 'Jesus of Nazareth'. But if this is so, then it is difficult to see how he can justify his claim that the biblical picture *is* an image of the Christ-event, that it is in some way analogous to its subject and *not* an idealistic reconstruction of a life deduced from an analysis of man's estranged predicament. How can Tillich demonstrate, first, that the New Testament does manifest to faith a fully concrete, past and personal, reality with which it is not itself identified; and second, that the reality thus revealed *is* the Christ-event, the existentially independent presupposition of the portrait through which it is now manifested and made presently actual to Christian faith?

It is in response to these questions that Tillich introduces his concept of the *analogia imaginis,* wherein he claims an analogy between the biblical picture of Jesus as the Christ and the concrete, personal life from which the biblical picture has evolved. 'There is', he writes, 'an *analogia imaginis,* namely, an analogy between the picture and the actual personal life from which it has arisen. It was this reality, when encountered by the disciples, which created the picture'.[116] Or, as A. T. Mollegen expresses it, the New Testament confession of Jesus as the Christ 'means not only that a human individuality existed, but that he was such as supports the Biblical picture'.[117] Faith, that is to say, can guarantee not only the factual basis of Christianity, but also an actual personal life whose concrete characteristics were such as to give rise to the biblical picture. And this it can do without recourse to the verifying techniques of historical research. Why so? Because, says Tillich, the analogy itself is not determined by the adequacy of its historical representation of the actual life portrayed in the gospel portrait of the event 'Jesus as the Christ': its significance lies rather in the continuance of the *transforming power of the New Being* between that portrait and that event. It is this 'transforming power' which vindicates the analogy, so that the theologically important character of the biblical picture does

---

[116] *ST,* 2: 132. The following account of the *analogia imaginis* is based on my article, 'The Certainty of Faith and Tillich's Concept of the *Analogia Imaginis*', *Scottish Journal of Theology,* XXV, No. 3 (August 1972) pp. 279—295.

[117] Mollegen, 'Christology and Biblical Criticism in Tillich', *The Theology of Paul Tillich,* ed. C. W. Kegley and R. W. Bretall (New York: Macmillan, 1964) p. 234.

not reside in its historical detail concerning the man called 'Jesus', but in the *power* which it mediates.

> The power which has created and preserved the community of the New Being is not an abstract statement about its appearance; it is the picture of him in whom it has appeared. No special trait of this picture can be verified with certainty. But it can be definitely asserted that through this picture the New Being has power to transform those who are transformed by it.[118]

Tillich's argument, therefore, is that, despite the unreliability of the biblical narratives—an unreliability which extends, we repeat, even to the naming of Jesus—the biblical portrait of Jesus as the Christ is nevertheless analogous to its subject because the transforming power of the New Being, which the first disciples encountered when they met Jesus and which led them to calling him 'Christ', is similarly encountered by present faith through the medium of the picture. In this sense, so the argument runs, there is an analogy between the personal life of him who *was* received as the Christ and the New Testament portrait through which the New Being is *now* received. None of the traits of the image of Jesus to which this portrait refers can be verified beyond any reasonable historical probability. All that faith can guarantee—and this is implied both in the disciples' original interpretation of Jesus and in faith's later acceptance of this interpretation through the New Testament's presentation of it—is the immediate encounter with a personal life that has grasped and transformed the faithful; and 'no historical criticism can question the immediate awareness of those who find themselves transformed into the state of faith'.[119] In his published conversations with students, Tillich clarifies the point he is making here.

> *STUDENT:* Suppose, somehow or other, science could come and expose St. Paul, Christianity, and all these things as just a big hoax. My understanding of your theology would be that this would in no way invalidate Christianity as a religion.
>
> *DR. TILLICH:* Now what do you mean by "a big hoax"?
>
> *STUDENT:* If they could prove that Christ, or Jesus, never existed.
>
> *DR. TILLICH:* Oh, then he had some other name! That wouldn't matter. I want to say that if we were able to read the original police registers of Nazareth, and found that there was neither a couple called

---

[118] *ST*, 2: 132.
[119] *Ibid.*, p. 131.

Mary and Joseph nor a man called Jesus, we should then go to some other city. The personal reality behind the gospel story is convincing. It shines through. And without this personal reality Christianity would not have existed for more than a year, or would not have come into existence at all, no matter what stories were told. But this was the great event that produced the transformation of reality. And if you yourself are transformed by it, you witness to the reality of what happened. That is the *proof*.[120]

According to this view, then, the *analogia imaginis* is independent of historical enquiry because it is confirmed by each individual's participation (in faith) in the 'transforming power of the New Being'. This experience of the New Being's power is based on the actual encounter with the new reality which was and is mediated through the event 'Jesus as the Christ'; and it thus includes 'the affirmation of the event and of the way in which it is continuously effective, namely, through the biblical picture, however the event came empirically into existence as fact and in its interpretation'.[121] In this respect, Tillich's use of the analogy undergirds and evolves from his earlier position that faith can, of itself, guarantee the factual basis of Christianity. If the power of New Being can be actualized *only* in and by an historical individual whose being exhibited no 'mark' of estrangement, and if this power *is* made apparent to faith through the biblical picture of Jesus the Christ, then there *must* have been an actual person whose concrete characteristics correspond to the meaning attributed to Jesus in that picture, even though 'Jesus' might not have been his name. While faith cannot therefore guarantee the empirical factuality of the concrete biblical material, it can, by this means, ensure that this material is an adequate expression of the transforming power of the New Being in Jesus as the Christ. 'Only in this sense does faith guarantee the biblical picture of Jesus'.[122] If faith implies response to him who, as the bearer of the New Being in existence, has the 'power' in him to conquer existential disruption and ambiguity, then to say that a man *now* has faith through the biblical portrait of the Christ entails that this portrait

---

[120] *Ultimate Concern: Dialogues with Students*, ed. D. Mackenzie Brown (London: S.C.M. Press, 1965) pp. 146—147 (my emphasis).

[121] 'Interrogation of Paul Tillich', *Philosophical Interrogations*, ed. S. & B. Rome, p. 366.

[122] *ST*, 2: 132.

is a sufficient and satisfactory expression of the New Being's transforming power, and so, in turn, of the *reality* of the New Being's bearer
upon which this power depends. It is faith's *experience* of the healing
power mediated by the picture that guarantees the New Testament's
adequate representation of a *past* life in which old being was actually
transformed into new being. Again, Tillich is quite emphatic on this
point:—

> If I am asked: "Does Christian faith guarantee that the synoptic
> picture of this man is guaranteed as historically correct—including his
> name?" I would say "No"! If I am asked: "Does Christian faith
> guarantee that this picture is an expression of the bearer of the Spirit
> who, through this picture, creates and recreates human beings spiritu-
> ally?" I would say "Yes"!
>
> If the Christian faith can guarantee as much as this it does not need
> to call for the support of human work, namely, historical research.
> And it does not need to be afraid of it. Suppose the bearer of the Spirit
> had another name than Jesus and did not come from Nazareth, and
> the New Testament picture of Jesus is essentially a creation of Mark
> (as has been said), then "Mark" was the bearer of the Spirit through
> whom God has created the church and transformed (in terms of "in
> spite of") many in all generations, somehow including myself. Then
> this "Mark" has expressed the inner events he has experienced in the
> symbolic image of the Christ story. All this is an historically absurd but
> logically necessary consequence of the attempt to liberate Christian
> faith in its very center from the bondage to scholarship. Theology, of
> course, is very much in this bondage, and it is the glory of scholarship
> that it has produced the question of the "historical Jesus". And insofar
> as theology has an indirect influence on the formulation of faith, it has
> influence on the life of the church. But there is one point where faith
> cannot be influenced by scholarship: the state of being grasped personally
> by the personal bearer of the creative Spirit through the message of
> Bible and church through his living picture. For without this picture the
> assertion that God has sent his Son to die for our salvation is an intel-
> lectual statement which could be accepted only by an act of wilful
> subjection to authority. But this is far away from what faith means.[123]

Tillich compares his use of the *analogia imaginis* with the *analogia
entis*, which he describes as not 'a method of knowing God', but 'a way

---

[123] 'Rejoinder' to D. Moody Smith, *The Journal of Religion*, XLVI, No. 1,
Part II (January 1966) pp. 192—193.

(actually the only way) of speaking about God'.[124] He maintains that these two analogies are comparable to each other because in both cases 'it is impossible to push behind the analogy and to state directly what can be stated only indirectly, that is, symbolically in the knowledge of God and mediated through faith in the knowledge of Jesus'.[125] It appears, then, that historical investigation cannot get behind the biblical picture to discover the empirical truth about Jesus of Nazareth because the *analogia imaginis* does not provide the means for such an approach.

> This "picture analogy" is, like the analogy of being, not a way given to man whereby he may "naturally" or empirically know the Christ, but a way through which he may speak about the one who makes himself known through that picture.[126]

Thus, just as 'symbol' is the determinative form through which God is cognitively approached by means of the *analogia entis,* so faith is the form through which a knowledge of Jesus as the Christ is mediated through the *analogia imaginis.* Consequently, it is faith's reception and experience of the 'transforming power of the New Being' which alone vindicates the analogy between the individual existence of the bearer of the New Being and the biblical portrait. It is not substantiated by the 'historical truth' of the correspondence between the details of the

---

[124] *ST*, 2: 132.
[125] *Ibid.* Tillich often refers to this equation of the *analogia entis* with 'symbol'. See, for example, *ST*, 1: 266; 'Reply to Interpretation and Criticism', *The Theology of Paul Tillich*, p. 239; and 'Reply' in Gustave Weigel's 'The Theological Significance of Paul Tillich', *Paul Tillich in Catholic Thought*, p. 23. In a letter to Weigel, cited in Weigel's 'Contemporaneous Protestantism and Paul Tillich', *Theological Studies*, XI, No. 2 (June 1950), Tillich writes: 'I speak of symbolic knowledge and mean by it exactly what St. Thomas means by *analogia entis*' (p. 201). However, J. Heywood Thomas argues that, in omitting many ontological distrinctions made by Aquinas, Tillich 'is quite wrong when he says that he means by symbolic knowledge what St. Thomas meant by analogy'. *Paul Tillich: An Appraisal* (London: S.C.M. Press, 1963) p. 198. In this criticism Heywood Thomas largely follows Edward O'Connor, 'Paul Tillich: An Impression', *Paul Tillich in Catholic Thought*, pp. 25—41. For an extensive comparison between Tillich and Aquinas, see Donald J. Keefe, *Thomism and the Ontological Theology of Paul Tillich* (Leiden: E. J. Brill, 1971).
[126] A. J. McKelway, *The Systematic Theology of Paul Tillich* (London: Lutterworth Press, 1964) p. 159.

picture and the form originally taken by the Christ-event. The biblical picture of the Christ is, that is to say, analogous to its subject not because it provides information about what 'actually took place', but because the power encountered through it by faith here and now is the *same* power mediated by the man called 'Jesus' to those who first acknowledged him to be the Christ. While there is therefore no certainty in the accuracy of the New Testament's narration of the past, there yet remains an absolute certainty in the *analogia imaginis* on the part of those who experience, through the medium of the picture, the transforming power of New Being in their own being. It is, in other terms, the power thus mediated which guarantees the picture *as* an image of the Christ for those who are themselves consciously aware of their own transformation by it. Thus Tillich concludes:

> The assertion that the New Testament portrays Jesus as the Christ is a matter of immediate awareness. It is actually a tautology. There is no possible doubt, conjecture, alternative to this assertion. It is logically completely different from statements about the actual occurrence of some events told in the New Testament. These statements are more or less probable or improbable and never can become certain. The stories concerning the foundation of Rome in a book which has come to us under the name of Livius are largely improbable. But that the book which I have in my hand tells these stories is a matter of immediate awareness.[127]

It is at this point in his argument that Tillich describes the biblical picture as an 'expressionist portrait'.[128] This he does to refute once more the claim that, if the gospel image of Jesus is not an empirical description of an historical person, then it must be a work purely of the imagination. Expressionist pictures, he says, are 'real' pictures, that is, they presuppose the independent existence of the reality depicted. In this approach, the painter tries 'to enter into the deepest levels of the person with whom he deals', and this he can only do 'by a profound participation in the reality and meaning of his subject'. What is here expressed is therefore neither a naturalistic nor idealistic representation of 'surface traits', but the use of such details 'to express what the painter has *experienced* through his participation in the being of his

---

[127] 'Interrogation of Paul Tillich', *Philosophical Interrogations*, p. 365.
[128] *ST*, 2: 133.

subject'.[129] And it is precisely this feature of expressionist art, Tillich continues, that is being alluded to 'when we use the term "real picture" with reference to the Gospel records of the Christ'.[130] The validity of these records is not, in other words, determined by the objective accuracy of their biographical content, but by their effective mediation of that 'power' originally perceived in the individual portrayed by those who created the scriptural image. 'A picture imagined by the same contemporaries of Jesus would have expressed their untransformed existence and their quest for a New Being. But it would not have been the New Being itself. That is tested by its transforming power'.[131] With this criterion established, it is possible for those who have been transformed by this power through this picture to guarantee the truth of the ultimate meaning there ascribed to Jesus. They know, first, that Jesus *as* the Christ lives *in* the biblical portrait because the power of New Being is expressed in and through that picture. They know, second, that the actual figure there called 'the Christ' lived *apart* from his portrait because the transforming power now experienced by the faithful must have a correspondence to the real life of him whose power it was to overcome existence in existence. These are the two conditions, necessary for the veracity of the gospel picture, that faith certifies in its immediate awareness of its own transformation.

---

[129] *Ibid.* (my emphasis).

[130] *Ibid.*

[131] Elsewhere Tillich writes that, if the biblical portrait had been the creation of existentialist thought or experience, 'it would be as distorted, tragic and sinful as existence itself, and would not be able to overcome existence'. 'A Reinterpretation of the Doctrine of the Incarnation', *Church Quarterly Review*, CXLVII, No. 294 (January—March, 1949) p. 146. Thus it is the 'power' mediated by the biblical picture that guarantees it as an image of the 'real' Christ. This argument, we should add, is almost certainly indebted to that presented by Tillich's teacher, Martin Kähler, in his *The So-called Historical Jesus and the Historic Biblical Christ*, trans. and ed. C. E. Braaten, with an Introduction by Paul Tillich (Philadelphia: The Fortress Press, 1964). Kähler similarly denies that 'such a realistic picture of the sinless One could be a poetic creation' (*Ibid.*, p. 79), and later maintains that the 'historic' *(geschichtliche)* Christ is encountered 'within a tradition which possesses the inherent power to convince us of its divine authenticity' (*Ibid.*, p. 122). It is this power which not only makes the reality of the Christ 'directly accessible', but which also renders any differentiation of the 'historic' from the 'biblical' Christ impossible *(Ibid.)*.

At one level, this description of the biblical picture as an 'expressionist portrait' tells us nothing new—and this despite the fact that it remains the only occasion in Tillich's theology where an aesthetic concept directly impinges upon an explication of the Christian message. For since he has been at pains to show that the christological validity of the gospel picture does not depend on the historical accuracy of its account of Jesus, it seems only natural that he should associate it with a style notable for its reduction of objective content or subject matter in favour of meaning or import. Here, then, we find a repetition of the argument, by now familiar, that the existential meaning perceived in a thing is not governed by the naturally given appearance of the subject portrayed; and, to this extent, Expressionism is doing no more than providing Tillich with a ready-made example of an argument already adduced.[132]

Taken at another level, however, Tillich's description introduces us to a further, and final, criterion by which to judge the validity of expressive art. This criterion, we have seen, is *identical* with that established in the *analogia imaginis,* namely, whether a picture does or does not mediate transforming power. The question is: Does Tillich intend that we should apply this criterion to religious art in general? That he does is, I think, apparent from his remarks that *all* revelations are manifestations of 'shaking, transforming, and healing power', and that the *authenticity* of a religious symbol is determined precisely by its capacity to express this 'religious experience' and retain its 'experiential basis'.[133] To put the matter the other way round, if something *is* a genuine religious symbol it *will* mediate to us the transforming power of the revelation it is expressing. Following this, we may say that religious art, in similar fashion, is deemed religious on the basis of *what it does:* that nothing can be received through it that does not involve a transformation of the existence of the receiver; and that a picture

---

[132] This point is reinforced by the fact that Tillich's first statement concerning the christological validity of the biblical picture is contained in the fragment of an unpublished address, 'Die christliche Gewissenheit und der historische Jesus', delivered by Tillich in 1911, and thus pre-dating his discovery of Expressionism by at least three years. The fragment is in the Paul Tillich archive in Marburg University.

[133] *ST,* 2: 192; and 'The Meaning and Justification of Religious Symbols', p. 10.

that does not, accordingly, shake one by its transforming power is not a religious picture.

If faith, therefore, is that condition of man in which what *is* our ultimate concern is 'immediately known' under the impact of the ecstatic and transforming experience it evokes, then the statement that a man now has faith in relation to a picture *entails* that that picture mediates this power, and that it is, in this sense alone, 'analogous' to the original experience that led to its creation. In this way, faith guarantees that religious pictures—those that elicit the response of faith—are 'real' and not imaginary pictures; that they are correlated to real events or situations in which a miracle was given and received in revelation. But here, to repeat, it is not the concrete character of these events that such pictures make known to us, but rather the actuality of their power as induced in us. The analogy between religious art and what it portrays is not, therefore, one of form but function: *both mediate the same power.*

CHAPTER FIVE
CONCLUSION: A CRITICAL
APPRAISAL

Throughout these chapters I have attempted to 'construct' Paul Tillich's philosophy of art; and, in so doing, I have for the most part deliberately avoided critical comments in order to provide a clear exposition wherever possible of his arguments. But in this final chapter I should like to adopt a more critical standpoint. Space forbids a comprehensive analysis of all the issues raised by Tillich; and for that reason I shall concentrate on what are, I believe, the principal features of his aesthetic theory.

Tillich's philosophy of art has a single objective, and that is that it should meet and exemplify the synthetic requirement of the theology of culture; that it should reveal, in other words, the truth of the claim that religion is the substance of culture and culture the form of religion. This objective, simply stated, exposes in turn one of the most prominent features of Tillich's discussion. Because his theory of art is based not only on his observation of art works and techniques but also on his own theological and philosophical thinking, it is necessary to understand the theology and philosophy in order to understand the theory. Indeed, to put the matter more strongly, so crucial is the theological-philosophical element to Tillich's aesthetics that its rejection entails a rejection of that aesthetics. Now this is not always the case with philosophers of art. We need not be committed to Aristotle's ontology to read and appreciate his *Poetics;* we need not succumb to Hegel's logic to accept a good deal of what he says about Greek literature and architecture; and it is not only pragmatists who believe that Dewey's *Art and Experience* contains many valuable insights into the nature of artistic creativity. But the same cannot be said of Tillich. Stripped of their theological and philosophical content, his accounts of Expressionism, of the meaning of art, of art's formal and epistemological structure, appear very bare indeed. Invariably we find that an aesthetic judgment can be explained only by reference to the theological or philosophical concept that stands behind it.

And this point leads to another. Tillich is not one of those philosophers of art who asserts that aesthetics must begin with a contemplation of the art object; that this object encompasses a world of its own; and that this world is divorced from ordinary experience. By contrast, Tillich believes not only that the art object, like every other element of reality, is determined by the ontological conditions of estrangement —that it is governed by the universal consequences of the Fall and shares in the equally universal hope of salvation—but that it is only through the proposition of a general theory of reality that the ultimate meaningfulness of artistic activity can be sustained at all.

Whether Tillich is right or wrong in this will be a matter of later debate. What results from it is, however, an immediate focus of criticism. This is Tillich's tendency to generalize apart from the art object to the point where he is either careless of or oblivious to many warranted artistic jugments that are not so amenable to the categories adduced by him. In Chapter One I dealt with the most obvious example of this: Tillich's application of the concepts 'immanent mysticism' and 'belief-ful realism' to modern Expressionism. At first blush, such terms appear appropriate for those who, like Kandinsky, speak of the 'spiritual in art'; but they become less so when we later discover that what was meant by this was the 'affective' expressiveness of art, i.e., that a work is spiritual to the extent that it has an emotional effect upon its percipient. Take also Tillich's memorable remark that, from the middle of the 17th century to the year 1900, there is 'no important religious art'. What, then, are we to make of Goya, Cézanne, Van Gogh and Gauguin? If these are exceptions, then they are of such stature as to impugn the rule. Or consider what Tillich has to say about Titian and Rembrandt, each of whom is said to indicate the gradual trend away from theonomy towards autonomy. Quite frankly, given the extraordinary range of Titian, this seems an absurd classification of a painter who could move from the introspective tenderness of his early Madonnas to the tragic depths of his later works like *Entombment* and *Christ Crowned with Thorns*. Nor is Rembrandt's 'unique bourgeois individual-

ism' an entirely accurate description of an artist who, on the evidence
of the unrivalled self-portraits, broke with public images of man, and
who possessed the power, as one art historian puts it, 'to penetrate the
world of appearance, to lay bear the quickening spiritual forces that
lie beneath'.[1] The dialectic interaction of autonomy, heteronomy and
theonomy may help to explain the steady dissolution of religious art
from the early to late Middle Ages or its redevelopment in the shift
from Impressionism to Expressionism; but it does not tell us how to deal
with the many obvious exceptions.

As a last example of Tillich's tendency to generalize, let us turn to
Giotto. Tillich praises Giotto. His pictures of St. Francis are, we are
told, the clearest expression of the theonomous ideal dominating the
high Middle Ages. Such a painter never for a moment doubts that
religious concepts ought to form the intellectual content of his work.
But this is very hard to take, and such remarks as these serve only to
obscure Giotto's extraordinary achievements in pictorial form. Indeed,
perhaps it is nearer the mark to say that the revolutionary character of
Giotto lies in his restoration of naturalism and in his belief that the
visible world must be observed before it is understood. If anything,
therefore, he *replaced* the medieval inward vision and inaugurated an
age that we might even call early scientific. Giotto, writes Alastair
Smart, conjured up 'a world of the imagination created out of a desire to
visualize an event as it might have appeared to the sense of sight'.[2] This,
I need hardly add, is a long way from Tillich's metaphysical speculations.

One suspects, in fact, that Tillich would find favour with very few
art historians. This is not simply because he is given to grandiose
generalizations, but because his aesthetics is, as I have indicated, so
largely dependent on a conceptual framework which is rarely informed
by any analysis of particular works of art. Where a picture is specifically
mentioned—like Picasso's *Guernica*—it is invariably cited as an instance
of an argument already adduced (in this case, the correlative use of
estrangement). Otherwise Tillich is totally uninformative about those

---

[1] William Fleming, *Art and Ideas* (New York: Holt, Rinehart & Winston,
1970) p. 372.
[2] Alastair Smart, *The Assisi Problem and the Art of Giotto* (Oxford:
Clarendon Press, 1971) p. 89.

paintings from which he says he derived ideas (for example, Nolde's *Pentecost*). One might suppose that Marc's 'Turm der blauen Pferde' is an exception in this respect; but even there it is an open question whether the significance of Marc is in his demonstration of symbolic form. For myself, I think it is better to say that, if these paintings are influences, they are such in the sense that any confirmation of an idea is an influence.

What, then, of this conceptual framework? Undoubtedly its most important and pervasive element is that first introduced by Tillich: the theory of meaning. This theory, we remember, sought to show that every act of meaning—and so every cultural science—depends on the presupposition of an unconditioned meaningfulness, of an unequivocally valid ground of meaning, which, in traditional language, we call God. That being the case, the only way in which we can distinguish between religious and non-religious art is in terms of intention: by deciding between those artists who set out to reveal the unconditioned ground of meaning and those who do not. Yet even this distinction, although true in fact, is false in principle, since every aesthetic expression by any artist of any subject in any style is an expression of meaning in its ultimate dimension. Hence the truth of the claim that religion is the substance of art.

We should be clear about what Tillich is *not* asserting here. He is not saying that the revelation of ultimate meaning is but one of the many different purposes that art may serve, or that (like the naturalistic reproduction of reality) it can be used as a means of interpreting styles like early Gothic or German Expressionism. He is saying, however, that ultimate meaning belongs to the essence of art, so that we cannot properly speak of art if no such meaning is presumed. This explains Tillich's use of the concept of import. For without the supposition that import is a separate and definable element literally 'in' aesthetic objects in precisely the same way that subject matter and form are in them, he would have to agree that some such objects may exist independently of ultimate meaning, which is contrary to the theology of culture. Tillich's assertions about import are not therefore assertions of aesthetic taste, expressing a liking or disliking for its presence in art objects: they are rather of (alleged) universal validity. The difference here, we might say, is between a perceptual judgment and an objective empirical judgment. If I say that a picture *seems* meaningful to me, I am not implying that another person to whom that picture does not seem meaningful is mistaken. If, however, I state that the picture *is* meaningful, I am saying that anybody who holds a contrary opinion is in some way wrong. It is in this second sense that we should approach Tillich's claim about the essentially religious character of art.

Now perhaps the most damaging criticism of Tillich at this point is that this claim is tautological; that it tells us nothing that is not already contained in the earlier definitions of religion and culture. The first practical indication we have of this comes when we set about trying to sort religious from non-religious pictures. We soon discover that this cannot be done, and that the proper distinction to be drawn here is between the more religious and the less religious. For this distinction we require the category of realism. But so comprehensive is this category—extending as it does to include the concepts of essential being, existential being, and the quest for salvation—that it becomes difficult to conceive of any picture that cannot somehow be construed in terms of it. For example, even an ink blob on white paper could be interpreted to reveal the separation of the particular from the whole. What, then, is left of the meaningfulness of Tillich's opening claim if nothing can be taken to count against it?

For another example, let us look at how Tillich deals with the autonomous and heteronomous forms of meaning, neither of which, he says, are ultimate meanings. Both forms result from the interaction of thought and being, and both contribute to the construction of culture. Meaning is here attributed to some aspect of the world, and accordingly every such act of meaning has an existential reference. To take two instances: in the extreme case of autonomous art, this reference is the artist himself (art as autobiography); and, in the extreme case of heteronomous art, it is an independently describable perception of reality which the artist is constrained to adopt (art as dogma). For Tillich, these are examples of meanings created within a 'system of meaning', which is itself limited to and determined by the finite structure of reason and being. Such meanings are thus beset by all the self-destructive conflicts natural to their existential state.

Now it is this feature of autonomy and heteronomy, our author continues, that demonstrates their *logical inadequacy* as possible can-

didates for the foundation of all meaning: neither can attain that level
of eternality which is the sole criterion of ultimate truth. But what
does Tillich mean by this? If he is saying that all existential propositions are contingent propositions, he is doing no more than uttering
the truism that they are not of such a kind that it is logically impossible
for them to be false; he is, in other words, criticizing autonomy and
heteronomy for never reaching a level of truth that would be impossible
for them anyway. If, however, and more importantly, he is saying that
ultimate truth should only be credited to that sort of proposition that
is applicable to any actual or possible existent state—such that it will
explain A if A occurs and not-A if not-A occurs—he is stating that
this proposition is a necessary one; that, like the propositions of logic
and mathematics, it is essentially hypothetical and unrestrictive, being
applicable to any state of affairs whatsoever. But if this is so, then the
ultimate basis of meaning can make no assertions about existence and
hence no assertions about the validity of the meanings construed in
existence, other than those that deal with their logical coherence.
Ultimate meaning is, as it were, limited thereby to the parts of speech
and their relation and has no separate ontological status of the sort
Tillich suggests. I am not arguing, at this juncture, that Tillich is wrong
in what he says about the principles of honesty and consecration; but
I am maintaining that their use is not rendered any more meaningful,
or saved from meaninglessness, by their orientation towards ultimacy.
Rather less so in fact, given that we must somehow contend that a
necessary proposition is the presupposition of a contingent one. If
Tillich insists on having it this way, expression will have nothing
(ultimately) to express, and reference nothing (ultimately) to refer to.

But this by no means exhausts our difficulties with Tillich's theory
of meaning. Another, though related, problem arises with the claim
that import—the religious element—is one of the three elements
constitutive of *every* aesthetic creation, such that the term 'art', properly
applied, will designate objects so constituted. Analysis reveals, however,
that no necessary and/or sufficient conditions can be found to justify
any definite and general description of anything that may be called
a work of art. To clarify this point, we should recall Friedrich
Waismann's notion of 'open-textured' terms. Waismann taught us that
open texture is a fundamental characteristic of most empirical concepts,
and that it is this texture that prevents us from 'verifying conclusively

most of our empirical statements'.[3] Open texture is not therefore
something like vagueness, which can be remedied by giving more
accurate rules, but is something related to the *essential incompleteness
of empirical descriptions.* Try as we might, says Waismann, we can
think of no definitions of open-textured terms that are not *always*
corrigible or emendable. But this is precisely what Tillich denies when he
supposes that art is constituted by subject matter, form, and import. If
art has these things as *essential* qualities, it must be said to have them
in all circumstances. This is to remove the margin of uncertainty that
belongs to statements about material objects (and hence about art
objects). Tillich is thus forced into the untenable position of having to
affirm, first, that he has here completed a description of a material
object which foresees completely all the possible circumstances in which
that description is true and in which it is false; and second, that his own
factual knowledge of art is complete to the point that there is no
chance of something unforeseen occurring (e.g., a new discovery or new
experience) that could upset or modify his description. This, however,
is to assign to empirical knowledge the complete or 'closed-textured'
character that is associated with the *a priori* knowledge of, say, geometry,
in which, if I describe a triangle, I give a complete description in the
sense that nothing can be added to it that is not included in, or at
variance with, the data.

The two criticisms offered so far have done no more than point
to the difficulties involved in general propositions of the sort 'all cows
are black', or 'all art is *gehaltlich*', or indeed in any empirical proposition
that includes words like 'any' or 'every'. I am not saying by this that
the proposition 'religion is the substance of culture' is actually meaningless, because there is a sense in which it remains intelligible to the point
that it can be debated and understood (or even misunderstood). What
does however emerge from this discussion is that, whatever else it may
be, this is not the kind of informative and conclusive proposition that
Tillich supposes it to be.

---

[3] 'Verifiability', *The Theory of Meaning,* ed. G. H. R. Parkinson (Oxford
University Press, 1968) p. 38. See also 'The Resources of Language', *The
Importance of Language,* ed. M. Black (Englewood Cliffs, N.J.: Prentice-
Hall, 1962). A similar position is adopted by Wittgenstein. See Richard
J. Sclafani, '"Art", Wittgenstein, and Open-Textured Concepts', *Journal
of Aesthetics and Art Criticism,* XXIX, No. 3 (Spring 1971) pp. 333—341.

Before leaving the theory of meaning, one final and no less substantial point of criticism should be mentioned. This appears if we turn away from Tillich's concept of ultimate meaning and consider instead his analysis of culture and cultural meanings. This analysis is, I suggest, similarly much less informative than it appears to be at first, and this because Tillich, unhappily for us, appears to think once again that a definition is better than an argument. Now it is certainly true that he tells us a good deal about the origin and structure of culture. We learn, for instance, that culture is born of the relation between *Denken* and *Sein;* that it is constituted by acts of meaning proceeding from the generative activity of man as the 'individual "spirit-bearing" form'; and that what is thereby created falls into the theoretical and practical divisions of the *Geisteswissenschaften,* such as epistemology, aesthetics and metaphysics on the one hand, and jurisprudence, political science and ethics on the other. Thereafter it is a short step to saying that the presupposition of an unconditioned meaningfulness is 'alive in every act of meaning'.[4]

But what is lacking here? It is not so much that we require an account of these disciplines detailed enough to illustrate the variety of ways in which such acts of meaning occur; it is rather that we require an account sufficient to determine whether these acts are as Tillich defines them, namely, whether they *are* acts of meaning requiring ultimate meaning. In other words, it is not enough to say that all cultural acts are susceptible to theonomous tendencies; for what we really want to have are more specific instances of these acts in order to judge whether a concept like theonomy, as a concept designating the presence of ultimacy, is appropriate to the particular case at hand. Indeed, I think it is a feature of Tillich's theology of culture that, so concerned is he to establish the ultimate reference of the cultural sciences, he overlooks the prior (and logically prior) question of the extent to which these sciences are produced by and productive of meaningful acts in which ultimacy is *implied.* Are we to say, for example, that the receptive function of *theoria* entails such acts? Tillich's answer at this point is not nearly as cogent as he believes. Not least it asks us to accept that certain meanings exist in things before we have determined those meanings in relation to those things.

---

[4] 'The Philosophy of Religion', *WR:* 57.

Let me begin by telescoping a large area of contemporary discussion of the theory of meaning and say that, for most parties to this dispute, meaning is a property of propositions; that a proposition is always verbal and descriptive of some state of affairs in the world; and that a proposition is true (or false) when what it asserts does (or does not) correspond to the facts it purports to describe. Now there are, I believe, good reasons for supposing that Tillich, when estimating the significance of a particular artist or picture, does so in part by analysis of the art object's propositions. This is, I admit, a much broader use of 'proposition' than the one just given, and a somewhat curious one. For if a proposition asserts something, then it seems hard to determine what, in the case of colour and sounds, is being asserted. For Tillich, however, *propositions may be expressed as well as asserted.* This is an important qualification since it allows him to describe aesthetic activity as something akin to a cognitive enterprise; as something which can reveal to us otherwise inaccessible aspects or 'qualities of being', and which can be judged 'true' or 'untrue' in relation to what its images purport to describe.[5] Thus is it possible to 'decipher' works of art and to derive from them independently verifiable assertions about the artist's thematic preoccupations, his cultural environment, his artistic tradition, and so on. Nor should we forget that Tillich's surveys of art proceed in this manner. In saying what the meaning of a particular style is, he invariably presents us with a proposition which, he believes, has some sort of equivalence to the artistic expression: propositions of the sort that 'the human situation is estranged' (Picasso), or that 'cosmic dread is present in nature and mankind' (Munch).[6] In these instances, we might say, art is rescued from triviality by its connatative and denotative functions, and may accordingly take its place beside science and philosophy as an activity, unique to itself, from which we can gain a knowledge of the encountered world.[7]

This estimate of art's meaning and cognitive value is, however, open to one very powerful objection brought by the so-called emotivist

---

[5] See *ST*, 3: 68.

[6] See above, Ch. I, p. 6.

[7] It is worth noting that this is a position similar to that of Theodore M. Greene, Tillich's co-author of 'Authentic Religious Art', *Art Institute of Chicago* (Chicago, 1954). See Greene, *The Arts and the Art of Criticism* (Princeton: Princeton University Press, 1947) Chaps. XXIII—XXIV.

theory of aesthetics. This is that Tillich appears oblivious of the fact that there is another great category of artistic style in which *no* such descriptive or cognitive function can be ascribed to art. The emotivist theory does not deny that art can, and frequently does, have the kind of cognitive function described by Tillich; but this, it maintains, is neither its primary nor even its distinctive feature. On the contrary, the function of art is neither to connote or denote anything, or even to help to do either, but to do such things as give voice to feelings or wishes, or to evoke certain attitudes in others, like fright, amusement or admiration. So I. A. Richards, speaking of poetry in his book *The Meaning of Meaning*, shows that we use linguistic symbols not only to talk about the facts of the world but also 'to express or excite feelings or attitudes'.[8] Richards is not denying that the words of poetry do have 'referents' in the empirical world, but that where such referents are intended or included they are not 'used ... for the sake of their truth or falsity'.[9] Any referential function that the words may have is thus instrumental only and subsidiary to the evocative function. The poet may describe correctly an existing state of affairs; but it is not in order to give or attain a knowledge of the world that the poet writes or is read. This is why Richards calls the assertions of poetry 'pseudo-statements': it is 'merely a form of words whose scientific truth or falsity is irrelevant to the purpose at hand' (this purpose being to arouse and organize the reader's feelings and attitudes).[10]

Although the category of 'emotive language' has been widely criticized[11], Richards' basic insight has remained, and innumerable studies have subsequently shown that language possesses a variety of uses all of which cannot be reduced to the description of facts and the

---

[8] I. A. Richards (with C. K. Ogden), *The Meaning of Meaning* (London: Kegan Paul, 1936; 4th ed.) p. 149.

[9] *Ibid.*, p. 150.

[10] I. A. Richards, 'Science and Poetry' in Rader, *A Modern Book of Esthetics* (London: Kegan Paul, 1926) p. 292, n. 2. See also Richards, *Principles of Literary Criticism* (New York: Harcourt, Brace, 1950).

[11] Cf. Allen Tate, *Reason in Madness* (New York: Putnams, 1941) and John Hospers, *Meaning and Truth in Arts* (Chapel Hill: University of North Carolina Press, 1970).

communication of information.[12] This has two serious implications for Tillich's account of religion and culture. The first is that Richards has here marked out an area of cultural activity which is not so easily susceptible to Tillich's theory of meaning. Certainly we need say no longer that *every* act of cultural meaning requires an awareness of ultimate meaning, because, in certain artistic instances, this act may be of such a kind that to suppose this connection *misreads* the act; it may, in other words, be of a type (viz., the decorative art of Matisse) in which the *whole* meaning of a picture is contained in its use of light and colour to evoke a response, or in which subject matter is a pretext for design, or in which the meaning of a canvas consists in the degree to which it widens our visual experience by presenting us with an arresting geometrical pattern.[13] In these examples, we can say, import is irrelevant to the meaning that form itself engenders; and that, following this, there may be cases in which there is something about the perceived object itself—the vigour and direction of its lines, its bodily posture, etc.—which is responsible for its expressive significance and thus *for its initial selection as a subject by the artist*.[14] The entire omission of this possibility is, I believe, a fundamental error of Tillich's aesthetic.

---

[12] Two examples of this approach may suffice: C. L. Stevenson, *Ethics and Language* (Yale: Yale University Press, 1943); and J. L. Austin, *Philosophical Papers* and *How to do Things with Words* (Oxford: The Clarendon Press, 1961 & 1962).

[13] This raises the question, entirely omitted by Tillich, of whether the form of a painting, as a configuration of lines, shapes and colours, has the *inherent* capacity to produce certain effects in its percipients. For two very different arguments in support of this view, see Kandinsky's *Über das Geistige in der Kunst* (München: R. Piper, 1912), and Rudolf Arnheim's *Art and Visual Perception* (London: Faber & Faber, 1956).

[14] An argument associated with the 'formalist' school of Clive Bell and Roger Fry and their concept of 'significant form'. In his book *Art* (London: Chatto and Windus, 1947), Bell defines 'significant form' in relation to the 'aesthetic emotion' it arouses. This emotion is 'peculiar' and totally unlike the emotions of 'life'. To apprehend form, and thus to feel this emotion, 'we need bring with us nothing from life, no knowledge of its ideas and affairs, no familiarity with its emotions ... (We) need bring with us nothing but a sense of form and colour and a knowledge of three-dimensional space' (*Ibid.*, pp. 6—7, 25—27). Bell continues: 'if a representative form has value, it is as form, not as representation. The representative element in a work of art may or may not be harmful; always it is irrele-

The second implication of Richards' theory is no less damaging to Tillich, and concerns those works of art from which are extrapolated propositions *denying* the autonomy of meaning (e.g., all those propositions that affirm the metaphysics of 'belief-ful realism' and 'immanent mysticism'). Here, says Tillich, import is brought to aesthetic expression, and it is impossible to apprehend the significance of these works without presupposing the unconditioned ground of significance and meaning which 'pulsates' in their 'aesthetic shaping'.[15] But this, Richards argues, is precisely what we can do *when* these propositions are aesthetically shaped. For when, in the act of art appreciation, we assent to such propositions, we do so *not* because we recognize their truth —these propositions being in fact 'pseudo-statements' and so aesthetically irrelevant—but because our beliefs here function as 'provisional acceptances ... made for the sake of the "imaginative experience" which they make possible'.[16] Interestingly enough, T. S. Eliot makes the same point in his famous essay on Dante. Eliot, like Richards, recognizes the importance of the cognitive element in art: 'You cannot afford', he says, 'to *ignore* Dante's philosophical and theological beliefs'; but he distinguishes nevertheless between aesthetic and non-aesthetic belief. The reader is not obliged to believe what Dante believed, there being 'a difference between philosophical *belief* and poetic *assent*'. Dante's world-view is derived from Aquinas, but we are 'not to take Dante for Aquinas or Aquinas for Dante, even when it is the same man, and that man a Catholic'. To this Eliot adds the observation that 'one probably has more pleasure in poetry when one shares the beliefs of the poet', but he considers this aesthetically 'irrelevant'.[17]

We may dispute what Richards and Eliot affirm—that truth is aesthetically irrelevant[18]—but not, I think, what they deny: that no

---

vant'. Accordingly, when people or objects are depicted in painting, we should 'treat them as though they were not representative of anything'; rather are they to be seen as patterns of line, mass and colour. (*Ibid.*, pp. 25 & 225).

15 'The Philosophy of Religion', *WR:* 66—67. See above, Ch. III, pp. 96—97.
16 Richards. *Principles of Literary Criticism* (London: Kegan Paul, 1925) p. 278.
17 Eliot, 'Dante' in *Selected Essays* (New York: Harcourt, Brace, 1950) pp. 218—220 & 231 (italics in original).
18 See Hospers, *op. cit.*

necessary relation exists between an awareness of meaning and an awareness of ultimate meaning. This, indeed, cannot even be claimed of those works which 'aesthetically express' this necessity. For even if we were to suppose that a work of art has a determinable meaning—a controversial view in itself—and even if we further supposed that this meaning is that 'ultimate meaning is the presupposition of all meaning', this would not prevent us from saying that our assent to this proposition was given in order to enter into the artist's 'frame of reference' and to enhance thereby our own emotional responses. Here, in other words, we could say that the concept of 'belief-ful realism' is not applied to an *awareness* of the unconditional character of every meaning but to an *acceptance* of this awareness 'provisional' for the sake of the aesthetic experiences that accrue from it.

I said earlier that Tillich's theory of meaning, since it is intended to establish the universal synthetic principle that all art is religious, is not designed to account for the variety of ways in which art can be more religious and less religious. For this we must turn, above all else, to Tillich's discussion of artistic 'form'. In religious style, we remember, artistic form acts as the medium by which import is revealed; but for form to act effectively in this way one major condition must be fulfilled: that no equation be made between that which is expressed and the means of expression. Form, in this sense, must become 'transparent' to, but not identifiable with, the ultimate meaning it reveals. Tillich repeats this point several times, and on two occasions gives it special prominence: the first, when he speaks of the 'formbreaking' methods of the Expressionists; the second, when he analyses the structure of religious symbolism. In each of these, however, we meet further difficulties.

In the case of Tillich's account of the expressionist method, the difficulty is an art-historical one. I do not propose to repeat here my earlier objections to Tillich's theological evaluations of Expressionism[19], but want instead to concentrate on what I believe to be his mistaken assumption that there is in art some sort of polarity between Naturalism and Expressionism, so that any deviation from the former will be taken as a progression towards a 'form-breaking' style and hence towards an increased amenability to religious expressiveness.

---

[19] Ch. I, pp. 25—32.

Tillich's narrative of the transition from Naturalism to Expressionism may be rendered thus: Naturalism, in construing art as the faithful, literal imitation of the objects and events of ordinary experience, denies that our perceptions of the world can move beyond those aspects of reality that we experience empirically, and hence excludes what Tillich considers a 'religious' perception of reality. So the Impressionists, believing in the neutrality of vision, sought to capture the momentary impressions of external nature without cognizance of nature's 'depth'. With the Expressionists, however, this positivistic attitude towards the world breaks down, and we become aware that there is no pure, innocent sensation of visual reality and that reality itself contains 'dimensions of being' which cannot be rendered according to the laws of verisimilitude. Expressionism thus becomes the opposite pole of Naturalism's objectivity; and because the latter constitutes the standard of photographic imitation in painting, the Expressionists can offer only distorted or 'form-breaking' pictures of reality by comparison. This, Tillich concludes, absolves Expressionism from the charge of 'idolatry': it avoids any supposition that the ultimate meaning it attributes to reality has anything to do with the representational accuracy of its pictorial images.

But accurate representation and Expressionism are not the two mutually exclusive forms of art that Tillich supposes them to be; and when a particular style is considered 'distorted' or 'form-breaking', it is not on that account any less objectively real or truly representational. To support this point I should like to refer briefly to three major theories of artistic perception, each of which has enabled us to extend the concept of representational art beyond that of naturalistic description.[20] The first is associated with the work of the distinguished psychologist Rudolf Arnheim and appears in his book *Art and Visual Perception*. Arnheim explains that we can assume no identity in the perceptions people have of reality because the act of perceiving is itself not a mechanical recording of the external world but the grasping of significant patterns or *Gestalt*. This is due to the necessity of the brain to abstract and organize the myriad light impulses received on the

---

[20] In the following analysis I am particularly indebted to Carol A. Donnell, 'The Problem of Representation and Expressionism in Post-Impressionist Art', *British Journal of Aesthetics*, XV, No. 3 (Summer, 1975) pp. 226—238.

retina of the eye. And in the same way an artist does not mechanically record what his eyes see. For Arnheim, 'here was scientific support for the growing conviction that images of reality could be valid even though far removed from "realistic semblance"'.[21] Representation cannot therefore be measured by the standards of Naturalism, or its approximation to a literal scientific description of objects (which is impossible anyway), since all retinal stimulations are subject to organizational processes, in which some predominant elements will determine the overall shape.

A conclusion similar to this is provided by E. H. Gombrich in his *Art and Illusion*. Gombrich begins with a question: Why is it that representational art, although intending to depict the visible world, depicts it in such a bewildering variety of ways (*viz.*, Rubens, Van Eyck and Monet)? The reason, says Gombrich, is not simply due to the endless succession of innumerable images on the artist's retina but to a host of other factors. Past experience, knowledge, learning, memory and individual expectation all contribute to the act by which a given phenomenon is perceived, and to these we must add other, more 'painterly' elements: that while nature can produce a vast range of colourful effects through the ever-changing activity of light upon objects, the artist is limited by the actual colours of his pigments; and that, because tone varies with size, the naturalistic ideal could be approached only by those paintings life-size with their subjects. Thus, for Gombrich as for Arnheim, all seeing is interpreting, all images are 'inherently ambiguous', and there is no such thing as a pure vision of reality. What Gombrich calls 'neutral Naturalism' is in fact a chimera.[22] So complex indeed is the information that reaches the artist from the visible world that there is no reason why he should not see it in terms of the simple shapes and colours and flattened space of the Expressionists. Given that there is perhaps no limit to the systems of forms that could be made the instruments of artistic perception, Expressionism may still depict a

---

[21] Arnheim, *op. cit.*, p. ix. Cf., 'The Gestalt Theory of Expression', *Psychological Review*, LVI, No. 3 (May 1949) pp. 156—171; and 'Experimentell-psychologische Untersuchungen zum Ausdrucksproblem', *Psychol. Forsch.*, (1928) II, pp. 2—132.

[22] Gombrich, *Art and Illusion* (London: Phaidon Press, 1960) p. 75. Cf. also *Meditations of a Hobby Horse* (London: Phaidon Press, 1963).

representation as valid and convincing to many as the naturalistic mode of rendering reality is to the convinced materialist positivist.

These ideas find further support in Suzanne Langer's *Feeling and Form*. She too rejects the distinction between representational and expressionistic art because, she says, *all* art 'has the purpose of making space visible and its continuity sensible'.[23] Even those artists who made the boldest departures from the 'actual form' of things believed they were faithfully reproducing nature. So Cézanne, recording what he saw, earnestly maintained that he painted exactly what 'was there'.[24] For Langer, this is further testimony to the fact that, however many possibilities may be open to the artistic imagination by the power of representing types, imitation is never (nor can it ever be) the criterion of aesthetic worth. Rather should we evaluate all art as *illusion,* as a metaphorical image having semblance to 'living form', in which the most immediate impression created is one of *otherness* from reality. The most literal instance of the illusion is when we see a face, stretch out our hand, and touch a surface smeared with paint; but at a deeper and more significant level the illusion exists when something, 'abstracted' from the physical and causal order, presents itself *purely* to our vision, i.e., as a sheer visual form detached from its actual setting in its material existence.[25] For example, in all plastic art the primary illusion is the illusion of space. Here every element of design and representation, every use of colour and semblance of shape, serves to produce and support and develop the 'picture space' that exists for vision alone; but this space, being only visual, 'has no continuity with the space in which we live; it is limited by the frame, or by surrounding blanks, or by incongruous

---

[23] Langer, *Feeling and Form* (London: Routledge & Kegan Paul, 1953) p. 77.

[24] Langer quotes from the following two letters of Cézanne to Emile Bernard:—
Nature reveals herself to me in very complex forms . . . One must see one's model correctly and experience it in the right way . . . To achieve progress nature alone counts, and the eye is trained through contact with her. It becomes concentric by looking and working. I mean to say that in an orange, an apple, a bowl, a head, there is a culminating point; and this point is always—in spite of the tremendous effect of light and shade and colourful sensations—the closest to our eye; the edges of the object recede to a centre on our horizon' (*Ibid.*, p. 78).

[25] *Ibid.*, p. 47.

other things that cut it off'.[26] The work of art, in other words, is an illusion not because it is a shape in space but because it is a shaping *of* space, a rendering of space as an entirely visual affair, even though space as we know it in the practical world has no shape. Herein lies the fundamental 'unreality' of artistic style; and the important point is that this applies to all forms of representational art as well as to expressionistic art. Thus, Langer concludes, we cannot judge Expressionism and its artistic form by the criterion of naturalistic painting, for this illusion belongs just as forcibly to the most representational canvases as to the most deliberately remote and non-objective designs. Put otherwise, all art is abstract art, whose visible character is its entire being, existing only for the imagination that perceives it, and creating a new dimension apart from the familiar world.

The three theories I have mentioned circumscribe some of the problems that arise when we attempt, like Tillich, to make absolute distinctions between Naturalism and Expressionism in art. For if we are to do as Tillich does—that is, to construct a heirarchy of religious styles with Naturalism at one level and Expressionism at another[27]—then we should begin by asking what it is that Expressionism has that Naturalism lacks. Now presumably, as I suggested earlier, it is some sort of method that directs our attention away from the empirical form of that which is being depicted. We must 'see' an object, but we must not see it in such a way that we identify its significance with its factuality. But are we able to say that Naturalism does not possess this method, or, conversely, that the method it does possess is such as to present a picture of reality whose value consists in copying a wholly fixed and determinate original? This, I think, we cannot do, given that the preceding arguments have considerably weakened any acceptance of Naturalism as the norm for representational accuracy, even to the point of breaking any connection that one might have supposed to exist between it and any specific or identifiable style, such as Impressionism. Indeed, once we have recognized the difficulties in determining the accuracy of artistic renderings of 'reality'—that people do not all see reality in the same way but idiosyncratically—there seems no good reason why we should

---

[26] *Ibid.*, p. 72.
[27] *ST*, 3: 213.

not accept Naturalism as a legitimate means of communicating religious insight, and why we should not rescind, or at least modify, Tillich's judgment about the 'revolutionary' character of Expressionism. The alternatives are in fact much more numerous than Tillich supposes. One need not be naturalistic in order to represent reality as faithfully as possible and according to valid perceptions; and one need not be expressionistic in order to avoid the so-called blasphemous exactitudes of photography. This does not in itself invalidate Tillich's belief that any aesthetic apprehension of the 'dimension of depth' will result in some 'distortion' of vision, in which nature is 'robbed of her external appearance'.[28] However, what it does do is to subsume the notion of distortion *within the act of perception itself,* thereby extending it to cover the whole variety of artistic styles and thus making it impossible to say *a priori* that there is one pictorial manner to which all religious paintings should aspire. To put the matter more bluntly: In the absence of any absolute norm of visual accuracy, the onus is on Tillich *not* to indicate those instances in which the destruction of form is apparent, but to indicate those instances in which, on the terms outlined by Arnheim, Gombrich and Langer, it is not *implied.*

With these remarks in mind, let us turn now to Tillich's theory of religious symbolism. Here we are introduced to the ontological and epistemological warrants for the division drawn between what art expresses and the artistic forms of such expression. The arguments presented by Tillich at this point span a wealth of interrelated topics —his doctrines of God, revelation, and religious knowledge—but we may, for convenience, reduce them to the following account. All religious artistic forms are, says Tillich, primary-immanent religious symbols: they are the finite media of revelation in the aesthetic sphere, through which are revealed the mystery of being, God as being-itself. We say that religious art *is* symbolic because it points to that which is unconditionally beyond its own conceptual and ontological sphere, namely, to that which, as the *prius* of subject and object, 'transcends' the subject-object schema of rationality; and to that which, as the ultimate level of reality, is not subject to the finite structure and its limitations. We say, on the other hand, that the statement 'God is being-itself' is not

---

[28] 'On the Idea of a Theology of Culture', *WR:* 169.

symbolic because, as the fundamental and most abstract ontological concept, it points to no higher mode of being beyond itself. Thus, in short, every statement about being-itself—other than the statement that God *is* being-itself—is symbolic. These are, in outline, the basic reasons why Tillich maintains that there is an infinite qualitative distinction between the religious-artistic forms of expressing ultimacy and that which is there expressed, the ultimate itself.

There are, however, several serious confusions in Tillich's argument. Let me begin by looking at his one non-symbolic proposition about God, that 'God is being-itself'. The literal status of this assertion, we recall, was admitted originally as a *logical* requirement safeguarding symbolism from circularity.[29] But I fail to see how this can be a literal assertion *about* God, given that the only assertions we can formulate thereafter remain symbolic assertions. If Tillich's non-symbolic statement is to have any meaning at all, it must surely have literal consequences, not least in requiring a corresponding and quite absolute distinction between transcendent and finite reality. For example, Tillich says that 'Being-itself infinitely transcends every finite being'[30]; and we are given to understand that this statement is symbolic. But this in turn raises the question: What can Tillich possibly mean by 'transcend' if his use of that term has no ontological implications, if it does not literally imply an equally literal distinction between what is possible for the transcendent and what is *not* possible for others? The relation between 'A possible to B' and 'A not possible to C' is exclusive, since under no circumstances could that which is possible to B be subsumed within the capacities or area of possibilities of C. To suppose otherwise is to fall into logical confusion. How else, then, are we to comprehend the claim that 'God is being-itself' is a literal assertion if the predicate does not here designate a mode of existence which cannot be surpassed?

Much the same criticism can be made of Tillich's remark that religious art discloses or points to the ultimate level of reality. He rejects the view that the ultimate, as the 'ground' of being, transcends reality absolutely. As such there is no supernatural God or transcendent world. But again, this conclusion only compounds our difficulties. For

---

[29] See above, Ch. IV, pp. 148—149, and n. 76 of that chapter.
[30] *ST*, 1: 263.

clearly in the phrase 'ultimate level of reality' we have the supposition, implied in the genitive case, of a particular level of existence (L1) which is distinguished from all others (L2) precisely because it is the last or final level of reality, beyond which nothing exists or is possible. This in turn suggests two things. If none greater than L1 is possible then it must embrace that which is contained in L2, since otherwise we could conceive of a greater by admitting to it that which is extrinsic to L1 but contained L2; and if L1 is the truly ultimate then it alone must possess some additional factor or property, since otherwise there would be two ultimates and so no ultimates at all. In this connection, therefore, the meaning of the term 'ultimate' depends on the absolute disjunction between L1 and L2. More specifically, while being-itself (L1) as the 'ground' of being must include the totality of finite reality (L2), and while there are thus obviously good reasons for conceiving God in terms of the categorical contrast 'ultimate-relative', it remains true to say that the sense of these two terms consists in there being an actual and quite literal distinction between them. The justification for maintaining that any use of this contrast must obey the laws of logic is simply that we cannot conceive of any other situation in which the contrast would remain intelligible.

This view, of course, applies equally to the phenomenological counterpart of Tillich's ontological definition of God, namely, that being-itself is the object of man's 'ultimate concern'. For here too the question is whether there can be any comprehensible and alternative translation of 'ultimate concern' that ascribes no literal meaning to the phrase. Admittedly, as I have indicated elsewhere, the phrase is ambiguous.[31] Does it refer to an attitude of concern or to the object of that attitude? Now if Tillich is stressing the ultimate object of concern, then, for the reasons just stated, this focus must be the truly ultimate, a singular reality literally distinguishable from all other areas of existence. If, however, he is emphasizing a particular disposition of the finite agent, then it must also be said that the admitted transcendence of the divine object cannot obliterate the literal contingency of the human attitude. For, as Charles Hartshorne has remarked, 'had certain conditions been different, God would have concerned me not at all, for

---

[31] Ch. IV. p. 140.

I should not have existed'.[32] To suppose, therefore, that *nothing* in the experience of being ultimately concerned (or in the artistic representation of that experience) can be defined literally is to ignore the relative ontological status of the individual who must exist to have that experience. It is in this way that the actual content of the divine life is, in a non-symbolic sense, conditioned—as literally conditioned as each individual is literally contingent. Being-itself, if thus conceived as the universal object of religious devotion and artistic expression, must embrace those finite, relative and changeable conditions upon which such devotion and expression depend. Accordingly, the logical consequence of Tillich's opening claim that God is literally being-itself, and so the ultimate focus of man's religious interest, is that the being of God must literally encompass the categorical elements of reality in *both* its aspects: reality conditioned and unconditioned, relative and absolute. Should this be denied, it is hard to know what other meaning Tillich's allegedly unique, non-symbolic truth about God could possess.

Tillich's objection to this kind of reasoning is that reason itself precludes the literal truth of any philosophical claim about God. If, he argues, all cognition is dichotomizing and relative—if, that is, we actively cognize or determine a thing only by juxtaposing it to that which it is not—then how can the conclusions of rational thinking be applied literally to a reality which, far from presupposing any categorical difference, forms the basis of all such contrasts? All that is indefinite and distorted within the structure of being is truly complete and unified in God, the *prius* of subject and object. All ontological statements about any aspect of this structure have a dual character which, when asserted of a reality which transcends the subject-object schema of rationality, *implies* the negation of the duality.

But quite what Tillich means by 'transcending the subject-object structure of knowledge' is hard to see. If he is suggesting that symbolic assertions, as utterances of the ecstatic reason, are simply expressions of numinous astonishment—rather like 'Oh, how wonderful!'—then clearly

---

[32] Hartshorne, 'Tillich's Doctrine of God', in *The Theology of Paul Tillich*, ed. C. W. Kegley and R. W. Bretall (New York: Macmillan, 1964) p. 167. For Hartshorne's criticism of Tillich at this point, see my article, 'Hartshorne's Critique of Tillich's Theory of Religious Symbolism', *The Heythrop Journal*, XVII, No. 4 (October 1976) pp. 379—394.

they do not imply literal statements. Yet he himself rules out this possibility when he says that the form of the artistic-religious symbol requires the presence of finite material in order to give cognitive content to the expression of faith. These symbols are not, then, descriptions of expansive feelings or mystical experiences, but are in some sense representations of the divine conceived and expressed in relation to concrete aspects of finite being. Tillich's point is rather that these finite elements cannot be regarded as symbols merely on the basis of a critical evaluation of their individual properties. The validity of faith's interpretation of an object as a symbol or 'sign-event' is not governed by any analysis of the correspondence between the meaning there ascribed by a picture to the object and that object's own empirical mode of being. But this conclusion only multiplies our confusion. For if the presence of this concrete element is necessary, how can *any* knowledge of *any* symbol be dissociated from the retrospective question of whether faith's interpretation was warranted in the first place? Here our empirical knowledge might well affect our judgment concerning the suitability of faith's description, even though we may agree with Tillich that this information can never add up to a knowledge of revelation. But conceding even this point does not require the *complete* disjunction of this knowledge from the subject-object form of knowing, since otherwise it becomes difficult to understand how the concrete assertions involved in symbolic language can ever be justified. For if all statements about being-itself are symbolic, then it seems impossible to distinguish the more appropriate statements about being-itself from the less appropriate. If no assertion is more true than another, then all assertions could be equally true, or equally false, and so meaningless. If the symbol's dialectic prevents us from saying what it is that is literally affirmed and negated in any statement about being-itself, then it would be impossible to determine, and so prevent, contradiction. Though one could distinguish between two assertions in terms of intent, one could never separate them in terms of their appropriate relation to their subject, being-itself. To suppose, therefore, that the literal statement 'God is being-itself' has no literal consequences debars that assertion from having any literal meaning. Thus we may conclude that to have a meaningful symbolic statement requires that it must have some non-symbolic criteria; and that there can be no sense in such a statement unless we know how it refers.

The criticisms I have mentioned here become still more acute when we consider another area in which Tillich's theory of religious symbolism plays a decisive part. This is his analysis of the biblical portrait of Jesus as the Christ. This portrait, like all religious pictures, belongs to the class of primary-immanent symbols and thus conforms to the non-literal structure of religious symbolism generally. Upon this fact Tillich constructs an important argument, central to his whole Christology. It is that the truth of this portrait *as* a portrait of the Christ cannot be determined by the objective accuracy of its biographical detail. What assertions this picture makes about Jesus' being as New Being are unrelated to the literal-scientific verification of the 'historical truth' of those self-same assertions. Thus, while the historian may be able to contradict the biographical information offered in this picture, he cannot confirm or deny anything of relevance to the 'theological truth' about Jesus which that portrait reveals.[33]

Now if we unpack this argument we can see that it depends on maintaining two propositions simultaneously:—

1) Belief in the truth of the biblical picture of Jesus as the Christ requires the belief not only that a human being, signified by the name 'Jesus of Nazareth', has existed in the past, but that his being was such as would support the christological interpretation which the picture ascribes to it.

2) Belief in the truth of the biblical picture of Jesus as the Christ does not require belief in the factual-historical accuracy of its stories about the man 'Jesus of Nazareth' whom it presents as the Christ. All that is required is that these stories should be understood as conveying a meaning equal to the meaning that man actually had.

Here we can see the dialectic of affirmation and negation at work. In the first proposition, Tillich asserts that the Christian confession of the biblical picture's truth *as* a picture of the Christ demands acceptance of certain factual statements about the nature of Jesus' historical existence; but, in the second, he refuses to stipulate what past state of affairs would count for or against the central claim that 'Jesus was the Christ', since according to him no empirical evidence concerning Jesus' life could conceivably confirm or disconfirm the Christian interpretation. But clearly both these propositions cannot be held at one and the same time. If all possible empirical evidence, whether adverse or not,

---

[33] See above, Ch. IV, p. 159.

is irrelevant to the truth of faith's interpretative statements about an event which faith itself agrees had an unquestionably empirical character, then all such statements are completely empty in that they imply no understanding of the circumstances which would verify or falsify the interpretation, and so no real appreciation of the nature of the event to which that interpretation is attached. And if this is so, *on what grounds* can Tillich claim that we would ascribe to a 'photographed Jesus' the same degree of importance as faith now ascribes to the 'portrayed Jesus' in its picture of him as the Christ? Either this is unwarranted speculation, or our author is here introducing a metaphysical assumption regarding the self-evident validity of the gospel testimony which he has not hitherto admitted.

Tillich's confusion undoubtedly arises from trying to get the best of both worlds. He wants, that is, to affirm the fully concrete, past-historical nature of the event proclaimed in the biblical picture, while yet refusing to make this event the possible object of critical study. Now while it may be one thing to warn correctly against improper attempts to get back *behind* the picture in order to secure some historical *proof* of its truth as a portrait of the real Christ, it remains quite another to insist upon the necessity of such undertakings for the purpose of making intelligible the continuity which is said to exist between the man Jesus and the picture's existential interpretation of him. For if, following Tillich, the quest for an historical Jesus behind the christological meaning of his being is truly irrelevant to theology, how can it be then maintained that the New Testament portrait of that man is not a fiction? Equally, how can it be argued that a material correlation exists between the earthly career of Jesus and the biblical picture when it is also held that the whole of the historical evidence for such a correlation is subsumed within scripture's 'interpretation'?[34]

---

[34] See above, Ch. II, p. 74. Gerhard Ebeling makes the same point very neatly. 'If the difference between the kerygma of Christ and the historical Jesus disappears, we shall not only have to fear that the church may usurp the position of the historical Jesus, we shall also have to ask whether in the end, in spite of the assertion of the real presence of Christ in the kerygma, it may not rather be the case that the kerygma has taken the place of something which is absent'. *Theology and Proclamation: A Discussion with Rudolf Bultmann*, trans. John Riches (London: Collins, 1966) p. 77.

Tillich, indeed, has here so divorced the *meaning* of the picture from all questions concerning its *historical validity* as a portrait of Jesus' actual life that, in the end, it becomes uncertain what historical claims, if any, he is making when he speaks of Jesus as the Christ. For if his assertion of an essential correspondence between 'historical fact' and 'biblical interpretation' is not a tautology, whereby the form of Jesus' existence has been presupposed in faith's *definition* of his meaning as New Being, then what we must have, and what Tillich never gives us, is the evidence on which this assertion is made, *the independent justification for the truth of that claim.* So long therefore as Tillich insists that the event on which Christianity is based is not a product of the imagination—that it is a *union* of fact and reception—he cannot avoid the conclusion that the risk of faith is *both* existential and historical, namely, that faith's picture of Jesus could be idolatrous in so far as it might have imputed to him characteristics he did not possess in real life.

Now it is largely in order to combat these sorts of criticism that Tillich, in the final phase of his philosophy of art, introduces his concept of the *analogia imaginis,* according to which we may speak of the 'realism' of the biblical picture—that it is a picture of an individual in whom New Being actually appeared—without recourse to some kind of historical test. Tillich's argument, therefore, is concerned primarily with the validity of the gospel portrait; but it may, as we saw, be applied to the whole range of religious art. On the strength of it, *all* religious pictures are creations not of the artist's imagination but of his ecstatic reception of a miracle that is *given.* How can this relation be guaranteed? It is guaranteed, says Tillich, by faith's own immediate awareness of transformation through the medium of a picture. This may be expressed as a syllogism: 1) Men of faith are transformed by a religious picture; 2) The revelation of the mystery of being, God as being-itself, is the source of all transforming power; 3) therefore it is the revelation of God as being-itself that transforms men of faith through a religious picture. In this way, faith can infer from its present experience of a transforming power mediated by a work of art that behind this work lies a reality which has caused this transformation.

The circularity of this is clear, and, as it stands at present, comparatively inoffensive since it implies no factual assertions about the individual characteristics of the revelation to which a religious picture refers. Nevertheless, the argument, even at this preliminary stage, is

highly dubious. According to Tillich, it is the *a priori* of faith that
its reception of transforming power be correlated with a finite event
which is itself constituted by two elements, miracle and ecstasy. Faith,
admittedly, cannot go into historical particulars about the nature of this
event, about the circumstances under which the artist responded to and
received the miracle; but it can know with certainty, and know *by
its own response to a picture,* that the artist concerned responded in a
certain way (i.e., ecstatically), and that what he responded to was a
revelation of the mystery of being. In other words, from the statement
that faith is the subjective state of one to whom the transforming power
of the mystery of being has been mediated through a revelation,
Tillich has here deduced that the affirmation of faith—the expression
of one's self-awareness of transformation—in relation to a picture
implies the actual occurrence of that revelation behind that picture.
As he remarks, the realism of these pictures is *tested* by their transforming power. But what he fails to see is that this is another tautology
—a deduction of a conclusion already implicit within the previous
definitions of faith and revelation—and so quite empty. On Tillich's
argument, to respond in faith to a work of art is to identify that work
as the consequence of an objective, two-sided occurrence because *faith
itself,* as the individual self-consciousness of transformation by the
power generated in the revelation of God as being-itself, presupposes
the *given-ness* of the miracle through which that revelation was ecstatically received. Thus, once again, X is Y because by X we mean Y.

Let us turn now to the gospel portrait. Here, we are told, faith's
experience of transformation *does* entail certain quite specific factual
assertions about a particular person. It is not just that the transformation
of people *today* is said to entail the existence of somebody in the *past;*
it is also that this individual was the New Being and that he exhibited
certain qualities in his actual life commensurate with his being the
New Being. As is to be expected, here Tillich's argument becomes even
more doubtful. If we had difficulties with faith's certification of an
event, it is hardly surprising that these should increase when to an
event we must now add characteristics.

So let us begin with these characteristics. Undoubtedly the most
powerful objection that can be levelled against Tillich at this juncture
is that these characteristics are in fact determined by the ontological
requirements of his own correlative method; that the correspondence

which is said to exist between the biblical picture and the concrete
historical existence of the Christ is governed by Tillich's own prior
ontological analysis of those existential conditions which *must have been
fulfilled* by the person whose portrait has occasioned faith's experience
of the transforming power of New Being. For how does his argument
proceed? According to the method of correlation, ontological judgments
cannot yield an independent account of that which is manifested to
faith in the situation of revelation.[35] What ontology can show, however,
is that the appearance of New Being, in historical and personal form
within the area of estrangement, is the only form in which salvation
could occur; it can, that is, provide warrants for historical conclusions
about the concrete nature of that revelation *should it happen.* Since,
therefore, faith's present experience of transformation through the
biblical picture *proves* that it is the Christ-event which is portrayed
there[36], this experience implies also that in this event all those existential
conditions necessary for the transformation of reality were fulfilled.
For if, as faith asserts, New Being was present in the man named
'Jesus', then he *must have exhibited* those characteristics which ontological analysis has shown are essential for the conversion of 'old being'
into 'new being'.

It is in this sense that faith can guarantee that the concrete biblical
material, if not historically accurate on points of detail, is yet
analogous to its subject in as much as it depicts a 'personal life' which,
though encountering serious temptation, real struggle and the tragic
ambiguities of life, lacked any 'mark' of estrangement from God.[37] And
precisely the same form of argumentation is used, we remember, to
establish the factual element in the gospel accounts of the Crucifixion
and Resurrection.[38] Faith cannot ensure the historical truth of those
stories which tell of Jesus dying on a cross and rising from the dead;
but it can guarantee that underlying these stories is the historical *fact*
that the man pointed to by the name 'Jesus of Nazareth' *did* surrender
himself to the finite consequences of existence, and *did* conquer the
death of existential estrangement. This claim is similarly justified by

---

[35] See above, Ch. II, p. 62.
[36] See above, Ch. IV, p. 169.
[37] See above, Ch. IV, p. 166.
[38] See above, Ch. IV, p. 162.

appeal to ontological analysis of *what must have been the case* for New Being to have entered the temporal order. Since these two sets of stories express symbolically what ontology has shown to be the two essential prerequisites for the transformation of reality, faith's immediate awareness of the power of New Being mediated by the biblical picture constitutes irrefutable evidence for the fact that these requirements were realized in the personal life it portrays. If Christian faith, in other terms, is the experience of being grasped by the power of New Being, then it is analytically true to say that these existential conditions, whatever the specific historical circumstances may have been, were fulfilled in the person whose portrait has evoked the response of faith.[39]

The first, and undoubtedly most problematic, feature of this argument consists in Tillich's view that ontological judgments can warrant historical judgments about the concrete nature of the bearer of New Being. From ontology's utterly general observations about the form of man and his world, Tillich has here deduced a few, but nevertheless quite definite, criteria of authentic revelation—his assumption being that the knowledge gained from contemplating the universal human situation can provide the key for understanding the 'factual content' of the biblical symbols. For example, since ontological analysis has demonstrated that the New Being must be without 'unbelief', *hubris* or 'concupiscence', and that he must 'suffer and die', such claims are therefore made about the person whose portrait has successfully mediated the power of New Being to the faithful.[40] Equally, since the bearer of the final revelation must become 'completely transparent to the mystery he reveals' and must 'surrender his finitude', so 'in the picture of Jesus as the Christ we have the picture of a man *who possesses these qualities* ...'[41] Yet it is precisely this form of argumenta-

---

[39] This is implied, for example, when Tillich speaks of the factual element in the symbol of the Resurrection: 'Faith can give certainty only to the victory of the Christ over the ultimate consequence of the existential estrangement to which he subjected himself. And faith can give this certainty because *it is itself based on it*. Faith is based on the experience of being grasped by the power of the New Being through which the destructive consequences of estrangement are conquered'. *ST*, 2: 179 (my emphasis).

[40] *ST*, 2: 144—145.

[41] *Ibid.*, p. 148 (my emphasis).

15*

tion which brings us to the principal christological difficulty that emerges from Tillich's correlative method. The difficulty is that the concept of New Being, if derived from a study of the *universal* predicament of man and his quest for salvation, cannot *specify* that actual historical event in which New Being appeared; for the study of history, dealing as it does with the order of becoming and contingency, is not amenable to discourse in terms of universals. Thus, even if we accept that faith's experience of the power of New Being can guarantee the picture's reference to the historical Christ—in itself a highly dubious assumption to which I shall return presently—ontological reflection on what *must have been* the concrete character of the human source of that power can provide no single historical instance in which the conditions necessary for its creation were realized. Here I agree with George Tavard that the main deficiency in Tillich's discussion of 'New Being' is that this concept 'conceived as a universal ... can never fully and exclusively be identified with any particular event'.[42]

This criticism, which is certainly one of the most common amongst Tillich's commentators, exposes the extreme formlessness of his interpretation of the gospel picture.[43] That is to say, his use of the ontological category of 'New Being' is characterized by a distinct lack of *specificness* concerning the so-called 'bearer of New Being'. Faith, it is held, can guarantee the actualization of New Being in *a* person; but it cannot ensure the historicity of any occurrence of which the existence of Jesus of Nazareth, or of any specified individual, was a constituent. On this reasoning, therefore, the notion of 'New Being' has become so generalized that it appears possible for faith to experience its religious transformation by the biblical picture without recourse to any

---

[42] *Paul Tillich and the Christian Message* (New York: Charles Scribner's Sons, 1962) p. 172.

[43] Cf. Wilfred O. Cross, 'Some Notes on the Ontology of Paul Tillich', *Anglican Theological Review*, XIV, No. 4 (October 1957) pp. 297—310; and Thomas E. McCollough, 'The Ontology of Tillich and Biblical Personalism', *The Scottish Journal of Theology*, XV, No. 3 (September 1962) pp. 266—281. A more general, but less critical, discussion of this problem is found in Nels Ferré's article review, 'The Fabric of Paul Tillich's Theology', *The Scottish Journal of Theology*, XXI, No. 2 (June 1968) pp. 157—169.

determinate and exclusive claim that any particular man, such as Jesus, was the one and only Christ.[44] But if that is the case, then this argument not only denies the scriptural assertion that the one whom God has made 'both Lord and Christ' is '*this* Jesus whom ye crucified'[45]; it also impugns those elements of factuality and uniqueness which Tillich himself sought to maintain in his discussion of the 'given' or 'miracle' side of the Christian revelation. For if, as we have said before, he cannot specify the particular individual in whom New Being is alleged to have entered existence, if he cannot know of any historical *instance* in which New Being appeared, then what possible justification can there be for the claim that estrangement has been conquered in '*a* personal life'? At this point, moreover, we should ask also whether there is not an implicit contradiction between Tillich's emphasis on the incomparable, unrepeatable form of this 'sign-event' and his subsequent derivation of its concrete characteristics from speculative conclusions about the nature of reality as such. For instance, should we not rather say that, in as much as this event signifies the advent of a 'new creation', it actually abrogates the ontological status of all prior levels of the created order as it transforms them?[46] Indeed, this suggestion indicates the most obvious fault in Tillich's juxtaposition of philosophical questions and the answers of revelation. It is that his correlative method has here so determined what the 'final revelation' can and cannot be that the *skandalon* of the gospel message is severely compromised. More exactly, it is that Tillich's conception of this revelation has been so controlled by the exigencies of his ontology that it is no longer compatible with his own notion of the Christian paradox as that which

---

[44] This lends weight to Killen's warning that there is a 'real danger ... that some of his (Tillich's) successors may find some other religion just as compatible with his ontology while rejecting the Christ whom he represents'. See R. Allen Killen, *The Ontological Theology of Paul Tillich* (Kampen, Netherlands: J. H. Kok, 1956) p. 265.

[45] *Acts* 2: 36.

[46] This is Bonhoeffer's criticism of Tillich's method: 'If revelation is essentially an event brought about by the free act of God, it outbids and supersedes the existential-ontological possibilities of existence'. *Act and Being*, trans. Bernard Noble, with an Introduction by Ernst Wolf (London: Collins, 1962) p. 75.

For if it is ontology that warrants faith's historical judgments about
'*contradicts* the opinion derived from man's existential predicament'.[47]
the concrete nature of the Christ-event, then this event has become, in
effect, the 'answer' already presupposed in, or anticipated by, man's
existential 'questions' *apart* from revelation. This makes it very hard to
accept Tillich's claim that philosophical questions determine only the
'form' of the theological answers, but not their 'content' which is
derived from revelation.[48] For surely when Jesus is called the 'bearer of
New Being' a quite definite 'content' is thereby ascribed to him—a
content wholly governed by ontological analysis of those conditions
required for the reunion of the estranged.

Tillich's *analogia imaginis,* therefore, far from involving a continuity
between the biblical picture and the historical manifestation of New
Being in Jesus the Christ, actually consists in no more than a correspondence between this picture and Tillich's own, ontologically derived,
conclusions about what the concrete nature of the Christ-event must
embody. This suggests in turn that Tillich's ontological interpretation
of revelation has resulted not only in a position directly opposite to
that intended, but in one liable to precisely the same criticism that
Tillich levelled earlier against Hegel and Marx. For though seeking
to distinguish theology from anthropology, he, too, has remained
bound to a preconceived philosophical doctrine of man's predicament,
from which he has deduced the concrete form in which New Being—the
paradoxical synthesis of essence and existence—must appear; and
though clearly concerned to uphold the universal validity of those
'concrete and special elements' in the Christian picture[49], his own subsequent use of ontology has not sufficiently safeguarded Christian
thought against the substitution of the distinctive historical existence of
the Christ for an idealistic notion of what the agent of salvation *must
be like* to effect the transformation of reality. For this reason, Gustave
Weigel can still ask,

---

[47] *ST,* 2: 106. For similar criticism, see Hendrik Kraemer, *Religion and the
Christian Faith* (London: Lutterworth Press, 1956) pp. 437—439, 445; and
Josef Schmitz, *Die apologetische Theologie Paul Tillichs* (Mainz: Matthias-
Grünewald Verlag, 1966) p. 271.

[48] *ST,* 1: 72.

[49] *Ibid.,* p. 12.

Is this an objective explanation of Christianity as it was and as it is, or is it a subjective reconstruction of a historical phenomenon? Does Professor Tillich explain what Christianity is, or does he propose to us what he would like it to be? Subjectivity is a golden word in existentialism, but objectivity has not lost its appeal for the human mind, and more objectivity and less subjectivity is the desideratum of our time.[50]

Not surprisingly, Weigel's charge of subjectivism becomes even more substantial when we move from Tillich's use of ontology to another, and equally questionable, feature of the *analogia imaginis*, namely, the role assigned to religious experience. With regard to religious pictures generally, Tillich claims that their authenticity as 'real' pictures can be guaranteed by the percipient's subsequent experience of transformation. According to him, therefore, such pictures, for those who are transformed by them, do refer to the actual historical appearance of a 'miracle'. Here, however, we must say that this appeal to experience, while it may direct attention to some human psychological state induced by the artistic skills of the artists concerned, remains totally unsatisfactory as an argument for the historicity of the events which are said to stand behind religious pictures. For it clearly does not follow that an historical judgment is true simply because somebody is convinced it is. A statement such as 'X is certain that E occurred' may be true in so far as it is a statement about the particular subjective disposition of X when he claims to know of E's occurrence; but the truth of the assertion that X was certain in this respect does not entail that he was correct in his judgment about E, that it did in fact occur. Subjective certainty is not, in other words, the measure of objective truth, nor is it a sufficient condition for the truth of an historical claim.

And the same, of course, applies to the biblical picture of the Christ. Are we to say, for example, that biography necessarily elicits more response from its readers than a work of the imagination simply because it tells of real events and real people? Very often the opposite is the case precisely because a fictional creation can weld together into one personality a much wider range of emotions and experiences than

---

[50] Weigel, 'Recent Protestant Theology', *Theological Studies* (Baltimore), 1953, p. 576. Quoted by J. Heywood Thomas, *Paul Tillich: An Appraisal*, p. 194.

those normally encountered by a single individual. The fact, therefore, that the figure of Jesus of Nazareth pictured in the gospels has been sufficiently forceful to transform the attitudes and actions of successive generations of Christian believers does not in itself guarantee that this figure was drawn from life. This does not, of course, exclude the possibility that the gospels do portray an actual person, and that it was 'this reality, when encountered by the disciples, which created the picture'.[51] But as I have indicated already, the claim that a correspondence would exist between a photographic record of Jesus and the biblical material can be upheld only if no historical evidence to the contrary is forthcoming. Were such information to be discovered, then this material, in so far as it purports to present the historical appearance of the Christ, would have to be declared false and so abandoned, no matter how profound the responses it may continue to evoke.

Indeed, if it is part and parcel of Tillich's philosophy of art that it asserts a correspondence between religious pictures and certain historical events *of a particular type* (i.e., the sign-events), should we not go further and say that the discovery of such adverse evidence remains a permanent theoretical possibility? In other terms, if faith's experience allegedly certifies the occurrence of the miracle behind the picture, then it is hard to see how this experience can abrogate that element of probability which is, according to Tillich himself, present in *every* claim to be certain about past facts.[52] Even if it were the case that historical knowledge could be reached on the basis of some kind of experiential evidence, Tillich's own understanding of the epistemological status of judgments about the past requires that no such judgment, however it is substantiated, can be absolutely certain because all such judgments are contingent. Since these judgments refer by definition to something which 'could be this or that', the logical possibility of their falsification remains, irrespective of how they were originally attained. And so it is with the gospel portrait. If faith can infer from its present experience of transformation that the man pictured in the New Testament was the Christ, then this claim, inasmuch as it involves historical claims about the nature of this man's life as a whole, can never be more than probable. Saying this, however, does not mean that

---

[51] *ST*, 2: 132.
[52] See above, Ch. IV, p. 161. Cf. *IH:* 256 & *ST*, 2: 120—121.

Tillich is wrong when he holds that knowledge of revelation cannot be reduced to historical knowledge; but it does indicate that he is mistaken—and mistaken in the light of his own remarks about probability—when he maintains that the confession 'Jesus is the Christ' transcends 'the alternative, "falsifiable" or "verifiable" . . .'[53]

But even if we accept, for the moment, that New Being necessarily implies an historical individual as its bearer, does this still allow the *analogia imaginis* the degree of importance that Tillich claims for it? For example, given his theological preoccupation with the condition of faith—*viz.*, the existential transformation of the faithful—what prevents us from saying that the process of transformation is primary, and the nature of its historical source merely the reflection of this experience projected back into history? If the analogy can be maintained independently of historical tests, can we rule out the possibility that Tillich has inferred from the *experience of transformation* that the intrinsic properties of the bearer of New Being, as pictured in the gospels, are true (i.e., that he did overcome existence in existence)? If, on Tillich's reasoning, every historical detail of the portrait *could* be false (except that an actual person existed), and if through that portrait we experience the 'transforming power of New Being', can we assume that the man depicted in the narrative was in fact the Christ, the one who did overcome the ambiguities of estrangement? Although we may grant for the purposes of this argument that the experience of transfor- mation presupposes an historical source, can we guarantee that the faith we have is distinctly Christian? It is by no means certain that the concrete historical character of the so-called 'bearer of New Being' is commensurate with his transforming effects in us.[54]

---

[53] 'Interrogation of Paul Tillich', *Philosophical Interrogations*, ed. S. & B. Rome (New York: Holt, Rinehart and Winston, 1964) p. 194.

[54] Tillich's remarks notwithstanding, therefore, one cannot exclude the view that in the *analogia imaginis* 'experience' does function as the source from which the contents of the biblical picture are derived, and not simply as the 'medium through which they are existentially received' (*ST*, 1: 48). This inconsistency has often been noticed by commentators. See Tavard, *op. cit.*, pp. 24—25; Robert C. Johnson, *Authority in Protestant Theology* (Philadelphia: The Westminster Press, 1959) pp. 133—134; and Willem F. Zuurdeeg, *An Analytical Philosophy of Religion* (London: George Allen & Unwin, 1959) pp. 156—157.

I therefore agree with John Clayton when he remarks that Tillich should have remembered his own warning against the dangers of subjectivism if the 'expressive' element in art (that is, the 'spiritual power' which comes to expression through artistic forms) is not held in check by other elements, notably by the empirical 'subject matter' or 'content'.[55] As Clayton continues, the inherent weakness of Tillich's aesthetic model is that expressionism cannot produce 'a criterion by which its product can be checked against that which it allegedly brings to expression'.[56] Indeed, so concerned is Tillich with the expressive function of religious pictures that it becomes doubtful whether his interpretation of their 'reality' can ever break out of the subjectivist circle. For though this account of faith's religious experience may provide an important description of what it is like to think and act *as if* these pictures were 'real' pictures—of the inner transformation which accompanies the reception of revelations—it yet remains silent on the crucial question of their validity: it cannot say, that is, whether the pictures on which this faith is based are historically justified or not; or whether there has ever existed an event or personality before which one could legitimately take up such an attitude; or even indeed whether there is, from faith's viewpoint, any substantial difference between pictures of the Christ and religious pictures generally.

This last point is worth underlining. Tillich is adamant that nothing can be excluded from becoming a bearer of the mystery of being because everything has an equal ontological status as elements participating in being-itself as the 'power of being'. Does this mean, therefore, that all religious-artistic forms are equivalent with regard to the *significance* of the revelations they mediate? Clearly not. For in the case of the biblical picture we are presented with the portrait of a man who is the final, decisive, and unsurpassable revelation of the mystery of being.[57]

---

[55] J. P. Clayton, 'Is Jesus Necessary for Christology? An Antimony in Tillich's Theological Method', *Christ, Faith and History*, ed. S. W. Sykes and J. P. Clayton (Cambridge: Cambridge University Press, 1972) pp. 162—163. Tillich's paragraph on the ambiguity of the expressive element appears only in the German edition of *Systematic Theology*. See *Systematische Theologie*, Bd. III, trans. Renate Albrecht *et al.* (Stuttgart: Evangelisches Verlagswerk, 1966) pp. 90—91.

[56] *Ibid.*, p. 163.

[57] *ST*, 1: 148—150.

The content of this picture is thus utterly distinguishable from the content of all other religious pictures. The trouble with this is that, if there is something absolutely distinctive about the biblical picture, and if what that is cannot be empirically established, we must suppose that there is something distinctive in the experience that accrues from this picture—something such that we can say, by inspection of our own transformation, that one picture is indeed revealing of New Being and another is not. But no such distinction is made by Tillich. No justification is here given for the juxtaposition of a particular experience with the particular reality that is said to cause it. All that Tillich does do is to *identify* the experience of transformation mediated by the gospel picture with the *presence* of the 'power of New Being' in that picture.[58] This, however, is to do no more than secure the distinctiveness of this experience by a re-definition of it. That said, I fail to see how, in the absence of an historical test and of any analysis of the variety of experiences to which faith is susceptible, Tillich can differentiate sufficiently between the *Christian* revelation in art and those revelations which are said to be mediated by *every* artistic creation.

At this juncture, it is worth reminding ourselves that this lack of specificness about the content of the Christian picture, if it is symptomatic of Tillich's general theory of revelation, is no less the product of the overall demand for synthesis. As I remarked at the beginning of this chapter, Tillich's philosophy of art is designed to fulfil the synthetic requirement of the theology of culture: to develop a 'unity' in which all the individual cultural parts—artistic as well as theological—find their place in accordance with the co-ordinating concept of religion. Now if this results in an aesthetic in which all absolute distinctions between sacred and secular pictures disappear, and in which any particular work of art can be viewed *sub specie aeternitatis*, should we be that surprised that this should also result in an account of the Christian picture in which the *skandalon* of the gospel is compromised? Tillich clearly does not intend to do this; but, given the exigencies of synthesis, he cannot, I think, avoid it. For when religion is taken in this universal sense, and when every artistic act is construed in terms of the unconditional, it becomes inevitable that the distinctiveness of

---

[58] *ST*, 2: 131.

any particular picture should recede, and that all pictures should be taken as so many instances of a single perception—single in that the variety of these pictures can never detract from their unanimity in revealing the dimension of depth. Thus Tillich speaks of differences in form and subject matter but never of 'substantive' differences. From the perspective of transcendent meaning, what distinctions there are here are of degree not of kind. No matter, therefore, what differences may be apparent in what artists seek to depict, or in what their pictures actually depict or in how they depict it, all pictures can be said to expose the same truth about the ultimate mystery of being; to refer to structurally identical events which manifest that mystery; and to have the same experiential effects on all those who perceive the mystery through them. I can only repeat that the longer Tillich proceeds in this vein, the more questionable his assertions become.

A final word. Tillich often speaks of the therapeutic consequences of synthesis, of a final healing of the psychologically damaging separation between religion and culture. Even in the absence of sufficient evidence, no one would deny, I think, that there is a measure of truth in what Tillich says. But it is nevertheless worth reflecting on the other side of the coin, namely, that synthesis may well contain its own disruptive possibilities. I can imagine, for example, that the constraints Tillich places upon us to view all artistic creation from within the perspective of religion, and to reduce accordingly the variety of interpretations to a single unit of meaning, could prove no less damaging, and lead to a dogmatic repression of artistic freedom. For creative inspiration, I should say, cannot be described simply as something bounded by theories and concepts held hitherto. It may come rather as a leap to a new level of apprehension, in the light of which is shown the inadequacy of our former ideas. And is there not something analogous to this in the experiences that Tillich himself describes as 'revelations'?

INDEX OF NAMES

INDEX OF SUBJECTS

THEOLOGISCHE BIBLIOTHEK TÖPELMANN

Herbert Neie

The Doctrine of the Atonement in the Theology of Wolfhart Pannenberg

Octavo. X, 237 pages. 1978. Cloth DM 72,—
ISBN 3 11 007506 7 (Volume 36)

John P. Clayton

The Concept of Correlation

Paul Tillich and the Possibility of a mediating Theology

Octavo. XII, 329 pages. 1980. Cloth DM 84,—
ISBN 3 11 007914 3 (Volume 37)

RELIGION AND REASON

Philip C. Almond

Mystical Experience and Religions Doctrine

An Investigation of the Study of Mysticism in World Religions

Large-octavo. X, 197 pages. 1982. Cloth DM 68,—
ISBN 90 279 3160 7 (Volume 26) Mouton Publishers

R. J. Siebert

The Critical Theory of Religion

The Frankfurt School

Large-octavo. Approx. 360 pages. 1983. Approx. DM 62,—
ISBN 90 279 3159 3 (in preparation) Mouton Publishers

Charles T. Waldrop

Karl Barth's Christology to Basic Alexandrian Character

Large-octavo. Approx. 248 pages. 1983. Approx. DM 52,—
ISBN 90 279 3109 7 (in preparation) Mouton Publishers

Prices are subject to change

Walter de Gruyter Berlin · New York

2007